Happy Mother's Day, Mom

your daughter

Sibylla

ONE STORY AT A TIME

Friend, Mother, Entrepreneur

A True Canadian Immigration Story

Astrid Peters, M.Ed.

Edited by Eric Muhr
Photos from family collection

First Edition
Published in Canada

For information regarding this book or its purchase,
contact the publisher:

www.sibyllaonestoryatatime.ca
peters_6@sympatico.ca

Library and Archives Canada Cataloguing in Publication
information is available on request.

ISBN 978-1-7779691-0-3 (paperback)
ISBN 978-1-7779691-1-0 (ebook)

Eric,

Enjoy!

Astrid

Sibylla

ONE STORY AT A TIME

Dedication

My mother, Sibylla, who promised me an exciting journey in writing this book

her loyal, loving family, who have contributed to the full and rich story of her life through friendship and assistance

her circle of friends, who continually made her happiness complete

all of you who appear in this book, who have touched her soul

all those who do not appear in this book, I assure you that you are all remembered and cherished.

Foreword

My mother lived two lives. She lived one life in the Netherlands and the other in Canada. In the Netherlands, her life enveloped remarkable and romantic adventures. In Canada, she experienced unpredictable hardships and extraordinary accomplishments. In *Sibylla, One Story At A Time*, I met my true mother, a woman of compassionate and vibrant spirit. Her life stories inspired her family, friends, acquaintances, and women entrepreneurs. Sibylla was one of the last links with the twentieth century. She lived through an epic historical time in the Netherlands, and discovered a land of vast opportunity in Canada.

As a young girl, she grew up in small-town Deventer, the Netherlands. She was educated in the Depression years of the 1930s, and sought her first job when the Second World War broke out. She worked in various cities in a war-torn country, and became a Sergeant under the British Army during the immediate aftermath of the war. Then she met my father, who changed her life completely.

Sibylla Janssen-Peters was probably best known in Canada for her accomplishments in the creation and development of the Humber Nurseries Ltd. (1948 to 2019). When she was twenty-nine years old, after arriving in Canada, she made the choice to join my father in establishing this business. She managed to forge her way into the competitive craft of horticulture in the

1950s. Her success was due to hard work, often at any price. In the twilight of her life, she even maintained a work routine at the nursery. Clients and personnel loved her and gave any excuse to sit and chat about gardening and non-gardening topics alike.

I was fortunate to share many afternoons with my mother in the dining room of her home, recording her voice on the tape recorder. Her life experiences were profound. But, as I transcribed the tapes, I came across many obstacles, one being the chronological timing of her life, and another, the fragmentation of the storylines. My challenge was to put them into a readable order, and that took a bit of work. Sometimes there were places and people that I needed to research, which, with the help of the Internet, I weaved into the stories. And this was how I came to the writing of this book, enjoying the ride, walking hand in hand with my mother, as she entertained me with all her lively narratives.

Sibylla's daughter, Astrid Peters

Dear Reader:

When I was a child, I took the train with my father, who invited me on family and business trips. I would dress up, place a bow in my hair, and wait for him to hold my hand and lead me to distant and faraway places. I grew up loving the adventures.

Sibylla

Dorothea Johanna Maria Janssen

I was on the left, age five; my sister Rie was seven, and my brother Andre was six. It was fashionable for little girls to wear huge white ribbons in their hair. (c. 1924)

At the age of twelve, I was all dressed up for my First Holy Communion.

Chapter One: Episodes of Youth

My family heritage dates back to 1377, in the region south of the Netherlands, in what is actually now France. My family tree was researched, and I was lucky enough to have family members recorded in the church registry and in the military records. Some of the records also showed what kinds of work they had done. That was how I knew that my ancestors came from entrepreneurial families. I was raised in the hustle of home business on both sides of my parents' families.

The Early Years

I was the third one born in a family of seven children, in the town of Deventer, in the beautiful country of the Netherlands. I spent my childhood living there, always accustomed to the crowded rooms of our house on the Niewstraat. In the early 1920s, we made weekend trips with our father. My mother was always too tired and even too sick to travel. So, we needed to first walk four kilometers from our home two the Diepenveenstraat, where there was a railway station. There, my father and two of my older siblings caught the train, and we went to places my father wanted us to go. It gave us all a chance to talk and travel. Sometimes we would see our cousins in the Netherlands. And sometimes we would go to Aachen, a town near the Dutch-German border, a journey of a hundred kilometres, to see my father's business associates. For children of our age, it was a real privilege to go on these trips.

I was always curious about our ancestry. Through research, and with the help of a professional genealogist, I found our family roots in church registries and military and town records. I traced our family back to the fourteenth century. I was a descendant of the land owner Johan Houba, born in 1377 in Flemelle, Luik, Belgium. My father had an aunt, Barbara Houba, whom he talked about when I was young.

I was only a child at the time, but I admired my grandmother because I had inherited her first name, although it was spelled differently. Her name was Sibilla Adelgunda Stinkes, born in Breyll, Germany, on January 16, 1842. She lived in Kevelaar, Germany, a small and religious town. After she married my grandfather, Josef Engels, they moved to the medieval village of Tegelen in the Netherlands.

In those days, there were many religious towns like Tegelen, which would present a Passion Play every five years during the Easter season to remember their fellow men who fell victim to the relentless plague of earlier times. The Passion Play presentation was how the inhabitants kept their pledge to God over the centuries, with few historical interruptions. The local people would be the actors, and in preparation, the men would grow their beards in time for the monumental occasion. None of this registered with me when I was growing up, but it did tell me about my grandparents and where they had grown up. My father wanted me to know all about this history, and I gladly listened. I would later participate in a Passion Play during my work years during the war.

The Pottery Business

My family meant everything to me in my youth. One story I especially liked was about my grandparents. We used to talk about the accident where my grandfather, Joseph Engels, died instantly. It was sad story, since he had ambitions from the beginning to build a prosperous business. First, he bought a plot of land from the merchant Gerard Jan de Rijk, a rich man from the Dutch province of Limburg. The land, registered as sheep meadow, was on the same industrial ground where my grandfather set up a pottery factory. His pottery business was doing well, and in 1874, he started to build an extension to his home and business. He hired a bricklayer, Conrad Steffels, and building was going smoothly at first. Then the construction site collapsed. Both my grandfather and his mason were buried and killed under the rubble of stone. My grandmother was left, three months pregnant at the time, to fend for herself and raise their son Josef Jacob independently.

My grandmother did not live that kind of life for long. Within two years, she married my second grandfather, Andreas Janssen, a potter at the shop. She was thirty-four years of age, and he was twenty-five. He lived in Tegelen. His father was a craftsman who had made wooden shoes since the early 1800s. He had only one sister, who died after nine months. Andreas Janssen and Sibilla Stinkes-Engels were married on May 28, 1876. They had five children together, all born in Tegelen, and my new grandfather took over the pottery business.

Tegelen was a town well known for its pottery-making in the seventeenth and eighteenth centuries. Historians discovered that the potters in Roman times had used tile ovens to make pottery from the local clay. While my grandmother took over the house duties, my new grandfather worked longer hours at the factory to learn more about pottery, terra cotta, and earthenware. Then he surmised that the pottery industry was much too competitive in Tegelen. Prospects declined in Tegelen. However, there was a lively activity developing in this field in the nearby town of Deventer, only 140 kilometres away. So both he and Sibilla agreed that they needed to move and take advantage of the business opportunity there, a market not yet inundated with pottery factories. The move would be a life-changing event for the entire family. They had their sixth and last child in Deventer. My grandfather established himself as an independent potter and applied for a parcel of land to start his own business. The timing and the place were perfect.

It would take years before I understood the impact of this move on our family. But I did not worry about it. I was more concerned, surprisingly, about remembering all the names of my aunts and uncles who established themselves in the town of Deventer. The truth was that I wanted to know more about my half-uncle Josef. I wanted to know why my aunts Maria, Margaretha, and Helene never married. I wondered how my Aunt Josephina met Uncle Arnold. And I was curious as to why two of my uncles were named Jacob.

The Jacob story caught my attention. Jacob comes from the Latin name Jacobus. It was this name that was given to the three sons of Sibilla Stinkes (Engels-Janssen). Sibilla used the name Jacob to identify her eldest son, Josef Jacob Engels. She had dropped the name Josef to differentiate him from her first husband's name, Josef Engels. Sibilla named her first-born son with her second husband as Jacob Josef Johannes Janssen, and she named her second-born son with him Jacobus Wilhemus Andreas Janssen. There was growing confusion in the family over these three names, so with this last son, a compromised name was created for him.

Choosing a compromised name evolved into a family feud. Sibilla wanted Wilhelm, a name of German origin. Andreas wanted Wim, a name of Dutch origin. Both of them did not get what they wanted, but agreed upon Guillaume, a name of French origin and translated to Bill, William, or Guy in English. This was how Sibilla and Andreas Janssen named their youngest son, my father, Guillaume Janssen.

My Parents

Guillaume Janssen was born on July 17, 1884, and in the genealogical records he was identified as J.W.A. Janssen.

My mother's name was Henrica Maria Koolhof and everyone called her Riek. She was born on January 25, 1893, in Deventer, about nine years after my father. She lived her entire early life on a huge dairy farm with plenty of cattle. She was one of six children who did not need to work at the farm, thanks to the craftiness of her parents. The farm produced enough milk and milk products to sustain a comfortable lifestyle for the Koolhof family. However, there was suspicion surrounding their high achievement. People called them "the water farmers" because Riek's father, Jan Koolhof, would add more water than was supposed to be added to the milk. He therefore produced and sold more milk than the usual quota. This upbringing all mattered in the grand scheme of my mother's life. Then came the Great War in 1914.

At the young age of twenty-one, on June 25, 1914, my mother married my father a month before the Great War started. Although the Netherlands was neutral in the First World War, it was nevertheless significantly affected by it. The army remained fully mobilized, and its economy felt the strain. During the war, all that mattered to Riek and Guillaume was making a living. Their dream was to carry on my grandparents' pottery business. If everything went well, the pottery industry would thrive in the restraining times of war. And indeed, in the beginning, all did go well.

They expanded the business to the Ooievaarstraat location in Deventer. Here, there was a store where they sold the pottery they made from their factory located nearby. Behind the store was a reconstructed house, where the employees lived and worked. Eventually, my father traveled to Germany to find different types of earthenware and crystal to sell at the store. The retail portion of the business grew rapidly and wholesale pursuits soon followed. The business grew to an enormous enterprise.

We, the seven young children, all grew up in the environment of family business ownership. We had daily chores, even though our housekeeper took care of most household jobs, since both our parents worked every day in the business. I loved observing all the activities that came with the territory. Some of my extroverted character wanted to meet all the new businessmen and customers, and I imagined all the stories that my parents could tell us about them. But neither did I meet any of these people, nor did I hear any stories. For some reason, my parents protected the girls from all outside business activity.

On the other hand, my brothers were introduced to pottery at a young age. They learned how to make clay pots all by hand, and after many hours of practice, they perfected the art. Through the 1920s and 1930s, Jan, Guillaume, and Arnold worked on Saturdays, Sundays, and holidays, until one by one, when they had girlfriends, my father allowed them to have an occasional Saturday afternoon off work. They all seemed to find a way to make it happen in a workable way.

I resorted, therefore, to getting to know my relatives. Although it was a challenge to understand my father's heritage, my mother's side was equally a test because she had a large family. There were five girls and one boy. First, Uncle Jan was married two times, because he remarried after his first wife died. There were ten children in that family, and while I did not know how many children there were with his second wife, undoubtedly there were many cousins to get to know. One of my favourite aunts, Aunt Jo, was the second eldest, and she became a nun. Aunt Marie remained single, probably because of her harsh and rigid character. My dear mother Riek came next. Aunt Mien had nine children, two of whom were twins and died at birth. And finally, Aunt Dien was blessed with four offspring. I was fascinated by them all, and looking back now, I thought my parents appreciated my enthusiastic interest in family as something they wanted to nurture as I was growing up.

My Education

I liked doing school homework at home, especially completing embroidery projects while sitting in my favourite living room chair. Needlepoint brought back memories about the nuns who taught me in my formative years. I enjoyed Sister Ludgerus, who pointed out the importance of doing your work neatly and correctly. But even at the age of six, I was distracted by the need to doze off. On one occasion, when I awoke, I noticed that I had disobeyed her commandment of getting things right and I, unfortunately, had misspelled my last name on my embroidery. After this incident, I never forgot that my surname (Janssen) had two letter Ss, not one. Thankfully, Sister Dygna came to my rescue and praised me for my designs on tablecloths, and my bed sheet repair work. I was probably no better than her other students, but she had a sympathetic heart when I felt frustrated like that.

There was magic in learning, and when it came to history and geography when I was eight years old, I longed to achieve high marks. But this was because my teacher, Mrs. Vink, who lived down the street from us, had taken a fond interest in me. She always remembered to write me a beautiful letter on my birthday. She told me once that she was not liked very much by her principal at the time, and I was sensitive to her disclosure of this fact about her life.

However, when it came to my French class, I needed to memorize all my words and sentences. One example was: "Je peux parler français un peu, mais c'est très difficile pour moi." ("I can speak French a little, but it is very difficult for me.") I kept this rescue phrase in my back pocket, for use when I could not understand the French conversation. My teacher used to look at me with curiosity because, although I studied hard, she knew that I would soon forget what she had taught. But in the depth of my heart, I loved school and felt driven to learn more each school day.

Friends, Relatives, and Siblings

Everything that mattered in my life was within a radius of five blocks—my relatives, the Catholic church that our family attended, and our schools. During my youth, I got used to visiting family who lived close by, because they were within walking distance. One of my favourites was Aunt Dien, the youngest in the family, who had a busy social life. Once I met her girlfriend from boarding school, whose last name was Verhaag. The Verhaag family took my aunt under their wing on weekends and holidays, and many times she was invited on their family vacations. After she married Jan Reyers, she continued her visits with the Verhaag family. Since I was her niece, the Verhaag family invited me to visit their home in Oldenzaal in 1922, and that was how I came to know the family. There were two Verhaag daughters about my age, whom I befriended, and I have great memories of spending my youth with them. Going forward in time and in a different country (Canada), I met other members of that same family and they became life-long friends.

My parents loved to go out to socialize and leave the children in the hands of a babysitter. They visited the families of the Klein Beerninks and the Hoogstratens who lived close by in Deventer, and there were other friends and families, too, living within walking distance. On these occasions, we knew that we could celebrate in their absence and have fun with the babysitters. On one occasion, a new babysitter, a woman who was at least ten years older than me, was descending the stairs as I ascended them. I immediately recognized her because she attended our school.

I asked her abruptly, "From where are you coming?"

To which she replied, "From my aunt's house from the Engels family."

I was in disbelief, because that meant that she was a half-cousin to me, a descendant of my half-uncle! It certainly was a small world.

"Tonight," she said, "We are opening the shelled peanuts bag. And you have my permission to throw the shells wherever you wish. You can make as much of a mess as you want!"

My siblings and I viciously removed their shells, throwing them everywhere and enjoying devouring all the fresh peanuts. In later years, I would walk around Deventer where I first grew up, and I would always remember the happiness that this peanut story brought to my mind.

Saint Bernard's elementary and high school were two separate buildings, not divided because of grade levels, but because the boys school was independent of the girls school. I walked daily to and from school with my older brother and sister, Andre and Rie. It was not long, however, before people noticed something strange about how Andre walked. He had an irregular limp and constantly gazed in different directions. Although one would call his health problems a result of meningitis, we were unsure if that was the problem, as his complications may have come from another type of brain disease.

I became quite close with Andre, as I spent a lot of time with him in the years he was growing up. He became dependent on my help, and I committed myself to walk with him, arm in arm, when he wanted to visit his friends or to run personal errands. Anyone who saw us walking together recognized Andre. And at school, the nuns enjoyed teaching him, where he excelled the most in mechanics class. Eventually, my father needed to send him to a special school for the mentally disabled in Apeldoorn.

My sister Rie seemed to be in another world, not in a strange way, but because she and I were three years apart in age and she seemed older and more mature. She took her responsibilities to help her mother in the household more seriously, mostly because she was the eldest sibling. As a good student at school, particularly excelling in mathematics and the sciences, she was also a supportive and fun sister. Playing with her, I would catch her in a game of tag, or we would ride our bikes outside of the neighbourhood. Hardworking and of a caring nature right from the beginning, she was destined to become a nurse.

An early family photograph of three family members showed us all dressed up. I was five, Andre was six, and Rie was seven. Photographed in black and white, Rie and I fashionably wore large white bows in our hair. On that Sunday afternoon, we took the train with our father to the town of Nijmegen, where Aunt Jo was celebrating her vow-taking in becoming a nun in the Dominican convent. On our journey there, we heard a shrill, screaming voice that somewhat sounded like Andre. He had caught his hand in the doorway of the train compartment! We took him immediately to the doctor in Nijmegen, and therefore we arrived late for the family party, all of us appearing dishevelled in appearance, especially Andre, with the saddest look on his face.

My three younger brothers, Jan, Guillaume, and Arnold, led mischievous and very restless lives. They did things that one would call boyhood pranks. In my opinion, these were serious situations, because the police knocked on our door at least once a month. I only found out many years later about the kind of mischief they created in the community. They were always under immediate suspicion from the authorities, and to my surprise, these mishaps included Andre.

For instance, my four brothers walked to the inner town of Deventer and victimized a targeted house. The goal was to create havoc while climbing onto the rooftop. The method was to run through the front door without knocking, quickly climb the stairs to the attic, exit to the rooftop, and reenter by running down the stairs or by sliding down the banister fast enough before anyone could catch them. Could you imagine if you were to see four boys enter your home, running up the stairwell, only to disappear momentarily and to reappear, all before your eyes in a quick second?

Other drama and intrigue happened on smaller streets with row houses. They would take a long piece of string and tie all the front door knobs together, then ring all the doorbells of each home, and finally, run away as quickly as possible before anyone could identify them. They did not do this only once, but repeatedly until the police would tell them to stop.

On one occasion, the police came to our home with three of my four brothers in tow, to tell my parents that they had been drinking out of discarded beer bottles. The boys thoroughly enjoyed the last drops in each bottle they had collected before being caught off their guard. Arnold, the youngest, who was four years old at the time, was not with them. The three others did not know where he had disappeared. No one knew where he was until the police arrived again with a little boy in hand and asked my parents if this was their son. The police guessed that he was from the Janssen family, the "Pottebakker" (pottery maker)!

My youngest brother Arnold always seemed to struggle to keep up with his brothers, as I remembered. Even when he was born, he was too ill to be brought home right away from the hospital after my mother gave birth. Also, he could not be baptized immediately after birth, as was the custom in Catholic families. Once, we went to see a homeopathic doctor on one of our adventures by train to Germany. My mother was not in favourable health, and she went to see this doctor quite often to help with her illness. My parents chose Arnold and me to go with them, with the hope that this doctor might also examine Arnold. The doctor detected Arnold's malfunctioning heart.

In growing up and living with our family, I recognized that there were always two sides to a story, or even more. Advancing into my teenage years, I learned more proof of that statement. However, when we learned of my mother's serious illness, each of my siblings would show their differences even more in response to the family situation. This affected the future balance of our family nest.

The adults, notably, middle row from left to right were my father, J.W.A. (Guillaume) Janssen, my mother, Riek Janssen-Koolhof, my grandfather, Jan Koolhof and my Aunt Jo, (Sister Romualda Koolhof). The children, notably, front row, from left to right were my sister Rie, my brother Andre laying with legs extended at the front, and myself, Sibylla, snuggled to the right of my Aunt Jo. The photo was taken on April 15, 1926, and we were gathered for a twelve and a half year celebration of Aunt Jo's commitment to being a nun.

Chapter Two: The 1930s: Our Mother and Life at Home

I faced many uncertain feelings as I reached my fourteenth year in life. What mattered most were the relationships within my family, but there was an underlying wish to make friends with the people with whom I attended school. We exchanged our support and trust as we shared our stories. I learned from one of my girlfriends that her mother died during the Spanish flu pandemic, and she said that her family was never the same afterward. I hoped that our mother would be with us always.

My Education in the 1930s

We moved to the Diepenweenseweg in 1929, after living eight years on the Niewstraat. The timing coincided, unfortunately, with my father's pottery business suffering financially. Our lives were humbled with fewer luxuries. The decline would be hard to measure, but my father either purchased too much earthenware from Germany, or made too many pots, or the market for pottery may have just been slowing down. My father was devastated to know that he needed help to pay off his accumulated debts. The financial rescue came from both sides of the family, the Koolhofs and the Janssens. Aunt Marie (Koolhof) offered one of the houses that she owned, for us to live in, and I was the person who always brought her the rent cheque.

There were not too many changes in our habits after the move. In the beginning, Rie and I remained at Saint Bernard's School, and the boys attended the new Parish School of the Blessed Heart Church. As I was maturing, ever since I could remember, my mother treated us as adults in a patient and ungrudging manner. In her wise opinion, she recommended that I study commercial business and languages, and attend night classes at the Commercial Evening School from six to nine o'clock, to learn how to improve my skills. That is how I decided at twelve years of age to take stenography, typing, French, English, and German during both day and night school, with the idea that the more diplomas I acquired, the easier it would be to get a better paying job.

My evening classes were small, and I grew up getting to know the other eleven girls. We used to go to each other's homes to study together, two weeks at a time in each home. We were a close-knit group, and we got to know each other very well, as we met everyone's parents and siblings and intermingled with each one's home habits. We discussed everything: parents, boys who were our age in each of our families, teachers who were boring and how we thought we knew better, our goals after graduating, and even politics. Without a clue to understanding the effects of the stock market crash or the long-lasting effects it had on society, we continued to enjoy each other's opinions, if we had any. My girlfriends and I graduated at the same time.

Developing such friendships was a source of strength during my school years, work years, and even later in married life. On the other hand, my brothers did not attend their high school daytime classes, as was true for many boys their age at the time. Instead, they worked at a paying job during the day and studied in the evenings at the Commercial School to receive their high school certificates.

My Mother's Counsel and Life at Home

My parents knew that we were not exceptional intellects. Therefore, they took on a diligent responsibility to teach us life skills at home. They taught us how to deal with daily life challenges as needed. For example, I was sure that my brothers knew that they were causing discomfort when the police reminded our parents about their unacceptable behaviour. By listening attentively to my brothers' extravagant stories, my mother would counsel not to repeat their disruptions to the neighbours. She would not absolve them immediately from their wrong choices. She and my father agreed to allow time for guilt to simmer, and they hoped that the boys would turn around independently. My brothers would need to choose between right and wrong on their own.

In my situation, my mother used to tell me to take pride in myself. This teaching filtered down to the way I chose to dress, always smartly, and how I learned to speak more articulately with others. Early parental lessons made lasting imprints on all their children. It was their way of pushing us out into the world, and teaching us to take ownership of the consequences for all our actions.

In my childhood, my mother counseled me to search for happiness, but I did not know what she really meant until I settled to believe that happiness was staring me right in the face. For example, the gift of laughter came in my discussions with my girlfriends. Or happiness was the feeling of contentment, walking with my brother Andre when he could no longer walk on his own. Or happiness was the beauty of nature, as I absorbed and gazed at a budding flower bush in the springtime. I had deep satisfaction in spending quality time with my parents, siblings, and friends. I felt that I was doing what I most wanted to do in my life already at this young age. I was learning to make decisions with confidence, and this proved a good thing for me when choosing what I wanted to do later in my life.

I remember some of my best girlfriends, Gerda Roebbers, Betty Wetveman, Sini Fifi, Betty Koster and Rie Krude. I would often compare the progress of my life with each of my friends' life stories. For example: Rie Krude's mother died during the Spanish flu pandemic, which spread all over Europe. We were told that soldiers, domiciled in closed quarters, fueled the pandemic towards the end of the Great War in 1918. Millions died. Rie lost her mother when was a toddler, and she never recovered. She grew up with that devastating reality. When we studied in our group every night, Rie found security with her girlfriends when discussing her situation. It was her way of coping.

After our move, we continued to visit our relatives. Not that we needed an excuse for a visit, but birthday parties were celebratory times in our family. On one occasion, my Opa (grandfather) Janssen was throwing a birthday party. His three daughters living with him organized a theatrical presentation. All the attending grandchildren had to create a personal poem, memorize it, and present it on his birthday. Every Sunday afternoon, for two months, we visited our aunts to oversee and correct the poems. I also had to practice the formality of bowing smartly before I started to recite. If I did not bend deeply enough, I needed to listen attentively and obey my aunts without any reservations on just how they wanted me to bow correctly.

Finally, the day arrived, and I was suddenly aware of people watching me from their chairs as I stared back at them. I looked around them, searching for the safe refuge of my Opa's face. And he nodded with approval, perhaps more to nudge me on than to simply hurry things up. I started, and there was no going back. Soon I was finished, and as I handed over my written poem to Opa, I gave him my biggest "Happy Birthday, Opa" hug. He was so pleased. I adored my Opa Janssen and remembered him very well. He died two years later, in 1932, when I was fourteen years old.

Six years after moving to the rented house from Aunt Marie Koolhof on the Diepenveenseweg, my youngest sister Greet was born on November 4, 1929. I never thought that I would have the opportunity to see a baby as adorable as my new sister, just about ten years younger than I. And there she was, beautiful and healthy.

We had some more good news, at least for me. We were going to move again, and I would not have to visit my Aunt Marie to bring her that monthly rent cheque. On my last visit with her, I did not care to wait long enough, suspecting a mortifying expression on her face. We moved to the Hoge Hondstraat, where part of the street was still farmland which also belonged to the Koolhof family. But then, the Janssen territory came with four mischievous boys who would jump and romp in the hay stocks, joining all the other neighbourhood children. They invented new pranks to play on people, and before you knew it, everyone got to know the four Janssen boys again. They were always together. And the police, without fail, would arrive at our doorstep, blaming one or all of them for the unfriendly trouble they were causing.

My Beloved Mother

It seemed my mother had cancer for quite a few years. She perhaps knew her time on earth was shorter than expected, as she was in and out of the hospital many times. Once when I visited her hospital room (I found it easily because it was the first room to the right of the hospital entrance), I had an interesting request from my mother, and a disturbing incident shortly thereafter.

My mother said to me, "Here, here are a few pennies. Buy whatever you want from it."

Not much later, after my visit and leaving the room, the nuns, who were the nurses, overheard what she had said to me, and they demanded I give them the money. I never understood why they would do that to a young girl whose mother was dying. I was unhappy, and the incident lingered in my memory for years to come.

The cancer was corroding inside my mother. Her last piece of advice was her show of humility in acceptance of her pain in her battle with life. She was lying in bed in our living room, and her sister, my Aunt Marie, stayed with her every night. Early one morning, in January of 1933, my father called us immediately to come downstairs and sit around my mother's bed, because she would not live much longer. While we prayed, I heard my father say that she had taken her last breath. We immediately darkened the room so that it was almost black inside, as was the custom in the Netherlands. They held the funeral at the Blessed Heart Catholic Church in Deventer. Andre was too sick to go, and Greet was too young to attend. The funeral marked the beginning of a new journey in my life. At the age of fourteen, was I grown up enough to weather the first storm of my life?

Our motherless family created disturbances in our lives. We had many changes. It began with my father experimenting with the help of a lady he hired to do the cooking and cleaning in the household. All did not go well, and after a month, my father decided to split us up: four of the seven children would go to the relatives, who agreed to give the needed support. Three of the children, Rie, Andre, and Greet, would stay at home. Rie was seventeen years old, and she would take on a motherly role for Andre and baby Greet.

Within a month, Andre became too much for Rie, who tried her utmost to take on a leadership role in the family. My father, who desperately aimed to put things back together, struggled with the decision to take his eldest son, Andre, to a home for the mentally disabled at Saint Josef's Stichting in the town of Apeldoorn. Being away from home caused Andre's mental and physical health to deteriorate quickly. Andre died within six months, in October 1933. His exact illness was not recorded, and we all knew that he died of the pain, the sorrow, and the feelings of helplessness over our mother's death. A reversal in the happiness of our home was slowly taking place – an inevitable split-up.

My brother Jan went to Uncle Jacob Janssen and Aunt Dorothea, and he felt at home playing with his two cousins, one of whom was about my age. The other was about six years older than me. The three unmarried

Janssen aunts spoiled Guillaume. All three aunts lived together on the Kromme Kerkstraat, where they owned and managed a sewing workshop. Because of their frugal lifestyle, they had accumulated a considerable fortune, money to purchase land and a few houses. Arnold felt at home at Aunt Dien's. She was my mother's youngest and kindest sister.

Of the four of us, I would be the least happy, because my father sent me to Aunt Marie, with whom I did not have a good relationship. Living on the Powelandstraat, I would wake up in the mornings shivering, having spent sleepless nights during the cold and damp spring mornings. Aunt Marie refused to put on the furnace on the upper floor, where I had my bedroom. She would occasionally make homemade bread for me, but most of the time, she did nothing else to help better our relationship. Aunt Marie preferred to stay in bed all day long. During this period, I spent a lot more time after school with my girlfriend Rie Krude.

The experience that followed next changed my life forever. I think the pain of my mother's loss was too overwhelming for me. I must have gone through shock for a long time, and from there to disbelief and then to profound sadness all at different times during the five months that I was at Aunt Marie's. I had no one to talk to except my dear friend Rie Krude, who had gone through the same feelings when growing up in a motherless family.

After half a year, my siblings and I were sent home for a little while. One day, I started to feel eerie loneliness while the entire family had gone out, except for my sister Rie. A pain was creeping all over my body, making it difficult for me to breathe or even think straight. I thought I was going crazy, having never felt this ill in my life. Finally, dizziness forced me to lie down on the nearest couch.

"I'm dying—I'm dying—!" I exhaled. I panicked with each breath of air.

Thankfully, my sister heard me and called the doctor immediately. Then, while I was still hysterical, my brothers came into the house, and I remembered hearing them screaming in fear, "Sibylla is dying!"

I was sure they had never witnessed anyone more frantic.

I was diagnosed with an anxiety disorder, and my recovery lasted six months. I was not even allowed to go to school. But while my health was improving, I still had bad days, where negative feelings were brought on by horrific nightmares about the untimely deaths of my brother Andre, my mother, and my grandfather. I questioned why God took them away all at the same time. I was troubled over what the future would hold for me.

Then, for the first time in my life, I was at a crossroads, and change was necessary. So I decided to put my idle negative thoughts of family deaths on permanent pause, to allow for my being to evolve. I was going to survive, and I committed myself to that wish. I could see a glimmer of hope. Before I trudged off to school in the late fall, I confidently thought of how I wanted to be and what I wanted to do in my life. I thoroughly convinced myself that achievers in life were those who did what others were afraid to do. I just needed an opening. So, while I waited, I planned to perform my normal daily activities, to trust my family, relatives, and friends, and keep the spiritual strength of my grandfather, mother, and brother in my prayers. I believed that life would resume to a new kind of rhythm and happiness.

New Home Life

Fourteen months after the death of my mother, I learned that my father was going to remarry. During my illness, he was dating someone, which explained why he was away a lot from our home. I thought my sister knew all about the relationship while I was sick. My new stepmother was going to be Gezina Klein Beernink. All my siblings arrived home two months before the wedding. There was quite an excitement, not only for the upcoming nuptials, but also because my siblings were happy to be together again after living separately with our relatives. My father and Gezina were married in the Blessed Heart Catholic Church, and we sat in the same pews, about the fifth row from the front, as we had for our mother's funeral in the same church. Rie and I were bridesmaids, and little Greet was the flower girl. Our father and our new mother went on a honeymoon for two weeks to Tegelen, where my father had been born. There was no extravagance, however, in that Depression year of 1934.

Home life began to change before my father and Gezina returned from their honeymoon. Life pulsed a different energy when Gezina delivered on her promise to her parents before they died. She had promised to take care of her eldest unmarried sister Riek, now of the age of forty. Gezina was the only one who could handle her sister's loud and expansive spirit, and that was how Aunt Riek became part of our family. But unfortunately, my brothers did not feel the same compassion for her, and they developed more confidence in pranking and teasing of their new aunt. For two weeks, they continually made fun of her. It first started with Aunt Riek's pet parrot.

Aunt Riek would say to her parrot, "Lorrie, Lorrie, my sweet little Lorrie, sing for me!"

My three brothers endlessly echoed, "Lorrie, Lorrie, my sweet little Lorrie, sing for me!" until she would be in tears.

My father returned home from the honeymoon to work at the pottery factory, and Gezina addressed and met her new family. I do not know what kind of married life she imagined for herself, or how she pictured herself suddenly as a mother to six children. I supposed I could have asked, but I did not. In any case, at that time, I was slowly distancing myself from my father and Gezina. I was becoming less inclined to disclose every thought in my head. As for my devilish brothers, Arnold, Guillaume, and Jan, now aged ten, twelve, and fourteen, they continued to make life miserable for Aunt Riek. Finally, after two years of intolerance in our home, Aunt Riek moved to her brother's house on the Groote Overstraat, and from there, she went to an institution in Diepenveen and later to Zutphen. It was peaceful at our home after Aunt Riek left.

Everyone in our family had their own means of healing after the passing of my mother. For me, I wanted to build a new foundation in my life, something like finding a new anchor to keep me focussed. I felt that the process of healing had already begun, with a strong feeling that my mother was personally guiding me with her heavenly counsel. I knew that I was headed in the right direction when I decided that education was the answer. I would learn the skills to make me job eligible.

These undergrads were my classmates in evening commercial school throughout the pre-war years. The date was July 26, 1934, a few days following our highly esteemed M.U.L.O. exam. I was in the back row, second from the left.

My youth was memorable because I took my education seriously. Education gave me the confidence to tell my father what I wanted to do and where I wanted to go in my life. I was determined to earn a living and bring home a wage that I could use to buy whatever I wanted— first, things needed for sustainability, and later, items of a more frivolous nature. I had the willpower and fearless attitude to move away from Deventer for a job, even though the politics and underlying tragic forces of Nazi Germany dictated that I should have been more careful in my choices.

Job Hunting

My high school experience cost nothing, because my father declined my request to go to boarding school. We could not afford that luxury, he told me. Routinely, every morning while getting up and preparing for school, I asked myself what I wanted to do with my life. At school, I would peek through the classroom window and watch men and women dressed in smart outfits of suits and skirts, rushing here and there with determined faces. They were the professionals going to work—the teachers, the nurses, or the lawyers my father suggested I became when I grew up. My father also said that I could stay at home to work in the family pottery business, or I could go out of town to Alkmaar, to stay with our family friends and go to school to learn about the floral industry. I collected and absorbed bits of information, sorting out where my strengths were, to see what was invisible to me. I finally decided to work in an established company or a government office.

At age eighteen, I was qualified in languages and commercial education. I built my confidence over the years, managing good grades, liking my teachers, and not being afraid to raise my hand to ask questions in class. I felt safe and smart. My freedom from uncertainty allowed me to stand up to my father. I asked for his blessing in my challenging search for a company job. The market was limited in options, since these were the Depression years of the 1930s, and I knew that employers were hiring only the best. I had some doubts, but I ground away.

One evening, as I was having dinner at home, the discussion led to my job-hunting progress. There were eleven graduates in my commercial school class, and when we saw an advertisement for a job opening, all eleven of us would stand in a line for the post. We all had training in a mixture of subjects and languages. When we all applied at once for a position with Noury and Van Der Lande, a research laboratory and chemical outfit with fifty employees in Deventer, no one received acceptance. We knew that the envied position was the reward of an inside connection. So, my father suggested speaking to my cousin Truus Janssen, who worked at a meat company called Lindhurst. This business was a half-hour bike ride from home. I applied, and true to the theory of knowing someone on the inside, I landed my very first job.

My Very First Money-Earning Job

There were five employees in the office, and I was the sixth. The job entailed accounts receivable and payable, and they wrote all invoices with pen and paper. Because there were no adding machines or computers to help make calculations, I needed to work out all the numbers in my head. Before we sent out the invoices, we would meticulously proofread each other's work. I liked it, especially when I could find a mistake made by one of my colleagues. I met some interesting people there, one person being Ep Pothaar, who lived a few houses away from where I lived on the Diepenveenseweg. He would weave in and out of my life as it unfolded.

I was the youngest employee in the company, and one would think that I would have more energy than the others. Everyone laughed that I would get exhausted while on the job, and I thought nothing of putting my head down on my desk to take a short nap. But then, one day, it was not so funny when my boss came into the office, stomping heavily on the floor, loudly enough to draw attention for all to hear.

"Which Miss Janssen needs an alarm clock?" he said.

Everyone laughed at his comment, appreciating his sense of humour. We worked hard, but we also had a lot of fun together. I stayed there for nine months.

My Second Job

My second job was at the department store chain Vroom & Dressman. In the office, I completed invoices again, in addition to the filing and the pricing of goods. They were quite strict there and would not tolerate errors, which would cost you your job. For that reason, I always double-checked my work. The office, located on top of the store, closed at six thirty in the evening. During the Christmas season, beginning at the end of November, the office employees would help in the store. My specific job was to sell books in the children's section, and on Saturdays, I worked as a cashier. During the off-season, I worked once every third Saturday.

Like many teenagers and young adults in the workforce, I moved around the neighbourhood with more independence, and I felt less tied to my parents and family. I would bicycle with a girlfriend to the local dance club to take ballroom dance classes. I also ran errands for Gezina to help with the household. With these new freedoms came new vulnerabilities, and I learned to keep my chin up if I passed a group of men, perhaps looking at me with interest. I knew to ignore their looks, and I learned never to walk or cycle alone at night.

My parents conceded that their children were growing up and that we needed more space to live. However, we remained to share our bedrooms because there was no space. We felt impingement on our privacy, but life was that way with most of my friends at the time. I supposed my parents were happy with my siblings and me, as we were ambitious enough to get out into the working world to bring in some money to help pay the family bills.

I made a few friends at Vroom & Dressman, such as Dickie Hoogstraten, who worked in the same invoicing department as I. Since we both had a two-hour lunch break from twelve to two o'clock, we would cycle together to our homes for lunch, and then she would stop by my house, from where we would bike together for our return trip, often taking the shortcut through the company's new garden.

Then I met Jasper Kijk, who lived in Nijmegen but moved to Deventer to volunteer in the community and board with the Winkels family. We somehow had decided we liked each other, and I enjoyed that feeling of my first love. I felt a zing of anticipation every time I saw him. However, there was nothing earthshattering about our first kiss. It was real and fun, and I detected that having a boyfriend was a rich and meaningful experience. However, there was a rule at work, and that rule was that you could not date anyone in the same company. Because both of us worked at Vroom & Dressman, one or both of us could lose our job if anyone saw us together, so we always dated in secret.

One day, a high-level boss in my department named Mr. Rebers, from a well-known Dutch family, aggravated me. There was a tradition within the company whereby the youngest employee had to pick up mail at the post office during their lunchtime break. Because I was the youngest of the group, I was supposed to do that job. Unfortunately, I did not always concentrate on my added workload, and so I would occasionally forget the mail for him. Perhaps I had my mind elsewhere, or I was simply tired and needed the lunch break. But messing up on this extra chore that particular day put me into the bad books of an important person in the company.

The long working hours were beginning to take their toll on me, and the work was way too busy in the store with so few employees working harder and longer hours because of reduced numbers. Wages for a beginning employee were low, at only fifteen to eighteen guilders monthly (thirteen to fifteen dollars). Since I had worked there for two and a half years, I received twenty-five to thirty guilders monthly (sixteen to twenty dollars). My boss thought that he paid too much, and that high school graduates could replace me more cheaply. Many of us "old-timers" were unhappy, and I was eager to move on at the age of twenty-one. During the early summer of 1939, I was not getting any further. I wanted a new job, and I also wanted to move out of Deventer. So I decided to look elsewhere.

My Post in Velsen

My father, flooded with worry, disagreed. He argued that I should not take the book-keeping job offer in a family business in the town of Velsen. The family invited me to lodge in their home, where I would be working as well. My father discussed with our parish priest the status of the Catholic family where I would live. He discovered that my new boss was a member of the Dutch Nazi Party. Our priest informed my father that Nazi members were not welcomed in the Catholic church, and soon, everyone found out that my new employer was excommunicated.

But I was determined to work for this man and his family. I went against the advice of both my parish priest and my dear father. I had many sociopolitical conversations with my boss when the fear of war was more pronounced and Hitler's politics were in the air. My boss would travel to his firm in Germany to buy raincoats and other clothing, and after his return to the Netherlands, we had our talks. He knew that I attended mass regularly at the Catholic church, and he asked once what the priest was preaching during his sermon. He also wanted to know what my view was on the new Nazi political thinking. It felt as though my future could take on a different turn, but I did not give too much attention to the politics of time.

It was summer, and I wanted to enjoy my weekends in the bustling city of Amsterdam. I could easily take the twenty-kilometre east train ride from Velsen to visit many friends and relatives. My sister Rie lived and worked in Amsterdam with a family of eight children. She planned to study nursing, but she found out that she had serious diabetes after much medical testing. Being that ill lessened her chances of being accepted at nursing college, so she settled to help take care of a family. Rie lived in an old house located across from the Amsterdam Central Railway Station beside the Saint Nicholas Church, which was close to the Amsterdam red light district. I used to wonder what the eight children were thinking when they gazed beyond the backyard to see some ladies behind shop windows dancing and showing off their "goods."

Life was wonderful during that summer, before the war officially broke out in early September. I made several train trips to go home to Deventer. I also purchased a beautiful bicycle from my own earned money and cycled many times to Nijmegen with my friends Bep Scheltinga and Gerda Roebbers, my classmates from commercial school. We cycled to Gerda's parents' quite often, and once, Bep and I met two young fellows along the way. I was immediately attracted to one of them, Joe Veils, but so were all my girlfriends. I bought a new jacket for my first visit with his parents at his family-owned jewelry store in Amsterdam. My friends and I always had exciting bicycle trips until we found out about an air raid from German warplanes that bombed the area of the jewelry store of Joe Veil's family. I never saw him again.

World War II was on.

I enjoyed working at the Amsterdam office of the Gerson clothing store for two years during the war (1941-1943). The picture was taken on April 7, 1941, and I was on the far right.

Chapter Four: Finding Work During World War II

Even though activities I took for granted became less safe, and the Netherlands deteriorated under German occupation, I took my jobs seriously, and I always found work posts. World War II brought many hectic situations, even to my hometown. The landscape of the war changed for the worse as each day passed. It was a war between life and death, and the end of the war was far beyond a sprinkle of hope.

Velsen and the Beginning of World War II

At about this time, the uncertainty of the political arena displayed itself with talk of war in northern Europe. Adolf Hitler and his Nazi Party had massively mobilized his armies to crush Poland and kept it under cruel occupation. After Christmas of 1939 and the beginning of 1940, the situation had already worsened. Unidentified planes flew over Velsen and Amsterdam, and alarms would go off.

There were shelters specially built for the citizens of Velsen. The privileged ones who entered the shelters first plunged to the deepest and safest part of the shelter. The last ones to enter had greater fears of debris falling on them, putting their lives in danger. I and the mother and two sons where I worked and stayed, were the last group of people always to enter. My boss was not allowed, because everyone knew that he was a member of the Nazi Party. We considered ourselves lucky to be there. After war was declared on Germany by Great Britain and France, we needed to enter the shelters more often.

Then one spring morning, May 10, 1940, there were German soldiers everywhere. The invasion of the Netherlands by the Nazi German army had taken place. The Germans bombed Rotterdam five days later, and the Dutch forces surrendered. However, that day, I noticed with wonder and confusion that many Dutch people were friendly, waving at the German soldiers, my landlady and her children included, but not my employer who was out of town that day. Then I became worried as

I asked myself: were there divided loyalties among the Dutch people, between the West of our country and the East and the North? I was from the East, so I did not understand what was going on. I had no idea why the Dutch people in the Northwest were so friendly to German occupiers. My answer came as a surprise. It was because of the location of the town of Velsen.

Velsen is a geographically divided town located on either side of the North Sea channel, in province of North Holland. Most importantly, it was easy to catch a boat here to cross over the English Channel and land on the southern shores of England. Since Velsen was the closest Dutch port town to the south shores of England, German warplanes used it as a target for bombing. The plan was to prevent people from immediately escaping to England by boat. I found out why the Dutch people were waving in a friendly manner. It was a disguise to protect the Jewish people seeking an exit from the country. The Dutch people invited the Jewish people to their homes and diverted attention away from the German army.

The many rich Jewish families who lived in Velsen and the families who arrived from Amsterdam by car hoped to escape by boat to England. Those driving from Amsterdam searched for garages for the safekeeping of their vehicles. One free garage was at the place where I lived. My boss had departed for Germany, and he was unlikely to return soon because crossing the border took much more time. Consequently, the garage would be available for an unknown length of time, and one of the Jewish families—mother, father and two children—

borrowed the garage to park their car. I remembered the conversation:

"Could I park my car here? Could I pick it up after the war?" the father asked.

My landlady replied, "Of course you can."

They joined other families who boarded small boats at the docks to take them across the Channel to the safety of England. The number of people was in the thousands during those first few weeks in the spring of 1940. However, all the boats that left the dock at that time never saw the shores of England. They were all torpedoed by Nazi German warplanes.

My Work at the Jewish Clothing Store

I saw an advertisement for office work at a Jewish clothing store named Gerson in Amsterdam, situated in the middle of the Jewish business area in the fashion district on the famous Kalverstraat. I was more than ready to move to Amsterdam after working in Velsen for only six months. In May 1940, my Aunt Eugenie Bernards, a teacher in Amsterdam, invited me to stay with the family with low rental costs. I felt comfortable moving because I also got along well with my cousin Pete living there. In Amsterdam, the Bernards lived on the Prinsengracht within a short biking distance to the Gerson store. I applied for the job, was immediately accepted, and my wage earnings increased from thirty guilders to seventy-five guilders.

I learned why they hired me so quickly at Gerson. Their Jewish employees were disappearing from their jobs, and they needed people to fill them. As each day went by, one or two more employees went missing. By the end of February of 1941, the Germans arrested several hundred Jews and deported them from Amsterdam to Buchenwald and Mauthausen concentration camps. The arrests and the brutal treatment shocked the population of Amsterdam. Could things get worse at the store? They did.

When I arrived for work, I noticed Gerson employees were standing at the entrance to the store, questioned by a group of people I later learned were Dutch communists and other worker organization activists. They were planning a general strike against the German administration. They questioned me as well. Our store and many other large factories, transportation systems, and public services came to a standstill on February 25, 1941.

But the Germans did not stand for it, and they suppressed the strike after three days, followed by more disappearances of workers. The Dutch city administration, railway workers, and the Dutch Nazi Party all cooperated with the final deportation. If you were an employee of the Jewish council in Amsterdam, the Germans immediately ordered you for deportation. Things worsened when many Jewish people did not comply with the suppression rule, and the Germans sealed off the Jewish quarter to round up the people. Some 25,000 Jews, including about 4,500 children, went into hiding to evade deportation. Nearly a third were discovered and arrested.

I worked at Gerson for two years, and I had an overall good experience there. In the beginning, I enjoyed the office personnel and living in the largest city in the Netherlands. Unfortunately, the war continually created problems, and in the spring of 1943, the Germans removed the store managers. I decided to leave Amsterdam to live with my family in Deventer. When I left the job, the remaining office girls gave me a memorable departure gift, a dozen silver "Advocaat" spoons. (Advokaat is a typical Dutch alcoholic beverage, a kind of eggnog too thick to drink. One uses a spoon to help consume it.) I continued correspondence with two of the girls there for a long time after. I was twenty-four years old when I left.

I Searched for Work in the Dutch Government

It was spring of 1943 when I returned to the Hoge Hondstraat, the street where my family lived in Deventer. I searched for work in the Dutch government, and I was successful. The job was within the small Deventer office of the price control department. Soon, I would be transferred to Groningen, a town in the north, where the bigger price control offices moved from The Hague, the capital of the Netherlands. However, before moving, I would experience impending danger in my hometown.

Deventer had deteriorated because of the German occupation. I had already realized that on my short trips to my hometown from Amsterdam. As a result, food became scarce, and my brother Guillaume traded clay sauerkraut pots that we sold in the pottery factory for eggs from the nearby chicken farmers. We received flour to make bread also through the bartering system. However, we were new at making bread, and we did not have the proper kitchen utensils to make it.

Meanwhile, my brother Arnold found a special apparatus at his girlfriend's, Gerda Haverkamp, whose family owned a hardware store where they sold this type of bread-making apparatus. Gerda decided to give the device to us. But things had worsened in Deventer, and there were many restrictions. German families needed supplies and other goods, so they took them away from the Dutch owners. We would not have this apparatus for long.

One day, two German soldiers rang our doorbell. I opened the door. My stepmother Gezina was standing at the end of the hallway. The soldiers ordered her to stay where she was and asked if we had flour in the house. Since she did not answer immediately, one soldier began a search on the ground floor, and the other searched the upstairs rooms. They were ruthless in their search, and when they finished, they showed us not the flour, but the bread-making apparatus. The Germans kept accurate records about everything that was bought and sold in our country.

Their records were so accurate because most workers who kept them were Dutch employees. Alcohol was also becoming scarce, and if you owned a bottle of gin, the Germans would first ask where you had obtained it, and then they would confiscate it. One of my jobs in the government price control department, under German control, was to record where and when they seized the highly prized Dutch Genever Gin.

It was becoming less safe to do the things we took for granted. An example was the "war garden." A bridge took you to the other side of the Ijssel River, where Deventer dwellers created gardens including vegetables, fruit, herbs, and flowers to supplement food rations and boost morale. People living on the city side of Deventer traveled over the bridge to their gardens. The trip became increasingly dangerous. Taking a bike would target you on two accounts: bikes were a valuable means of transportation, and bags of any food were a necessary commodity. Ria Peters, my future sister-in-law, risked her life with these errands. Sometimes she came home with food, other times not.

Our world, as we knew it, had changed. One day, while I was outside the house to get some fresh air, I saw a German soldier riding on his bike. He was not an ordinary-looking man. He must have weighed over 300 pounds. I unwittingly said aloud in Dutch, "Look at that fat one!"

The soldier sprang off his bike, ran towards our house, about thirty feet from where he dropped his bike, and yelled at me.

"Fat one? Oh! No you don't! If I wanted, I could send you to one of the concentration camps!"

My supposedly innocent remark filled my stomach with fear. I darted into the house as fast as I could, hoping nothing would come out of the incident. I was lucky, this time.

Moving to Groningen

After working in Deventer for four months, the government transferred offices to Groningen for security reasons, including the price control department. My job remained the same, and by this stage in my life, my skills had improved. I was meticulous in my work, skilled at invoicing, and I analysed financial spreadsheets quickly and accurately. I also spoke German fluently and was better equipped in translations because of this. Other employees typed more slowly, made many mistakes, were less fluent in German, and wasted time restarting their assignments. As a result, they chose me with four others, including two lawyers, to go to the Groningen office. I was proud to be working in my country's government.

What was currently happening in the Dutch monarchy in The Hague? The Netherlands was a monarchy. During the initial unrest in 1939, Queen Wilhelmina was forced to flee the country to stay in London, England, where she ran the Dutch government until after the war. Her daughter, Princess Juliana, with her two young daughters, were invited to stay in Canada. They lived in the capital city of Ottawa for the duration of the war. A third Princess was born to her there in the Dutch embassy, and she was declared a Dutch citizen. For many years in the future, the new Queen Juliana, grateful for how Canada welcomed her and her family, sent hundreds of Dutch tulip bulbs in gratitude to Ottawa every year. Her eldest daughter, as Queen Beatrix, and later the new monarch, King Willem-Alexander, continued the tradition.

The government found rooming houses for us in Groningen. I was lucky enough again in my life to meet and live with kind and accommodating people. There were ten of us in the rooming house, and we leaned on each other for support when we needed it. There was little in the way of entertainment, and going out to restaurants was out of the question. Making meals was a highlight of our day, with the minimal portions of food available. Fortunately, I had certain food privileges in the department where I worked. They freely gave me foods such as coffee, sugar beets, sugar, butter, and gin. These items were not always available to the Dutch, even if you had enough coupons to buy them. I would bring them to the rooming house and use them for trading for other foods. With Genever Gin, for instance, I traded four bottles for a pound of butter, which was extraordinary.

We were lucky to have a working coal-burning stove at the office. On that stove, I learned to make something delicious out of the sugar beets. I prepared them by cooking them until they were almost dry, which created delicious beet jam or beet butter. Even though I was never a good cook, I always remembered the recipe. I divided most of it at work, and the few containers left over, I gave to our landlord, my roommates, and my family, who were quite happy to have something to spread on their bread to give more taste. Incidentally, the bread was tasteless and mushy, because one mixed it with a lot of water. I was happy at the workplace, and our boss was kind to the five of us. We were grateful to have heat and enough food to survive.

It was my job to make deliveries of government papers throughout the Netherlands for the price control department. To do that, I used the train system for transportation to go to the designated cities. I was not afraid for my life, because I did not think about the reality of the war, and I trusted the safety of the train system in The Netherlands. I was wrong.

German soldiers were always shooting at the trains. They did that to prevent the trains from arriving on time to their destinations. Once I was on the Dutch train that was delivering food to Germany. The train was dirty and overfilled with many men and few women. At one of the train stops, German soldiers boarded unexpectedly and shouted at us to disembark immediately. We were to stay overnight at the train station, where we heard that the Allies were unexpectedly shooting at the train. But fortunately, the train was only impaired and not destroyed. The next day, we could embark and continue 120 kilometres further on to Deventer.

I used to carry gifts for my aunts and friends on my trips, and this time, I collected four bottles of precious salad oil, one for my girlfriend's parents in Groningen (Metje Kwakenbrug) and three others for my aunts in Deventer. I was lucky that the soldiers did not confiscate them while I was on the train.

It turned out that there were many things I had yet to learn in life, or at least life during this ongoing, miserable war. My eagerness to deliver government papers had diminished, and thoughts of quitting my job played in my mind. However, one more delivery job called me. The chief executive to the whole country's delivery system asked me to accompany him on the next German delivery train to Deventer. I decided to go with him.

Unfortunately, the train came to an abrupt halt. We felt a sharp hit by either flying V-1 bombs or V-2 missiles by the Allies. We were near Zwolle, a town centrally located in the Netherlands, and we were all rushed to disembark and stay overnight in a school. I remembered holding on tightly to my little overnight suitcase, looking at the old and faded coloured bulletin boards in the classroom where they sent us. The minutes turned into hours as I fell in and out of sleep. The only security that I felt was the sight of my boss, who was seated in the next row of desks, also trying to get some sleep. Early morning of the next day, we waited to embark on the same train and, to our relief, it continued to Deventer. I delivered the papers for my department, but I did not know about what the reports were or why my boss had accompanied me.

Then came another delivery mission. I would witness destruction from the bombings on my street where I lived in Deventer. I probably should not have taken the job, as I was completely alone. Unexpectedly, as the train slowed down before stopping at the station, a bomb from the air blasted one of the train cars. I saw a smoky cloud overtaking the train after the hit. Along with many other passengers pushing and shoving, I managed to get off the train. I sensed that more danger was about to come. My mind jabbed at the thought that I should have quit the job when I had the chance.

I was nervous about arriving at my parents' home, and I ran towards the train station and onward along the familiar path to the Hoge Hondstraat. I said a little prayer to Saint Jude to keep me safe. Then I arrived within view of my home. There was not a single person to be seen on the street. I called out names, expecting an answer. There was nothing. I noticed tree-like formations of dusty clouds where a bomb had hit the ground at the end of the street. I walked more closely to the shapes on the ground. I discovered that they were either injured or dead people. I did not know how many people were killed that day because of the bombings. I did not even recognize anyone where I stumbled. My mind went blank.

I never suspected that my job posts would lead me to witness such scenes of war. I innocently believed that I was truly protected, especially in my government job. However, my surviving family and friends had their stories to prove that war was a devasting stage in any one's life.

A family portrait on the Hoge Hondstraat in Deventer, the Netherlands (c.1946), where Greet and Arnold witnessed their neighbours killed by German soldiers on their last leg of fighting (April 10, 1945). From left to right were Rie (my sister), Arnold (brother), Guillaume (brother), Greet (sister), Frans Louis Peters (Jan's best friend), Gretel (sister-in-law), Jan (brother) and Wolfgang (Gretel and Guillaume's eldest son).

Chapter Five: Would the War Ever End?

The war would end, but not before the gunfire, bombing, and the human screams of fear exposed to the country that there had to be more suffering before there was peace. The final day of war had not yet arrived in our small country of the Netherlands, because the soldiers were still fighting—everywhere.

Mad Tuesday

Throughout the next year, until the end of the summer of 1944, I could only appreciate that I was lucky in the safety net of my government job in Groningen. On September 4, 1944, the Allies conquered Antwerp, a Belgian city close to the southern Dutch border. With radios, people could follow how the months of war were passing. Radios were supposedly confiscated by the Germans; however, as it turned out, a few people either hid and kept a radio or found one, despite the risk of being punished by the Germans. The Dutch people confirmed by radio that the Allies had entered Belgium, and were on their way to the Netherlands. Despite the threats, on September 5, 1944, many Dutch people in the southern provinces of Zeeland, Brabant, and Limburg celebrated on the streets while preparing to receive and cheer on the Allied liberators. The day was called "Dolle Dinsdag" (Mad Tuesday).

The Germans thought that the Canadians would walk through the Netherlands and imprison them immediately. All the German Nazis ran to Germany, literally ran with nothing but what they were wearing, in fear of the oncoming Canadians and Americans. Houses that they formerly occupied were left empty, and one of these Dutch Nazis from the north of the Netherlands bought the houses immediately from their German Kamarades, who left for Germany. This Dutch Nazi was my kind boss at the price control department. He bought several of the houses after the Dolle Dinsdag, and had the right to own them, since Germany still occupied the northern part of the Netherlands.

I remembered one of my conversations with this man very well, in which he explained why he believed in German supremacy.

"As you believe in your Catholic religion," he said, "I believe in Hitler, the head of the Nazi party."

At the end of the war, the Dutch officials picked him up, and I learned that he was in a prison camp for years. After that, I did not know what happened to him.

Operation Market Garden

As time marched on in the month of September 1944, the Allied plan was to advance across the Rhine River to liberate the north of the Netherlands. But it was also the plan of the enemy to overtake the same area. The Allied advance could not continue, as they had overextended themselves and, discouraged at the time, they had to halt in the south of the Netherlands. In their defeat, the liberation of the remaining Dutch territory was suspended until the next spring. The northern part of the Netherlands had to wait until May 5, 1945, for their liberation. The bombing and destruction from both sides continued terribly in Nijmegen, Arnhem, and in our hometown of Deventer. The Allies called their plan Operation Market Garden.

My cousin Wim Klein Beernink, living and working for the Red Cross in Deventer at the time, was caught in the middle of that ongoing battle. He was eighteen years old. He wrote a memoir for his grandchild Paul to read in his history class at school. In one part of the memoir, he referred to the bombings in Deventer. It read:

"The idea was to land behind German lines, reorganize and push onward into Germany. It just did not work out that way. The battle of Arnhem was a total disaster, and thousands of Allied forces died or got wounded. The book and movie *A Bridge Too Far* was based upon this last battle. Weeks later, I was near Arnhem and saw jeeps, cannons, and even parachutists still hanging in the trees. From then on, the trains stopped running, and transportation generally was at a standstill, so I could not go back to work.

"I became a member of the Red Cross, complete with helmet and armband, which got me to many places. I joined the Home Guard to protect our Catholic hospital. We also worked in a converted school, open to refugees mostly from the western part of the Netherlands.

"Our city, Deventer, was bombed quite often. American planes tried to hit the two bridges over the Ijssel River but were not successful. The result was that there were many civilian casualties. And then we were asked to assist the surgeons in the operating rooms, to help by holding down the wounded patients because there were not always enough anesthetics to give to them. The hospital nurses (Catholic nuns) were nervous, and the surgeons did not have much patience. They told the nuns to go instead to the chapel and pray. As young inexperienced men of war, one had to have nerves of steel and could not be afraid at the sight of so much blood."

I was in Deventer at this time as well. Every day, hundreds of planes would fly over my town. The Germans wanted to destroy bridges so that no Allied troops could walk over them. The English and the American air forces also wanted to destroy bridges so that no German troops could walk over them. I could see the planes as they closed in and grew louder when they flew lower. My first thoughts were always of worrying about my loved ones, and my second thoughts were of how I was going to place myself out of immediate danger. Fear would always settle in as I hoped and prayed that my life would be protected. I took the precaution of huddling near the closest building for safety and laying down as close to the ground as possible. When the planes were gone, I could stand up and walk away. That was quite a time.

In Deventer, we always questioned what was being bombed, while judging the direction of the planes. We never really knew. However, it became more obvious to us that the aircraft that flew during the afternoons were German. They were unsuccessful in destroying the two important bridges in Deventer.

After the Allies failed Operation Market Garden, there was continued deadlock in the fighting between the German and Allied troops. The frontline ran across the Betuwe region, a geographical area in the river delta formed by the Rhine and the Meuse River waters in Gelderland, where there was a small town named Tiel. Tiel was where my dear cousin Wim's future wife, Catherina (Tiny, pronounced Teeny) Vallinga, lived and struggled during the war. Tiel was in the middle of the Allied fire line for months, and the Allies needed to evacuate the people.

To prevent the Allies from moving any further, the Germans flooded the area by blowing up the dike. The rushing water submerged houses up to their roofs in the entire Betuwe region. Another dam had collapsed and gave the Germans their share of flooding. The winter of 1944-1945 was exceptionally wet and cold, and after three weeks, the Betuwe region froze and turned into a sea of ice. The production of food and crops diminished immensely during the German occupation. The Betuwe region was where you would hear about the Dutch citizens who were forced to survive by eating things like Dutch tulip bulbs.

The Nazis went so far as to restrict humanitarian aid coming into the country. This terrible winter, often called the Hunger Winter, was when thousands of people died. Although the fighting lasted through the winter, and generally it was more quiet than usual with only minor skirmishes, the situation in Tiel, still occupied by the Germans, had become unbearable for the Dutch inhabitants. Therefore, they needed to be evacuated to a safer place. Tiny, her sister Gonny, her brother Hein, and their mother were part of that evacuation. Tiny wrote a memoir also for her grandchild Paul to read in his school's history class:

"Trains stopped running; transports stopped going; the odd truck was still on the road until the gas ran out. My city of Tiel, close to Arnhem, then became the target for Allied shelling from across the river. Very sporadic at first, then more and more frequently. For protection, first, we went to the upstairs bedrooms to hide under the mattresses. Then we sometimes ended up altogether in the cellar, about ten of us. We laughed a lot, nervously, I suspected, about what we all were wearing, making sure that we had our warmest clothes on all the time. You never knew when you were going to be hit by those darn shells.

"They did a lot of damage to my little city of Tiel. There was no more electricity, and we made do with some hoarded candles, some coal, some wood, and less and less food. We played an awful lot of cards and Monopoly. We tried to get our rations of bread which was awful but edible, sometimes some milk or margarine, and some vegetables from farmers in the area. While taking the chance to get the food, we often had to dive into the side road ditches or doorways of peoples' homes when the shelling started up again.

"Every day we heard of people we knew who were killed or maimed. I was twenty years old at the time. My brother was seventeen and at this age, he had to disappear from this city. Otherwise, he would have been picked up to work in Germany. It was about the time also that good friends of ours, who worked for the Dutch underground, were picked up, put in jail and later shot for treason."

As the winter worsened and food became scarce in January 1945, the final decision was to evacuate the people in Tiel to the north of the Netherlands. Tiny, her family, and many other families boarded a hay wagon pulled by a lorry headed for the town of Zeist. Her mother suffered from rheumatism, and so they wrapped her up in blankets in the wagon amidst coats and suitcases. There was not enough room for everyone to sit in the wagon at one time, so they took turns to walk the thirty kilometres through deep snow and ice, a rare weather condition in the Netherlands. After camping out with others in a movie theatre in Zeist for about a week, they boarded a train headed for the northern province of Friesland. Lonely and weary from the train journey, they could lay down peacefully on fresh straw in the cattle barn of the family who offered them a place to stay for three more days. The farmer gave them fresh eggs, vegetables and better tasting bread, which was more than they ever could ask.

Tiny and her family moved on to stay with a family in the town of Heerenveen, Friesland. The Canadian Corps entered the province of Gelderland, which included Tiel, in early April. After many days of fighting, always resulting in deadly skirmishes, they managed to penetrate more cities in the area. But by April 10, 1945, the area was officially liberated. Only by early July, 1945, could all the evacuees return to their hometown. Like many other towns, Tiel had been largely turned into rubble. With their homes vandalized but still livable, life would go on. Tiny and her family were the lucky ones to come out alive from this sad part of history. They had to have been thankful to be in a small farming town to the north of the country while they waited for the Liberation.

In contrast, people suffered badly in that severe winter in the larger cities such as Amsterdam, Rotterdam, and The Hague. My aunt living in Amsterdam, who owned a house, rented an extra bedroom for two pounds of butter monthly. My aunt should have said she would rent for gold, as butter became a rarity in the city. Hundreds needed to go on foot to the farm country, searching for food or a place to live. Many of the Dutch who could not walk died of starvation.

Liberation Day in Deventer

What happened on Liberation Day in my hometown, Deventer? In the early spring of 1945, many German soldiers and Dutch sympathizers, all wearing civilian clothes, were still around in my hometown. No one could easily identify these enemy snipers. A typical fighting scene took place more inside the houses than outside in the streets. The Canadians would be first alerted by hearing or by seeing machine guns in the basement homes. Then, I saw the Canadian soldiers as they would go from one house to another, weapons always in hand.

Understanding the buildup to this scene demands a little background history. The railway bridge in Deventer was destroyed by Dutch engineers in the early spring of 1940 to prevent German armored troop train crossings over the Ijssel River. The German forces replaced it with a makeshift bridge, as it became part of the rail line passage for food and war materials. Only trains were allowed to cross, and the area around the bridge was considered a military area. Anyone who entered the area would be at risk of being shot. The Allied forces attempted to destroy the railway bridge around October 15, 1944. It was damaged, but it remained in usable condition. So bombs were coming down from the air, and there were bombs launched from the ground, many with inaccurate targeting. The result had a terrorizing effect on the civilians living in the vicinity of the bridge, particularly those living on the Hoge Hondstraat where I lived, less than a kilometre away.

During the final phase of the war, the reasoning for the bombing changed, because it was imperative now for the Allies to keep the railway bridge open for the path of the liberation armies. However, on April 6, 1945, the German forces thoroughly blew up the railway bridge with missiles from the ground.

The Liberation Day of Deventer took place on the 10th of April 1945. However, a lot happened in the early part of the afternoon of that day. The Canadian Liberation Army already secured the area of Schalkhaar, about five to ten kilometres from the old cemetery on the Hoge Hondstraat of Deventer. The Canadians arrived at Centurbaan Street, which crossed diagonally from our street to the northwest. They saw that the whole neighbourhood was standing and watching the Allied planes flying low overhead to bomb the German defence. The Canadians shouted at the Dutch people to get out of sight and run for safety because they were standing in a dangerous area.

At about two o'clock in the afternoon, loud explosions came from unexpected flying bombs or ground missiles. There were terrible screams from many people scattered on the streets and hiding in the house basements. Two of those people were my siblings, Arnold and Greet. Arnold was standing between Mr. van der Griendt (a father of fourteen children), and his friend Mr. Scheuter. Abruptly, Mr. van der Griendt and Mr. Scheuter both fell to the ground, presumably hit either by shrapnel or gunfire. They were both killed instantly. My younger sister Greet was close by, and she fell too, perhaps losing her footing and falling from weakness in her limbs from the site of the violent actions taking place around her.

Nevertheless, Greet miraculously fell under the protection of the bodies of the two men. She was alive. Arnold and others came immediately to the assistance of Greet and others who needed help. All were shocked and speechless. Would the survivors ever see life in the same way again? Eleven people died in this incident.

The fighting continued, my brother Arnold explained to us later, as the Canadian soldiers urged the people to take cover into the closest houses and warned them from wandering in the streets. They could hear and see the gunfire from the German soldiers, disguised as civilians, who were still shooting from basement house windows at random into the street. Many German soldiers bravely appeared on the road, running and shooting at Dutch citizens and Canadian soldiers.

Then the shooting stopped, followed by complete silence. Not a single sound. Slowly the Dutch citizens came out of their houses and basements to view the grim scene before them, a setting that would change their lives forever.

Liberation Day in Groningen

After eight months of fighting in the south, the Allied troops finally advanced into the northern provinces. I was still working in the government offices when we knew that the end of the war was nearing in April 1945. Groningen was one of the last places to be liberated by the Canadians. It was a difficult battle. Some say it was one of the largest urban battles of the war, with five times as many Canadian soldiers fighting directly in combat than in Ortona, Italy, in 1943.

Groningen is a city built in the late medieval period with narrow streets often limited to one-way traffic. It is completely enclosed by a wide canal, and most of the twelve bridges were destroyed or rendered inoperative by April 1945. The city had several canals entering from the south and west that posed obstacles to soldiers from these directions. Instead, the First Canadian Army moved northeast, supporting the flank of the British Second Army as they entered Germany proper. Enemy troops, numbering 7,000, were situated in the areas to the east. The Germans forced all Dutch males aged sixteen to sixty to build trenches, anti-tank ditches, and weapon pits along the canal banks. I was living more in the city centre, and it was a dangerous place to be.

Sporadic clashes of German and Canadian soldiers moving from one house to another were the norm of fighting up, until the specific date of April 16. Each day we lived in fear of the sound of shootings. Each day was a nightmare. The shootings everywhere made it impossible to walk or bike to work. If we did venture outside of the house searching for food, we would stay close to the walls of the ancient houses, and hide quickly in the basements if needed. The monstrously large German tanks on the roads would not find us there.

However, we needed to fear the soldiers who followed these tanks and inspected the narrow corridors between the houses. The enemy would run quickly through the houses to make it to the rooftops. Most shootings and killings took place there. On April 16, in the midst of all this, we could hear people singing and screaming for joy, softly at first, in the distance. We knew that they were the heavenly sounds of the liberation celebrations. However, liberation was still premature for my housemates and me, because we were still trapped in our home.

There were a few people on the streets in the area, other than German soldiers, when early on the evening of April 15, two of our young men decided to take a chance to find some food. They planned only to go a block away from the rooming house where there was a school, because earlier, they had heard that you could go to the schools and factories to find where the Germans hid jams, cigarettes, liquor and other preserved foods. So they went, and when they safely returned with hands full, they reported that you could still get more of these items left behind by the Germans. We had little to eat by this time of the war, so whatever was left behind would be welcomed.

I sincerely wanted to see for myself, because I dreamed of finding different kinds of food. Unfortunately, it was too late to leave the house that evening, and it was our house rule that everyone would lock down in the basement at night. It was too dangerous to stay on the ground floor, especially upstairs, while the German and Canadian shootings were taking place.

Early the next morning, while we were still wrapped in our sleeping blankets, German soldiers charged into the house with Canadian soldiers in pursuit. The action was too fast to comprehend. I did not know how many German soldiers made it to the rooftop and returned open fire at Canadians. Then there was silence. All the soldiers had disappeared as suddenly as they had appeared.

I decided that I was going to find some food later that morning. My girlfriend agreed to come with me. I thought that if the men could go out without mishap, so could the women. It was a cool and wet spring day, so I wore a warm dress and woollen overcoat, which I had bought just before the war broke out five years earlier.

Just as we stepped out onto the street, we were astonished at the new sight appearing in front of our eyes. There were two different-looking tanks humming slowly up the road towards us. The tanks belonged to the Canadians. They broke the great news of the city's true liberation, and it was clear that further resistance by the

Germans would be useless. While we were standing on one side of the street, five weary-looking Canadian soldiers sitting on top of the tanks saw us and recognized us as Dutch. We waved endlessly to them and blew kisses to them with our waves. What an indescribable moment of happiness and relief!

I do not know how long that moment lasted, but it felt ecstatically long. Then we remembered our mission. We found the school where we would find the goods. It was an old schoolhouse with a shallow basement and no steps. We needed to get on our hands and knees and reach for whatever we could get. Most of the jam jars were all strewn about, because people did not want jam. They wanted cigarettes and liquor, and there were none of those left for us to take home. The goal of my mission was to find something different to eat. I was unsuccessful, because I was specifically thinking of a jar of fruit cocktail. Perhaps symbolically speaking, I would always be reminded of an inner yearning to search for something with which to sweeten my life. I would adjust and overcome but I would never forget the sweet taste of a fruit cocktail. We returned to the house with as many goods as we could carry.

Two weeks later, after our Liberation Day in Groningen, I departed for Deventer. Because there were no trains anymore in operation, I had to resort to riding my bike. Unfortunately, most bikes owned by the Dutch had been taken earlier by the Germans. Therefore, the Germans left plenty of bikes around our house, but most were in bad condition with tires in need of repair. My girlfriend Gerda Roebbers had a brother, Martin, who was studying at the University of Groningen. He luckily knew where I lived, and he quickly learned what we needed to do first to get our journey started. When he arrived, I remembered that he said:

"Come on, Sibylla, let us take that bike over there and your bike. The tires are still good on both these bikes!"

He was a good companion to cycle with me to Deventer. I planned to return later to Groningen to pick up all my belongings.

Our journey was 150 kilometres on broken roads. What we witnessed was a traumatic and pitiful sight. We saw rows and rows of German soldiers and officers dressed in ragged and worn clothing. All of them were walking out, some with horses and wagons carrying food, all headed for the Dutch-German border, which was about seventy-five kilometres away. It was 1945, during the early month of May. When we finally arrived in Deventer near my family's home, there was still a German presence. We both were exhausted from traveling, and because it was dark by that time, Martin feared to continue to his family home, which was only a twenty-minute bike ride away. So he stayed overnight with our family.

Our endless conversation that evening was exciting news about my brothers Jan and Guillaume working in Germany. Guillaume had met Gretel Grafenhain in Germany, and their first child Wolfgang was born there. Jan was working with one of my father's business colleagues and made several artistic pieces of pottery. He made one specifically for the parents of his best friend,

Frans Peters, in celebration of their twenty-fifth wedding anniversary, on June 8, 1943. What I was comforted to know at the end of that day was that everyone was alive and safe and that the war had finally ended. A new life would surface in the morning.

A self-portrait taken in Peine, Germany in March of 1946, where I landed my first job with British Censorship. I sent the photo to my ever-supportive father and stepmother.

1946

Chapter Six: Working for British Censorship After the War

I was ambitious and I wanted to achieve. I was willing to take control of my life and do whatever was necessary to reach my goal. I was not sitting on an island doing all this by myself, as my women friends also had similar ambitions. We all wanted to work and find jobs with the British Army after the war. Armed with the talents of business and fluency in many languages, I sought out work in the British Censorship. I would meet a wide range of people in my travels throughout war-torn Germany.

Returning to the Hague

I was willing to control my own life and do whatever was necessary to get back to work. In May 1945, nearly all the government workers received a message to return to The Hague. I departed for the capital city with all my bags packed, where the government found hotel rooms for the outsiders to live. I met one of my friends, Metje Kwakenbrug, with whom I used to work, and we decided to room together.

Because food was scarce in the hotel, they gave us coupons to purchase any food we could find, and we were also provided with meals in the close-by canteen. Without much warning, I became sick with a high fever. My illness was not reported officially to the government office because there was no health department. Neither doctor nor nurse came to care for me or arranged to have meals brought to me. Metje was horrified but could only help by bringing me her leftover food, which she gladly shared daily. The situation worsened, and I felt melancholic, perhaps intensified as an after-effect of war recovery, perhaps not; but what I confirmed was that had Metje not cared for me, I would have starved. I did get better, but because of this adverse treatment, Metje contemplated leaving the government job. I agreed to join her.

As a lawyer, Metje wrote a convincing letter on my behalf to the Dutch government, declaring how badly the government looked after me. However, I did not want to lose my job at the price control department, and I did not know how they would react to Metje's letter.

We needed a back-up plan. Therefore, Metje and I researched the English newspapers for job ads, particularly in translation using the German and English languages. The job we found and that appealed to both of us was working with the British Intelligence Department. The jobs were immediately available and entailed censoring letters. We would need to move to Germany to do that job. For the interviews that weekend, we traveled to Tilburg, a town located in the south of the Netherlands. We stayed overnight in a hotel for three days.

In our interviews, they tested for German skills in speaking, writing, and comprehension. As luck would have it, we both passed and were accepted for the jobs. After only a few weeks in The Hague, we officially quit our government jobs. The British Army had already filled 200 censorship jobs and sent these employees to Germany. They moved us to a government housing unit in Tilburg with meals served at the Hotel Zomerhove. We were to stay there while officials processed and prepared what was required to live and work in Germany.

They postponed our departure from Tilburg many times. While waiting for our official departure time, and because few trains, if any, were running in the Netherlands, Metje and I decided to hitchhike to our hometowns together. We managed to make the 200-kilometre trip to Groningen and Deventer about five times. I had acquainted myself with Metje's parents and decided that I liked them both.

Have you ever had a strange feeling towards people who could make you inwardly feel uncomfortable? During my last two visits with Metje's parents, I experienced a suspicious mistrust, and that same feeling soon carried over while living with Metje for the next little while. They say that some people have unsuspecting double personalities. I soon learned the nature of my suspicion. Metje had another side to her.

I discovered something I had not known when I roomed with Metje. Her father, a professor at the Groningen University, sympathized and collaborated with the German enemy—a fact that would impede Metje's future.

Our jobs with the British Censorship had many secrets regarding the place or length of time for our work. In addition, our relatives were not to know about the job and our exact time of departure to Germany. One day in late September, we were amongst the 200 employees suddenly called, and we needed to depart within an hour. We were standing on the train station platform, all our belongings already on the train, when a voice calling over the P.A. system asked for five people to see the British Censorship departure office.

One of these people called was Metje. They prohibited her from going to work in Germany. The British Intelligence Service in censorship did not want the daughter of a German sympathizer to work for them. If Metje knew about her father, she had kept the information to herself all this time. They did not punish her in any other way. I gathered and returned her luggage, and departed in haste. I did not see her for a long time after that incident, but we kept in touch for many years through letter writing.

Working British Army Censorship

"Have you ever been to Peine?" Ilse Van Geuns, one of my four roommates, asked me at one point about our placement destination.

My answer was no. The small village of Peine near Hanover, Germany, was partly taken over by the British Army. The British Army built a housing compound consisting of new houses where groups of four people lived together. My group got along so well that we created memorable songs for our archives. But what kind of work or new life experiences were before us, we did not know. All we knew was that we were each chosen for our specific talents, mine being in business skills and fluency in many languages. Others in the compound, 150 men and 150 women, had other reasons for working there, including some wishing to return to German girlfriends and others wanting to be with German family and friends.

I spent my first post-war Christmas in 1945 in Peine, as we were not allowed to return to our hometowns. If I had stopped to think about it, I might have realized that I was homesick. Instead, I joined with the others in the traditions of the town of Peine. My friend Ilse and I decided to volunteer as actors in the annual traditional Passion Play of the story of Jesus Christ. We roleplayed the angels and ordered our costumes from Tegelen, where they also performed a Passion Play. The event essentially involved every member of the town and allowed us to socialize and make friends quickly. We prided ourselves on becoming involved, and before we knew it, the Christmas season passed quickly. We enjoyed a refreshed and positive attitude to our work.

Before I knew it, I was in the teeming heart of my job, reading letters confiscated by British or Russian intelligence. I sorted the content in each letter as a complaint, a family interaction, prison life, political commentary, business transactions, or any other reason for writing that letter. I identified the names of people mentioned in the letters, those who wrote the letters, and to whom they were written. Among the nearly fifty people in the German forces that I followed were Adenauer and Goebbels, and even Hitler's personnel.

The office was in the compound, and I loved the feeling of having office work to do there. I was learning how to write more efficiently and how to think more critically. I loved the sense of satisfaction I felt when I found some interesting and worthy information. As I saw it, my job was to be on the side of working thoroughly and pacing myself while reading the letters.

I accelerated in my work skills. After three months, at the end of February 1946, I was thrilled to be asked to censor phone calls. They also requested my roommate Ilse, and they moved our group of twelve from Peine to Münster, a much larger town, where we learned the work of censoring phone calls at the German post office. Eight people worked a twenty-four-hour workday, and we had the liberty to work out our schedules in eight-hour intervals. We liked the flexibility to change the times of this arrangement, because we could organize two or three full days off in a row. In this way, we created personal time to make short weekend trips.

My skills acquired at censoring letters flowed into the skills I needed for editing phone calls. Our terminals at the post office had a little box with a hearing apparatus and there was a Dictaphone. The back board of the terminal had eight lines attached to it, which clicked with out-of-town calls from all over Europe and Russia. We would connect our lines with the calls. The themes of each call would be categorised, as we had done in censoring the letters; however, the conversations could change quickly. For instance, a politically-related conversation would switch to a discussion about paintings or stolen articles. I had a list of specified names of people for whom to listen and of whom to especially keep track.

On one occasion, I needed to keep track of conversations initiated at first by Mr. Adenauer, an opponent to Hitler, and who had been imprisoned in 1934. He later became the First Chancellor of West Germany after the war. He spoke to an unknown person at his home, and I needed to find out who that person was. Although I did not find out who he spoke to during that phone call, I found out other information regarding an upcoming important meeting, such as its time and place. During another phone call that same day, after Mr. Adenauer had gone to work, his wife answered the call. I wrote down the question that she was asked:

"Where is your husband?"

And the answer that Mrs. Adenauer gave was: "Oh, he just went to the meeting at..."

I recorded the place of the meeting and its time. I discovered that the locations and times were the same. I needed to give this information immediately to the officer in charge, who continued further investigation.

Although the job was steady and stimulating, it was also intense. Every conversation needed transcribing from the Dictaphones, which took two hours after the eight-hour shift. The conversations needed a flow. I needed to be precise, so that the person taking my work shift immediately after me could, in the first place, understand what I had written, and secondly, move seamlessly into an ongoing discussion. It was especially challenging when on duty from twelve midnight to eight in the morning. Every conversation was proofread and inspected for any hidden messages. Calls continued night and day, and a person could have made more than ten calls a day on one of the eight lines. Because of the need for accuracy, we taped each conversation for a later thorough examination.

In the beginning, callers had no idea that we were taping them. As time pressed on towards the end of 1946, until 1948, we would hear more often the whispered words, "Oh, someone is taping us..."

The callers could hear the clicking sound on the system. They would know that something was up.

Censoring phone calls was especially helpful in finding and retrieving stolen paintings from famous art galleries in the Netherlands, Belgium, France, and Russia. The Germans stored many paintings in German factories. An international agreement allowed for all paintings that had gone missing during the war to be returned to their rightful owners. However, that did not always happen, and many paintings did not arrive at the agreed-upon location for retrieval. In a string of phone conversations, I discovered that the Dutch government was still looking for lost paintings by Rembrandt and Jan Steen. They either were lost, or sold to another country or someone privately, because they were no longer in Germany. Once on my weekend off work while in Münster, I had the occasion to meet up with what I thought was a suspicious vehicle carrying stolen paintings. Here is the story.

Missing Paintings

Corrie Corsee, a very dear friend I had made while working in Peine in censoring letters, was eager to explore Germany. She loved the countryside and the cities of Germany, and so we organized many traveling weekends together. But first, we needed to get our papers in order. Traveling throughout Germany was allowed for army officials in the British censorship, since we had the titles of army sergeants. By November 1945, the Allies reached agreements covering military travel among the four occupation zones (Great Britain, France, Russia, and the United States). With representatives of the

United States, Great Britain, and France, the combined Travel Security Board set up stringent regulations on procedures and necessary paperwork for travel by military personnel, which we applied for and received. But Russia was still in talks with the Allied Control Council to close all zonal borders on June 30, 1946. So we had to be careful to keep our inter-zonal passes updated because of the fluid changes amongst the countries.

For transportation, we would hitchhike, as there were so few trains. One weekend in 1946, we stood on the side of the highway waiting for a ride for about an hour. There was not a single vehicle on the road. Then came a tank with two American soldiers sitting on the top. It must have been an unusual sight for them to see two ladies in British uniforms hitchhiking in a war-torn country. They stopped, and we decided to accept their invitation to drive about ten kilometres down the road. The ride seemed to last a long time, but before we knew it, we parted ways.

We were on the same highway once again, and a decent-looking Jeep was coming up in the distance. It was time to put up our thumbs, and immediately, the Jeep stopped. Of course, again, seeing two ladies on a highway in British Army uniforms was an unusual sight. The soldiers were in Dutch uniforms, and we exchanged stories of who we were and where we wanted to go. Corrie and I always agreed that there would be no conversation about our jobs, as we were also under oath to say nothing.

While sitting in the back seat, I noticed some cylindrical art containers that I secretly suspected contained rolled-up paintings. At the time, and perhaps unfairly, my mind judged our drivers to be involved in mishandling the paintings. Unfortunately, at that precise moment, the conversation had mysteriously steered to the topic of paintings. A suspicious comment came from either myself or Corrie, and I would never remember clearly which one of us it was.

Instantaneously, our Jeep driver jammed on the brakes, and the two soldiers quickly asked us if we heard about any missing Dutch paintings. They got out of their Jeep and showed us six painting titles, and asked us if we recognized them. It was their job from the Dutch government to look for them, as the real ones were missing. They badgered us endlessly, and we insisted that we were obliged to give no information. Their destination was in Hanover, where there was a Dutch consulate, and if we changed our minds, we could contact them there.

We later discussed the situation with our officer in charge, and of course, he agreed that we could not give any information. We never said who we were at the time. After Germany's unconditional surrender on May 8, 1945, many war-related issues remained unresolved and perpetually under investigation from 1946 to 1947.

Entrepreneurship

In the early years of the war, money had depreciated to almost nothing. Bartering goods for food became the only means to make purchases. I had over 1000 German marks then, and in earlier days, I would have been considered rich. But not anymore. I could buy nothing. Because I earned many German marks from my present job, I needed, therefore, to obtain a rewrite into British bank notes. I then requested that the British government send some of my salary cheques to the Netherlands in my father's name for my savings. The rest of the cheques could be used for exchange into Belgian francs when I traveled to Belgium. With Belgian money, I had the means to buy a variety of goods and services.

Corrie, Ilse, and I made our cash transactions to British bank notes every two weeks with the British captains. Then we applied to go on a leave train to Brussels, Ghent, or another city in Belgium to exchange our money for the precious Belgian francs. While exploring our expanding options of purchases, we discovered new commodity money for trade, by acquiring Belgian cigarettes. Was there a reason why we were interested in purchasing cigarettes? Yes. Cigarettes were a means for us to earn extra money. Our market targets would be both in Germany and the Netherlands. We were now entrepreneurs.

As budding entrepreneurs, Corrie and I developed a method on how to proceed in our business. In the first place, we would depart from Germany with empty suitcases. Secondly, we would purchase the cigarettes in Belgium and fill up our suitcases with them. Thirdly, we would return to Germany with full bags to make our trades for goods and money. Many times, we pursued items that were not readily available in the Netherlands, as our post-war homeland was poor and needed to get its economy moving forward. Finally, it was important to keep our "Ausweiss," or our military passes, updated to officially leave from Münster. One small glitch was that Corrie, still working in censoring letters, could not enter the Netherlands from Peine. She needed to go to Münster first. But that was no problem to overcome.

Soon we discovered that many others were copying this kind of business, and we all did not realize that the new trade came with risk. At the Belgian train station, on a return journey to Münster, Corrie once said in a loud voice, "Sibylla, I need to rest and sit here in this seat. These suitcases weigh far too much for me to carry."

There were some Germans in uniform who boarded the train at the same time as us. They were alerted to Corrie's voice and saw our suitcases and then, in German, asked us what was in them. It seemed that they already knew the answer, because they immediately snapped up the three suitcases before we could reply. We lost three suitcases of cigarettes just like that.

At the same time, and without understanding the reason, that same train started to re-track, and we thought that the authorities wanted to take us in for questioning. Would we lose our jobs, be charged for bringing over the cigarettes, or worse, have our papers removed? We were shaken up for a frightening twenty minutes in a stopped train. But no one came for us. As the train restarted for Germany, we learned from others that those German soldiers used the cigarettes for themselves and shared them with all the people on the train. Truly, we were relieved to discover that they were not supposed to do this. Somewhat jolted, we continued with our cigarette business.

We searched for more markets where we could sell our cigarettes. Corrie suggested that we look at the industries and factories in Germany where the employers paid low wages in German marks. The workers generally were hard-working people but could hardly pay for food and living expenses. Corrie speculated that the factory owners wanted to pay some of the more industrious employees with cigarettes. One of these factories was in the camera-making industry. Here was our opportunity.

We wanted to work with a camera company in Braunsweig, a town in the British zone near the Russian zone in Germany. In business for over 100 years and now back up and running, the company made specialized parts for cameras. Still, the only parts that they had difficulty in procuring were a type of photographic lenses. Another factory within the Russian zone made and supplied them. The two companies were still on good terms. However, one was not allowed to enter the Russian zone, and if you were found there illegally, you would be jailed and possibly sent to Siberia. So, the owner's son decided to take the chance to purchase the lenses. He would use cigarettes for the trade, and Corrie and I were the ones who would supply the cigarettes.

We came to know the family well, and they always welcomed us to stay overnight on our visits. No one seemed to worry why two ladies dressed in beautiful civilian dresses with military overcoats came to visit so often to their home and factory which were almost ruined because of the war. I remembered that other family members lived there in the safekeeping of their dwelling. One was a disliked daughter, who had a child but no husband present that we could see.

Then one day, to my surprise, Corrie said to me:

"Did you not know that Herman tried hard and was going through great lengths to get the lenses for you so that you could sell them in the Netherlands every time we came to trade our cigarettes? Did you not know that that twinkle in his eye was a twinkle of love for you?"

"I never knew," I responded.

They also needed the camera lenses in the Netherlands, and we supplied the Dutch buyers. We would purchase the same lenses and conceal them in our clothing and baggage, because they were small enough to carry that way. After crossing the border to the Netherlands, we made secret arrangements with my younger brother Guillaume to help in distribution. He would meet Corrie on the Dutch side of the border, and both Corrie and my brother were responsible for circulating these lenses in the Netherlands.

After one of our visits to Braunsweig, the owner of the business pulled me aside and said:

“Sibylla, you and Corrie need to stop bringing cigarettes. My salesmen in the Netherlands discovered that there is an abundance of lenses in the country, and they do not know from where they came. The older salesman of our company suspects that the lenses are stolen and sold privately.”

The kind owner of the camera company confirmed his suspicion that it was too difficult for any civilian, other than an army official, to acquire a permit to go to Germany from the Netherlands. So, he narrowed down the suspects to us, as only the military was allowed to cross borders. He did not want any trouble. He always received us well, but after this conversation, he put up a sign at the outside entrance of his factory, which read: “Out of Bounds to Military and Civilians.” We stopped our lens trading business with the camera factory.

I was fully engaged in the working world in the British Army. I felt revitalized after my gruesome experiences during the war. I was completely focused even more on my new role as an entrepreneur. My exposure to business ownership pinpointed the direction that I wanted to further develop in my life. But as I kept one toe in my budding career, I felt my other toe stepping towards another adventure, that of exploring war-torn Germany. I knew I had the opportunity to do so.

“

Soon we discovered that many others were copying this kind of business, and we all did not realize that the new trade came with risk.

My friend Corrie Cossee and I were on our first visit to Berlin after the war (1946). I was standing between two Russian soldiers who spoke French.

Corrie and I were returning from a business trip to Braunsweig, Germany, in April of 1947 and traveling to Hanover, Germany. One could notice the destruction of buildings where I was sitting.

Chapter Seven: Weekend Traveling

Traveling could awaken my soul so much that, after my return from an adventure, I immediately craved another destination. During my weekend trips with either Ilse or Corrie, I fell into a routine where I would lodge at the YMCA, explore a town or site, and return with a fantastic story to tell the listeners at the compound. Through hitchhiking, my main source of transportation, I met a wide range of people from royalty in an overcrowded Mercedes car, to air pilots who would fly me to wherever I wanted or was allowed to go.

Thumbs Up!

One long weekend, Corrie and I, dressed in our British Army uniforms, managed to hitchhike to Copenhagen, Denmark. We spotted a vehicle coming down the road.

"Thumbs up!" I said to Corrie.

Upon seeing the unusual sight comprising two women in army uniform, the driver, also in uniform, needed no persuasion to stop his jeep. We greeted one another, and we learned that he was a pilot working also for the British Army. Surprisingly, he drove us all the way to our destination: the YMCA in Copenhagan.Before we parted company he asked:

"Would you like a return two-hour flight back to Hanover, Germany? That would give you extra sightseeing time in the city."

We thanked him kindly and agreed to meet him at the airport for the promised flight. Our departure day arrived but, unfortunately, so did inclement weather conditions that delayed our departure time at five in the morning. Sadly, we needed to decline the plane ride.

We were in a precarious position, as we would not arrive on time for our work shift because of the extra travel time needed to return to Hanover. The hitchhiking trip took us the entire day, and both Corrie and I were sure to lose our jobs. But unexpectedly, on the contrary, we drew people's attention to our engagement in our daring and romantic adventure to Denmark, and attentive audiences wanted to know more about us and our trips.

We first cited the stories of our business trips to Braunsweig. However, I felt that I could provide more drama if I recounted the story about our side trip to Berlin.

Berlin

Our opportunity to go to Russian-zoned Berlin had come a little more easily than expected. Corrie and I still took precautions about going, because we had heard a recent story about a girl who had gone there and never returned. Russian soldiers picked us up on that weekend. They entertained us with their Russian songs, which kept a happy mood in the vehicle. Along with the lyrics, we learned how to read a few of the road signs written in Russian. (After our ride, we confirmed that travel from Braunsweig to Berlin had become more common and much safer than when we had first started our cigarette business.) Although somewhat nervous at the beginning, we soon felt comfortable.

Corrie wanted to visit a colleague teacher friend that she made in West Berlin before the war. Before our journey, we obtained a privilege pass in Braunsweig to cross the British city border into the Russian zone of Berlin. It was my first time in Berlin, and what I saw was the same as what I first saw in Münster.

"Traumerhaufen," I sadly said under my breath. The expression meant that most buildings were bombed out, with only a handful of buildings still standing.

Berlin was divided into three zones: Britain, France, and Russia. Our passes allowed us to only stay in the British zone, and we needed to always be in uniform. The main streets were leveled to the ground, and there was no way to determine where the city's own borders existed. So Corrie and I decided to walk quickly to use our time more efficiently to find her friend and her family. We walked around a lot, and who would ever know if we passed by the bunker where Adolf Hitler and Eva Braun lived and took their own lives in east Berlin?

As we strolled, always in close sight of each other, we checked street signs and house numbers, always in fear of meeting with a Russian officer, who could deport us if we walked away into a forbidden zone. We hoped that our passes would give us enough protection if that ever happened. In the end, we were neither stopped nor questioned, but sadly, we could not find Corrie's friend. After hitchhiking back to the compound and telling our group what we had seen and done, they labeled this story as an unforgettable, sensational one to tell their offspring in the future.

The Nuremberg Trials

Corrie and I visited the Nuremberg Trials, otherwise known as the International Military Tribunal, extending from November 20, 1945, to October 1, 1946. Every country that participated had its number of seats depending on the size of the country. The Netherlands had six out of the 100 seats. When Corrie and I arrived in Nuremberg in the spring of 1946, we quickly identified the building where the trials took place, because the British military was guarding the front entrance. We later learned that we were two of the first Dutch women to have ever entered the building and to have witnessed the trials. If one inquired within the Dutch government, one might find no other Sergeant women on that list.

Because we worked with the British Military Censorship, we thought that that was our easy ticket for entry. It was not that easy. Initially, we needed to wait for one half-hour for the tribunal officials to accept our request. Many rooms were identified by country, and the officials were required to account for and do background research for everyone in these rooms.

They escorted us into the Dutch room, where a Dutch government official listened to our explanation about why we had come to the trials. The next step was to hand over everything in our possession, even our coats. After our initiation, they guided us to some seats in the courtroom, which had over 100 seats. On each chair's armrest was an earphone to dial in which language you wanted to hear. We wanted to listen to German, because it was the language of the court and the language spoken by the Nazi prisoners on trial.

Of the twenty German criminals, I recognized only one, the Dutch leader for Hitler in the Netherlands, whose name was Mr. Seyss-Inquaat. We listened to one of the other criminals on trial that day, whose name was Mr. Sauckel. At ten o'clock in the morning, the interrogation had already started with more than one interrogator. There were four or five sharing the same questioning. I listened with heightened interest as one of the questions asked was:

"You ordered, in that city, that all the men had to get out of the house to be transported into concentration camps. Did you know about it?"

"Ich habe es nicht gewust," Mr. Sauckel answered. This translated to, "I did not know anything about it."

The other interrogators asked the same question, and Mr. Sauckel gave the same answer for the rest of the morning.

During the lunch hour, which started at noon, the prisoners were to leave under the guard of two military police for each one prisoner. The police escorted the prisoners to private prison chambers located in another building. They also guarded the open corridor between the two buildings, to protect the prisoners from snipers who would shoot at them if they had the chance. They all entered and exited at the same doorway.

In the afternoon session, we sat in the gallery. During our lunch hour, we had found some names of the prisoners who were close military members to Hitler: Goering, Ribbentrop, Doenitz, and von Papen. Below us were the judges located in front of the twenty prisoners. Behind the prisoners were twenty military police.

The interrogations began, and they read different citations of accusations or situations. It eventually became very monotonous to hear the same questioning and the same answers. For example, we knew that Mr.Sauckel had signed papers of commitment, and yet throughout the day, while the interrogators questioned him about all his wrongdoings, he always answered, "Ich habe es nicht gewust."

I did not know from which country Mr. Sauckel came, and it may have been days or weeks that this same man was questioned repeatedly. They held the trials in the British zones of Nuremberg, which, because of its location, gave us the great opportunity to attend them, and a fabulous story to recount.

After our long day at the trials, we hitchhiked to Vienna and stayed at a hotel that served as the officers mess for British occupation forces. Several raids and bombings on the city had caused severe damage to the nearby famous Parkhotel Schoenbrunn and the Schoenbrunn Park itself. But Vienna was still beautiful on that spring evening, already budding into a new life. The calmness of Vienna was a sharp contrast to the seriousness of Nuremberg and to our emotional experience of witnessing the tribunals of Nazi criminals.

The Eagle's Nest

Konigsee is a natural lake in the extreme southeast land district of Berchtesgaden, in the German state of Bavaria, near the Austrian border. It is a stunning area, and a unique village called Berchtesgaden lies high up in the mountains, with 10,000 inhabitants. Higher in the mountains and overlooking the village is a summer home, well-known throughout Germany, called the Kehlsteinhaus, or by the Allies' adopted name, the Eagle's Nest. Ilse and I were traveling together to see it.

The Eagle's Nest was inaugurated by Adolf Hitler on his fiftieth birthday, April 20, 1939. However, he visited the villa only fourteen times, because of his fear of heights and the risk of bad weather. Here, Hitler conducted his private life with mistress Eva Braun, and secret political meetings with Hess, Ribbentrop, and Goering.

If you were with the British Army, you were allowed entry to ascend on the elevator, built in Hitler's time, to get to the SS Defence level where the highest fanatic SS German officers had lived. At this level were their armouries, intended to be used to protect their ruler. Ilse and I took in the beautiful view, but there were another 500 meters to climb to get to the actual Eagle's Nest.

The construction of the small house was built on two levels. Inside was a conference room overlooking the entire region. The place was "Traumerhaufen," with many bricks and other debris strewn everywhere, much too dangerous to walk on. In the midst of the destruction, I took a picture of the bathtub lying on its side, and another picture of Ilse standing in the remains of the living room windowsill, so that you could measure how high the window was.

I could not remember if the "Eagles' Nest" was bombed before Hitler was gone, or if it was bombed because the Allies wanted to destroy the area because of Hitler's existence there. However, it remained in the history books, known as an incredible construction built in a stunning setting high in the mountains.

The Battle of Remagen

The real story about the Battle of Remagen was retold when Corrie and I met American officers who spoke fluent German, whose job was to investigate battles in the Netherlands and Germany. Their stories stayed with me because it was word-of-mouth history. It was confirmed that the bridge of Arnhem needed to be saved to get the Americans over to the Netherlands. It was also confirmed that the bridge needed to be destroyed to prevent the Germans from going over. The Americans even had military who were familiar with the area and knew where to send troops in the spring of 1945, in case the Germans blew up the bridge. However, the battle in Arnhem was a failure. On the other hand, the battle in Remagen on the west side of the Rhine River was a remarkable success.

The Battle of Remagen involved the Germans blowing up its bridge to prevent the Americans from crossing over to the Netherlands. The Americans succeeded in crossing over the bridge before it was partly destroyed because they battled with the Germans and prevented them from blowing it up completely. This action brought the Americans two weeks ahead in their planning, and therefore brought them four days closer to the Liberation of the Netherlands. This detailed information they gave to us came from their private investigations only about a year after the battles.

Belsen-Belsen: Concentration Camp

Bergen-Belsen was a sad story about the Nazi concentration camp in northern Germany. Corrie had a list of names and addresses of people who never returned to the Netherlands after the war. She wanted to search for people who might have been sent to Belsen, where not only Jews were killed, but also anti-government people from the Netherlands, France, and Belgium. We hitchhiked with two Polish army officers, who knew their way to and around the camp. When we arrived, I was surprised by the size of the camp, with hundreds of buildings everywhere. Our Polish friends pointed out a wooden cross, the huts where the prisoners lived, and the gas chambers. Behind the huge building containing the gas chambers, you could see a large hole dug out by the prisoners, where the bodies had been laid. More than 1,000 prisoners could be killed in a day and not be missed. The prisoners did not know that this building was a gas chamber, and because there were so many prisoners, no one knew who was missing.

Our Polish friends showed us the inside of one gas chamber. First, there was a place to undress and hang up clothes. Then, the prisoners went through another door and were gassed right away. Close by there was the huge gravesite for the bodies. All the gas chambers resembled this one that we saw.

Placed at the entrance was a list of people killed, thousands of names, but Corrie could not find the names written on her list, and she never found out where they did die. Some other visitors we talked to were returning because they had worked in these camps and wanted to find out about relatives or friends. For them, it was quite emotional. I remembered that one woman was crying near one of the gas chambers, and she related to us how horrible it was. During the end of the war, typhus had spread. Anne Frank had died because of it. She was buried at Belsen, and a memorial was laid in her memory.

"Death Triumphant"

Ruth Nussbaum and her family were friends of mine. They were born in Germany and immigrated to the Netherlands in 1935. The family was taken up by a Dutch family who took the risk to keep them safe. I did not know how many members were in that Nussbaum family. When the war broke out, they had no freedom, they could not leave the house, and they received no coupons since they were not registered with the government. But thanks to the Dutch underground, they were fed and well taken care of. If the Germans had discovered them at that time, the family and their Dutch caregivers would have been killed.

Many years after the war, I watched a German television show illustrating the reaction to the persecution of the Jews during the war. The answers of the people interviewed ranged from knowing nothing to everything about the concentration camps. Sometimes they said just enough to allow the viewers like me to know that friends and relatives had disappeared and were never seen again. When the name Nussbaum came up, I watched carefully since I never did find out what had happened to the family immediately after the war.

The program discussed a painter named Felix Nussbaum, born in Osnabruck, Germany, where there was a Jewish community. He was a Holocaust artist whose last painting in 1944, titled "Death Triumphant," depicted skeletal musicians playing music on various instruments with no one left to listen. Nussbaum's surname was common, but many years after seeing this TV show, I found an address to my lost friend Ruth Nussbaum. I decided to go to Tel Aviv, Israel, where she lived, to meet her and get caught up with her life.

Dortmund, Germany

During my employment after the war, I worked in Peine, Münster, Hanover, Hamburg, and Dortmund. In Dortmund, I spent my last three work months with the British censorship. When I first arrived, there was no place officially for women to lodge among the male officers, and I was the first and only woman working at the post office of Dortmund to present this new problem. I would be saved neither by my military rank, nor by my gender. Where were they going to have me live? Nobody knew the correct protocol.

Eventually, they decided to put me into the same hotel complex as them, which meant that I lived with "the boys." When I thought about it later, I could not believe my naïveté. Somewhere along the way during that first night, I had missed something. During my first morning where I had breakfast sitting in the officers' mess with about ten other officers at the same table, one officer jovially asked me:

"Miss Janssen, how was your sleep last night?"

I innocently replied with embarrassment:

"It was terrible because, on both sides of my room, I heard a thumping noise through the walls that continued all night long!"

All the officers cracked up laughing. I instantly figured out that they were sleeping with German girls at the hotel.

While I was living in Dortmund, Corrie and I continued our cigarette trading system. Corrie found another factory in need of paying their employees with cigarettes, as Germany was still under impoverishment. With her connections in Peine, we found an address to a factory that made raincoats. Plastic raincoats. No one had heard of a plastic raincoat, and our market, therefore, was wide open. We would depart from Dortmund, each with two empty suitcases, and head to the factory, where we would pay for as many raincoats as we could fill into our bags. They became so heavy! Then we would travel towards the southern border of the Netherlands, where we would transfer them to two people: a family friend from Deventer named Jack Hoogstraten, and my brother Guillaume. Both distributed the raincoats to the Dutch market. It was a prosperous business.

Some Sad Family Stories, and One Very Happy One!

During my stay in Dortmund, I learned of a sad family story. The war had its effects on all families, and there were repercussions in my family because of its Dutch and German heritage. Well before the war broke out, my father had grown up with cousins living across the Dutch-German border. During the war, those social connections changed. The risk of deportation or being put to war work became a reality for those who continued their social connections.

My Dutch cousin worked as a nurse in the Netherlands. She had married a man of German birth and became a naturalized German citizen. They were living in the Netherlands when the German army called him to fight for his country. She often visited her mother and socialized with our Engels family cousins who lived in Hengelo, a town on the Dutch side of the border. One day, she visited this aunt in Hengelo. She rang the doorbell, and upon opening the door, her aunt saw only a woman dressed in German uniform. Her aunt decided to slam the door in her face without saying a word. She and one of her cousins who also witnessed the scene immediately left together for Germany, and both were never seen again for over forty years.

During my visit about forty years later, I spoke with my cousin whose aunt slammed the door. At first sight, I did not know that she was the same nurse of so many years ago. It only came about as we coincidentally discussed the incident when her aunt slammed the door in her face. She explained to me that she was so hurt that she would never have anything to do with the Engels family or any more of the Dutch relatives living in the Netherlands. The rift remained unhealed for forty years. And here I was, a Dutch relative visiting from Canada, greeting my German cousins in Germany, on a friendly visit. The healing was finally taking place in our family.

There were other family stories, one of which also resulted in a sad ending. Being in the pottery business, my father enjoyed the camaraderie of other pottery factory owners, specifically one in Germany. This German colleague would frequently cross the border to visit us and instruct Jan, my brother, in our factory about the making of pottery. The problem arose when the neighbours reported:

“Look at that, they are collaborating with the Germans.”

As it turned out, this colleague found out that there was a lot of clay around my father’s factory. One day, he asked my father if he might hide his German army clothes in the clay of the factory. He wanted to desert the German army. My father was easygoing and replied that he could do what he wanted to do. However, the colleague never did it. We did not see him again until after the war, when he explained that he desperately wanted to get out of the German army at that time. He disliked Hitler's rule, but he could not bring himself to desert the German army. He survived the war, and he never discussed his life as a German soldier during that time.

When given the opportunity, Dutch citizens made time to enjoy nature despite the destruction of war. For instance, even before the Great War, our government had encouraged people to plant victory gardens. One day, an established Deventer family purchased a squared-off piece of land on the other side of the Ijssel River. One of the children of this family worked there often and had the opportunity to purchase clay flower-pots from my brother Jan, who was selling them from our father's factory. That child's name was Frans L. Peters. Jan and Frans soon became best of friends. One day after school, Jan brought him to our home, and I recognized him immediately. My life was about to change completely.

“

During the end of the war, typhus had spread. Anne Frank had died because of it. She was buried at Belsen, and a memorial was laid in her memory.

On April 12, 1948, Frans and I were married at the Blessed Heart Catholic Church in Deventer. We first went to the city hall, each of us traveling there in separate horse-drawn carriages, and from there we traveled in one carriage to the church.

During the war years, I remembered seeing an image in an outdoor visual advertisement of a woman dressed in army uniform, flexing her muscles. It was supposed to inspire women who would be looking for new liberation. But what happened to her after the war?

I knew that I exuded confidence in the workforce during the war, and during the years immediately following. I also knew that travel inspired my senses. And then I knew that, in love, I searched for someone who would respect my self-supporting way of life. I searched for trust in that someone I loved, to be married to him and plan a future together.

Meeting Frans

Because I was a member of the British censorship in the British Army, I benefitted from the experience in many ways. First, I was earning my living. Second, I liked working at something much different than most of my high school and college friends. Third, I discovered within myself a smart, ambitious, and innovative thinker for a woman of the times. For instance, I realized on my own that I needed to move on and learn to put aside the effects of war. I needed to leave the British Army without feeling that I needed it or that the army needed me for survival. My next job had to promise me challenges and rewards. These were the goals that I set to motivate me to move on with my life. Then, without warning, I found someone. I discovered that I could make good on my self-promises lying in the name Frans, the person with whom I fell in love.

In the beginning, Frans was just a name. But I had come to realize that he meant more to me. I thought that I did not regret buying a Christmas candle for him, worth hundreds of German marks, in 1947. I unwrapped the packaging tissue and rubbed my fingers over the smooth wood of the candle holder, the way I might have touched his hand. Then I placed the candle on top of it. I decided that I had become the woman I wanted to be, and it was finally time to light the candle and move on.

I was driven not only by love but by some inner wish to do something great during the next phase of my life. I had survived many risky adventures and knew that my self-confidence looked impressive to many who could not even step outside their home's doorway. So it was a casual acquaintance as friends when he came over to our house on the Hoge Hondstraat to visit my brother Jan, and I could say yes when he asked me to accompany him when attending his family functions.

Because I was three years older, I never associated with Frans in school. At that time, we attended the same elementary school, and after that, the odds of meeting him lessened even more because all schools were segregated. As a teenager, while I was working at Vroom & Dressmann, Frans worked in his father's jewelry store during the day. We both went to night school at the same commercial school, and I knew Frans also attended because we took the same classes, one being French class. But although he was interested in and clever in learning languages, I learned later that he was more passionate about gardening and could distract himself with hours of meaningful labour in the family garden across the Ijssel River.

During pre-war activity, Frans's thoughts were not directed towards the political arena Frans felt more secure in volunteering to work in the family garden, his parents' business, and a nearby garden centre. He felt more in control of his life in fulfilling his home front duties. Then, he applied and was accepted to Horticulture College in Arnhem.

We had had our first date and soon we were dating regularly—attending dances, movies, and family gatherings. I would cycle to the family jewelry store where he lived, and he would cycle to my house. Our lives carried on this way for a few years, and in the family pictures and sometimes pictures of just the two of us, one could tell that we were happy together. In 1940, however, our dating was abruptly interrupted by the German occupation in the Netherlands. This was when I moved to Velsen, near Amsterdam, to work and live in the home of a trusted family.

Frans and Jan always remained friends. During the war, Frans and Jan went to Germany to work. Jan worked with our father's friend and colleague in a German pottery business, and Frans made deliveries for his father's jewelry business. Both jobs allowed them to enter Germany while the border was still unrestricted. Frans made a lot of German friends at this time, and even lived there with them. As the war continued and the years marched by, Frans was spending more and more time in Germany, and he made less contact with his family and my family. It almost seemed that he had disappeared.

Frans's mother repeatedly said that she could not understand why he was not returning home or sending letters. There was little to no postal service during these years, and I worried too because I had not heard from him either. Was he working at the pottery factory with Jan? Or was he caught by the Germans and compelled to do war work? Was he fraternizing and living with German friends? Or a combination of all the above? No one knew, and when he returned in July 1945 to Deventer, he did have a story—but more about that later.

Frans's Family

I learned to like Frans's parents and his three siblings, Ton, Ria, and Lou. His parents were third-generation owners of their jewelry store. His grandfather, Frans J.C. Peters, born on April 6, 1857, had learned watch-making in Rotterdam. He moved to Deventer to open a watch and repair store. To immediately attract customers to his new store, he kept the shop open on Saturday nights until ten o'clock or later, as was the custom for most shop keepers in those days. By socializing after their workday, customers would linger and drop into the shops to enjoy a comfortable ambiance with drinks and food. Most owners and their families lived in their shops, and the doors were always opened to people, stranger or not, who would be interested in buying their products. In his case, he advertised watches and other pieces of jewelry.

Frans J.C. Peters married Maria Grada van de Beld from Deventer, and together they continued the jewelry and watchmaking shop. They were something of an odd-looking couple: Maria was a very tall lady, and he was much shorter. Their characters differed as well, because she had business wisdom, and he had a much softer temperament. She was also so frugal that once she snapped away the weekly almsgiving from the plate at the Catholic church, complaining that her husband was much too generous.

In the early 1900s, Frans and Maria relocated the store on Spijkerboorsteeg Street to the Langebisschop-straat 44. The renovated building contained a store on the ground floor and living quarters on the second and third floors. The business grew quickly, and after thirty years, they passed on the company to their twenty-seven-year-old son, Frans Caspar Johannes Peters. Frans and Maria retired in Arnhem and lived in a large and beautiful home, with balconies on each of the three floors.

Frans used to tell me about his visits to his grandfather, who became one of the well-to-do residents living in Arnhem. His grandfather would send a horse-drawn carriage to his house on the Langebisschopstraat in Deventer to pick him up and bring him home from his visits to Arnhem. To be in a horse-drawn carriage was an unusual sight at that time, and he thoroughly enjoyed being the centre of attention. Frans used to visit him often, and during one of these visits, someone took a picture of all three generations of Franses sitting on a bench in the garden: his grandfather in his late seventies, his father in his mid-forties, and he in his teenage years.

Frans J.C. Peters, Frans's father, soon had the opportunity to purchase the building next door, number forty-two. The purchase allowed for expansion to the store that covered the entire corner block at the intersection of the two central streets of Deventer.

Frans's Work after the War

Luxury businesses did not get off to a prosperous start in the Dutch economy, the Peters family business included. One day, by chance, Frans's mother connected with a salesman in the jewelry business named Mr. Humberg, who made and sold his jewelry pieces. She encouraged Frans to work with him. Mr. Humberg said to Frans:

"If you want to sell some jewelry that I make myself, different and unique bracelets, and other pieces made from silver and gold, you can do that for me."

Frans agreed, and cycling on a bicycle at first, later upgrading to a motorbike, he traveled to potential clients all over the country. I asked Frans if I could recruit customers for Mr. Humburg, too, because it gave me a chance to show how I could influence people in his business. It also gave me an excuse to see Frans more often, and Frans agreed that I could do that. Mr. Humburg later made me an elaborate gold bracelet, an artistic piece designed with three beautiful diamond settings on it. I would wear it every day in memory of my work in the jewelry business.

Our Engagement

Postal service recommenced in 1946, and working with British Army personnel gave me privileges of sending and receiving letters from Frans. On weekend leaves, I would write Frans to let him know when I would meet him. We agreed on the time and place to meet, usually at the Dutch-German border train station in Hengelo, where the leave trains were most reliable, or in Deventer or at my parents' home.

On one occasion, I invited Frans to a family celebration. I managed a few days off, organizing a ride from someone at the compound to drive me from Münster to Deventer. My father and Gezina were married in April 1934 and on October 5, 1946, they would be married for twelve and a half years. In keeping with the Dutch tradition that would be the date of the celebration. Although sweet food items were scarce at the time, Frans purchased a gift of some chocolate candies using his coupons. He won over their warmth and respect. Then everyone lit their Belgian cigarettes, which I had provided for the celebration!

Frans had passed the family test, and then I knew that the game was on. I decided to stop analyzing my life and live for the moment. It was a warm day in September 1946 when Frans L. Peters asked for my hand in marriage. Any worries that I had concealed about my life and career fell away and were replaced by my urge to get to know him better. We were going to formally announce our engagement on Christmas Day 1946.

I was working in Germany during the Christmas season, and I was uncomfortable about still being in Dortmund on Christmas Eve. How would I ever navigate over 150 kilometres to return home in time to prepare a party reception for twenty people? I had already filled my bags with specialty foods I had purchased with coupons at the army canteen, and my overnight bags were packed. But there was absolutely no transportation on Christmas Eve. Everything had to be put on hold for one more day.

Finally, after a ride from someone at the compound to the border, and then a train ride to Deventer, I arrived on Christmas Day. The following day, on the Second Christmas Day (December 26), as it was called in the Netherlands, my father and Gezina arranged a dinner for us at Longayroux Restaurant on Grote Overstraat 21, followed by a reception party at my home Hoge Hondstraat 12. By the end of the day's celebrations, I was smoothing over the coral beads embedded on a gold cross, handmade by Frans, as he said:

"I love you, Sibylla."

I placed it next to my gift to him of a unique cigarette lighter. They were our first gifts to each other. I placed them on top of all our congratulatory letters.

Life Would Not Be Dull

Frans was no longer content with working in his father's jewelry business. He said to me one day, "I want to seriously get back into gardening. Also, I am not getting along with my father right now, and I want to move out of the house."

In an unusually raised voice, I responded, "Pardon me? Where are you going to live, and what are you going to do?"

"Just give me some time," he answered. And shifting in his chair, he added, "I have saved enough money for a small place in Amsterdam."

Inherently, I suspected two things: that life would not be dull with this man, and that quite possibly he would earn enough money to make a substantial living. He was exuberant about trying new things, but was also greatly unsettled for the next couple of months, because he later piloted himself to live in Amersfoort and then in Utrecht. He found out that there was not enough business to make a living in the jewelry business. This was true in all luxury industries, considering that, so soon after the war, one could still not find enough food to feed a family or even responsibly buy new clothes.

Aimless as it seemed, he intended to find an answer, which was when it hit me that Frans wanted to immigrate to another country and use horticulture to get him entry to that country. It was clear that he adored me and seemed most eager to sit down and talk with me, describing his plans for our future. Something was comforting about the procedure, and I agreed with what he wanted to do.

We applied to three countries. Canada and South Africa needed farmers and horticulturalists. Peru was our third choice because a cousin from the Peters family used to live there. This cousin's wife had died, and he returned to the Netherlands at the beginning of 1945, where he met someone new. He married her and returned to Peru. We might have gone there, had his cousin answered our letters. But finally, we chose Canada, as they had first responded to accepting immigrants in agriculture and horticulture, as well as Dutch war brides with their immediate families.

Our Wedding

I poured myself into planning this day. The elegance of the entire affair had somehow mattered to me, and there was a lot of preparation. First, I wanted to purchase specialty foods for the celebration. Because there was nothing to buy in the Netherlands, I needed to go to Germany. I took the leave train to my army unit, where I was allowed to purchase the items that I wanted: cookies, butter, sugar, chocolate, and many other similar foods that I could not get in Deventer. I could not use money to purchase these items, but I could trade with my coupons at our YMCA. When returning, I would get a ride to the border and take the train from the border to Deventer. Frans would be standing at the border train station, patiently waiting, when I could not get the train on these errands. We would drive to Deventer together with all my food parcels.

Secondly, of course, I wanted to buy a wedding dress, which I could neither find in the Netherlands nor in Germany. So, I went to Belgium, and with my Belgian money, I bought some dress material. The plan was to have the dress made in Münster, Germany. When I saw the finished dress, I could not believe the seamstress's attention to detail. It was so beautifully made.

Then on my return train ride, I ran into difficulty because, in 1948, there were more stringent rules in border crossings, even for those in the military. Border officials inspected my suitcase and saw what I had packed. Would they spoil my dream of walking down the aisle in my dream wedding dress? I found that my heart was pounding as they asked many detailed questions about where I had purchased the material, who made it, and how I had paid for it. I remembered thinking that if my heart stopped beating, they would never forgive themselves for their entire lives. After the wretched ordeal was over at the border, I made a hasty return home.

But I did not want to make this my last trip to Germany as a member of the British Army. I had one more plan up my sleeve.

Before I was ready to depart from my past, I wanted to bring over Philips radios. I had heard a rumour that many Philips radios were stored in one of the factories in Hanover, Germany. Hundreds of them had been stolen from the Eindhoven factory under the German occupation in 1940. I wanted to buy one for the YMCA, one for my family in Deventer, and one for myself. I needed to take the three radios with me as baggage, but I knew that I needed formal Dutch government papers. Without thinking it through, I tried to hide them in the train with an army blanket covering them up. The border officials found and took them away, but they agreed that I could pick them up later after they were inspected and released. I obtained all three radios, and I took my radio with me to Canada.

In researching Phillips radios, I discovered that they needed a unique type of light bulb to keep them operational. The radios, however, came without these light bulbs, and one could only purchase them in the Netherlands. So I decided to buy them in the Netherlands and sell them in Germany! I used my British bank notes to make it a legal purchase, and I put the profits that I made in the sales towards paying for the wedding and our upcoming trip across the ocean.

The twelfth of April, 1948, was the most beautiful day of my life. At eight-thirty in the morning, a horse-drawn carriage came to the Peters's residence on the Langebisschopstraat to pick up Frans. After that, another carriage came to pick me up on the Hoge Hondstraat. We had a procession of five horse-drawn carriages in total. I remember seeing many familiar faces in the crowd looking at us, one of them being Frans's former boss from the garden centre where he once volunteered. At nine o'clock, we went to the town hall to be married by the civil official and sign our marriage contract. We were in the Blessed Heart Catholic Church in Deventer on the Zwolseweg for the religious ceremony at a quarter to ten.

I felt it then, the power of what we were doing and the significance of the whole marriage ritual. With our futures still unwritten, we stood there before our friends and family in the church while three priests recited the mass. Frans and I gripped each other's hands as we said our vows. We later went to the statue of Maria and prayed for her blessings for our marriage.

Between two and four o'clock in the afternoon, we had a reception in my parents' home. We sent out twenty invitations to family and friends, so we had forty guests in addition to the wedding party. We had dinner at the Maison Longayroux Restaurant in Deventer, the same place as the celebration for our engagement. We were surrounded by the love of both our parents and bridesmaids, Ria Peters, Lies Gotink (who later married Frans's brother, Ton), and my sister Rie Janssen. My younger sister Greet was supposed to be a bridesmaid, but she became sick at her boarding school only a week before the wedding and needed to be hospitalized. Gerda Haverkamp, my brother Arnold's fiancée, would replace her. The ushers were Ton Peters, Arnold Janssen, Jan Janssen and Lou Peters.

At the church, Pa Janssen (my father) walked with Oma Peters (Frans's mother), and Pa Peters (Frans's father) walked with Oma Janssen (my stepmother). They took photos at the church and at my home. We received many good wishes, flowers, and gifts. I had my wedding flowers dried and embedded in our wedding photo album. The guests' names and what they gave as gifts were written in this album, too. Finally, we spent our first night at the Hotel van Wely near the Deventer train station.

Preparations for Our Departure

The SS *Tabinta* was a transport ship for army troops in the army during the war. It weighed 8,100 tons and could carry 750 passengers. The vessel made five trips to Canada, carrying many immigrants, who were mostly farmers leaving their homes in the north province of Friesland because there was a shortage of land there for them to farm. However, there were others who all had differing reasons for departing. For us, we had connected with and were sponsored by a nurseryman who grew roses in greenhouses, and trees and shrubs on a large piece of land. He lived in the small town of Sheguiandah on northern Manitoulin Island in the province of Ontario, Canada.

We were supposed to be on the ship's first voyage. Unfortunately, because of a health issue, our departure date was delayed. A large tumor had grown on my neck, which needed treatment before arriving in Canada. After a visit to the doctor, I had it removed at the end of January, but we had to wait for medical permission to leave the Netherlands. The first voyage of the SS *Tabinta* was already solidly booked, but we successfully purchased tickets for her second voyage.

During the two weeks before our planned departure from Rotterdam on April 27, 1948, we visited many relatives, including cousins, aunts, and uncles from both sides of our families. We left Deventer by train that morning with some of our family members. Frans's mother did not want to go with us because it was too emotionally difficult for her to say goodbye at the port of departure. The prevailing thought for all of us was that Frans and I would never return to the Netherlands or ever see the family again. And to both our surprise, Frans's father said while we were sitting on the train that if we did not like living and working in Canada, we would always be welcome to return to live with them in Deventer. We were comforted to have his father's kind blessing in this way.

We sailed from the Rotterdam port at four o'clock in the afternoon to depart for Canada with two large baggage containers addressed to Sudbury, Canada. We also had 100 Canadian dollars in our pockets.

Our Accommodations on the SS *Tabinta*, and First Sights of Canada

On the first day on the SS *Tabinta*, we learned that all the men and women would be separated and sleeping in segregated quarters. The women were to have their children with them. Bunk beds were assigned, and I had lucked out with a bunk bed on the third level. Truly this was not what we had expected. We knew that a certain level of comfort would be sacrificed on the war transport ship across the Atlantic Ocean, but nothing like this!

I could not even describe how terrible the conditions truly were, and they progressively went from bad to worse because, by the third day, most of the women and children became seasick. However, in my specific case, I was learning about a new and surprisingly beautiful reality. I may have been seasick for part of the time, but I also felt sick more from morning sickness. I was pregnant with Sibylleke, our first daughter.

On his first day, Frans met someone he recognized, Ep Pothaar, who was also planning to work in the gardening industry. He was married to Rita, and they had a four-year-old son. The ship's personnel asked if any men wanted to help with kitchen duties by peeling potatoes. Frans and Ep both volunteered, and they earned the limited amount of one Canadian dollar a day. Frans also met Mr. Sloot, who had five children, and whose wife was expecting a sixth. Mrs. Sloot gave birth to a girl on the ship, and they named her Tabinta. We kept in contact with the Pothaar and the Sloot families for many years in Canada.

Several highlights of our twelve-day voyage were the times when husbands could rejoin their wives and families. One celebration that I remembered clearly took place on our ninth day at sea. The date was May 5, the day the Canadians had liberated the Netherlands. It was called Liberation Day and was considered an official holiday in the Netherlands. In merriment, we all danced to and sang old Dutch songs. Then, on that same day, we had our first sighting of Canadian land, the coast of Newfoundland. We sailed on through the St. Lawrence River. Finally, on May 7, we landed at Quebec City. Our journey into a new country was about to begin.

Frans and I were on the high seas, aboard the SS Tabinta, in April/May, 1948, en route to Canada.

I was at the rose greenhouse area and my first job was budding carnations for five cents an hour. Frans worked extra hours ploughing the fields on the Sheguiandah farm.

Chapter Nine: Initiation in Canada

Canada was a beautiful place and had evidently been a favourite of many people. How I wondered what fortune this new country would bring to us. Our lives seemed so tiny here.

I cut out a clipping from an anonymous newspaper that I found in Sheguiandah. It read:

Hollanders Now At Sheguiandah

A party of eight or nine Hollanders passed through Little Current on Tuesday on their way to their new home and employment at the Manitoulin Gardens, Sheguiandah. Youngest of the party was a baby born at sea on the way to Canada. The party landed at Quebec and came directly to Sudbury by train. The trip to Little Current was made by bus.

One English-speaking immigrant is said to have expressed his pleasure at the appearance of the local country, and the amount of water. He planned on eventually having a boat as he did in Holland.

Quebec City, Sudbury, and Little Current

In the distance, Frans and I saw the port of Quebec City. As the ship prepared to dock, we prepared ourselves for final goodbyes. We would not see our traveling acquaintances again, as some would travel as far as Alberta and British Columbia. There was no one else except for the Sloot family and us who were headed to the small town of Sheguiandah on Manitoulin Island in northern Ontario.

Before we were to set out, we walked around the old Quebec City, where I suddenly noticed an ice cream stand. Ice cream was an item unavailable in the Netherlands because of food shortages after the war. I could only allow my mouth to water at the ice cream cone in my hand that Frans bought in Canadian money, our very first purchase on Canadian soil. I allowed the sweet dessert to slowly melt in my mouth so that I could relish every delicious moment. With spirits lifted, I could now concentrate on my new stage of life, my pregnancy with our first child. I alone could think about my little secret inside of me as Frans and I strolled around the city.

Frans and I, and the Sloot family, traveled fifteen hours by train with the Sloot family to our second stop, the town of Sudbury, Ontario. Once there, fatigued from the long ride, we spotted a man waiting for us at the train station. He guided us to a bus, which would take us to Little Current, a town on Manitoulin Island, our third stop.

Frans and I were the only Europeans on the bus. The rest were Indigenous peoples who were not shy about asking Frans for cigarettes. Frans gave them a cigarette here and there to be friendly, but then the situation got out of hand, with everyone on the bus asking for cigarettes all at once. Finally, the bus driver shouted something in a language that I could not understand. Instantly, the passengers moved away from Frans and put their hands in their pockets. The driver also politely asked Frans to stop giving out cigarettes.

At the end of a four-hour bus ride, we arrived in Little Current in the late afternoon, where an employee from the florist greenhouse business picked us up to continue the final leg of our journey to the small town of Sheguiandah.

Sheguiandah, and Our Peters House

We traveled in a station-wagon-like vehicle, or perhaps it was a transformed truck with an added roof. The vehicle could hold the entire Sloot family plus the two of us. After we fussed and squeezed with our luggage into the vehicle, we were finally on our way. We passed by countryside dotted with farmhouses on huge pieces of farmland. Some had one or two cars or even two trucks parked in front of the houses. I had a mixture of unpleasant feelings at these sights.

Was I disillusioned or disappointed? Or was I too tired to even think of how I felt? Did I feel let down because most farms I saw were in a state of disrepair? I realized that this would go into my file of things I was learning quickly—that Frans's job would take on a different form than his previous work in the gardening business in the Netherlands. And my life would change with his life. I was beginning to suspect this plan of ours was leading into something of a trap, or at least that was how I felt it was initially playing out for me.

When we arrived at our destination, we stepped out of the vehicle, looked around, and immediately were confronted with two sagging old farmhouses in need of repair. The driver of our vehicle said the larger one was for the Sloot family, and the smaller one was for us.

We all trampled first towards the Sloot family farmhouse, which appeared to be normal-looking on the outside, but as we stepped inside, we discovered that there was not a single piece of furniture, not even a bed. What were we going to do? Frans immediately offered to help make beds out of the straw nearby. Never in his life had he made beds out of straw, but he persevered with the hope that the children would have a sound sleep. Exhausted after building benches with some bricks and boards nearby, we sat down and talked about our new surroundings.

Frans and I were tired, and we finally departed from the new home of the worn-out Sloot family to whom we so dearly attached ourselves during our three-day journey in Canada. We would see them in the morning and search for better furniture. We had yet to open the door of our own new home.

Our farmhouse was called Peters house. Upon entering, I almost threw up from the smell of manure and wet leaves. We could believe neither sight nor condition of the building where we were to live. How did we agree to this situation? It was like entering an oversized dog house, uninhabitable to human beings. For the single window, if you could call it that, was a hole in the wall. The floor was hardened ground, and we had no straw to make beds on which to sleep. We walked back to the larger farmhouse, and we asked to sleep the night there. We would not call the dog house our first home.

Mr. Johnston, the florist and owner of the greenhouse where we were to work, was absent when we had arrived. He owned a florist store in Sudbury, and because it was Mother's Day weekend, he was too busy with his business to be in Sheguiandah to greet us. I did not understand it then, but I learned soon enough that in the flower industry, all florists were at their busiest at this time of year in Canada—another item in my file of things I was learning.

We spent three days of inconvenienced living in subhuman conditions. We had to build our own straw beds in which to sleep, and construct our own furniture with the bricks and wood planks we found near the larger farmhouse. We explicitly told Mr. Johnston we would not live in the dog house for much longer. He then offered a room in his summer house, where we lived the rest of the short time we were there.

Our Jobs, and Our Accommodations

We started work the next day, the Thursday after Mother's Day weekend. Frans worked in the rose greenhouses during the day, and at night, he offered to plough the fields with a huge plough drawn by a tractor. Frans saw the work that needed to be done, and he could earn extra money by doing so. I could get the job of budding carnations in the greenhouses and earn five cents an hour. I would learn to do anything, as I did not want to sit idly and alone in this summer house room.

Therefore, my first job in Canada was to work with beautiful carnation flowers by cleaning them up before sending them to market. I had never done that work before in my life, but it was an easy job. The symbolic meaning of the carnation, I learned, was gratitude and affection, which I translated as blessings from God for our future lives in Canada.

One night, we decided to visit our Japanese neighbours, who were also working at the farm. In conversation, they mentioned that many Japanese were working in the tobacco fields during the month of May around the town of Simcoe in southern Ontario. One family recently left Mr. Johnston's to work there. Our neighbour added that he did not know if they made it there safely. We asked him why, and he replied:

"We fear that the Canadian government officials are sending the Japanese to internment camps in Western Canada because of the war."

We knew little about this part of the war, and they did not know much more either. We then asked about their need for more money and food, and they answered that there was work in the tobacco fields that provided much better pay than their present greenhouse work. We departed that evening, and in the next week, we did not see them anymore. We believed the government sent them to internment camps in Western Canada. We also thought of a new plan for our future.

In the meantime, we needed to purchase daily food, and since we had little money with us, Mr. Johnston allowed us to buy food items and other personal supplies at a little grocery store he owned to service his employees. We wrote down our supplies, and at the end of the week, the cost was deducted from our salary. We had few clothes with us, because we had packed most of our clothing in two larger baggage crates sent to Sudbury for storage. (But we did not need to buy any new clothes at the time, since we did not have the money, nor were there any clothes to buy there!) We had sent them there for safe keeping because, in the first place, we did not know how to transport them with us to Sheguiandah, and secondly, we did not know about the certainty of our jobs there. Were we destined to live in Sheguiandah our entire lives?

Growing Dissatisfaction

After each day, I felt less inspired in my job, and I battled unhappy emotions because I missed my European friends and the closeness of my family. Mostly, each day blurred into the next, and I was beginning to feel trapped in a place where I did not want to be. The days grew into weeks, and when six weeks went by, I thought I had lived for six years in this lonely part of northern Ontario.

We were not the only dissatisfied arrivals in Sheguiandah. One day, as I was sitting on a tree stump in front of Mr. Johnston's summer home, I just cried and cried loudly enough for everyone to hear. My physical state brought the attention of a young mother, pregnant with her second baby. Her name was Mrs. Touw, and she revealed that she and her husband were also growing uncomfortable with the living and working conditions. She admitted they were more attracted to work in the tobacco fields in Simcoe, where they needed help and the pay was higher.

Meanwhile, knowing the situation was not getting better for our family's future, Frans sought information from a magazine called *Canadian Florist* that he found on Mr. Johnston's coffee table. (*Canadian Florist* magazine has been the voice of the Canadian floral industry for over 100 years.) When flipping through the pages, he came upon a section titled "Job Advertisements." We both knew we needed to do something soon about our situation, or we would have to search for better prospects back in the Netherlands. So, for a start, we figured out how to place an ad in the same magazine, and it read:

"Dutch florist. Fourteen years of experience. Occupied leading positions in the Netherlands. Desires a good position, preferably in city suburbs. Horticultural College degree. Married. Home essential."

While waiting for a response, Frans and I decided to search for work in the tobacco fields with Mr. Touw and Mr. Sloot. We needed to leave Sheguiandah for Simcoe County in southern Ontario. We packed our bags with all our clothing, toiletries, and some food, because we realized we would not be returning if we found an immediate job worthy of our goals. To travel to our destination, we planned to take a bus, although we had little money to spend. If we could not get a bus, we thought to hitchhike to the tobacco fields, a trip of over 500 kilometres. I was not afraid of hitchhiking because I was already a seasoned veteran. Traveling in the Netherlands and Germany seemed like a lifetime away, but I was now in my niche, which made me feel strong and useful to our group.

Our Departure

It was early Sunday morning, and without rousing Mr. Johnston, the four of us departed for the first time from Sheguiandah. We took the first and only bus to the town of Little Current. From there we needed to get to Sudbury, a two-hour car ride. Our timing was not right, and there was not a single bus. So we decided to hitchhike. There were very few vehicles on the road, but we had to try.

Being the only woman in our little group, they chose me to put out my thumb to attract a ride while the other three would hide in the bushes to the side of the road. There I was, standing all by myself, feeling self-important with a big smile and my thumb turned up. And what a sight to see—a European-looking woman hitchhiking on a Sunday morning in the direction of Sudbury! Was I going to church? Was I going to visit family? Was I going to a funeral or a wedding? Who would know the answer? And the driver who would stop and pick me up would not know there would be three other passengers.

After one beautiful-looking car stopped, the driver opened his window to speak to me. He must have detected my European accent and asked from what country I had come. I was not in the mood for idle conversation, so I politely answered his question and hastily explained in English:

"I am interested in going to Toronto, and I need a ride," I said. I knew I had to tell him I was not traveling alone, so all in that same breath, I continued, "and I have three Dutchmen who are traveling with me as well."

At that moment, Frans, Mr. Sloot and Mr. Touw came running out of their hiding places and presented themselves to our next mode of transportation. We were in luck, because this kind driver was heading in our direction, and he agreed to let us off at the Sudbury bus station where we planned to take the five-hour trip to Simcoe. With luck working for us, we caught a bus that would leave in half an hour. We never saw our kind driver again.

We wanted a substantial meal after our long day of traveling. Finding a restaurant that would be open in the small town of Simcoe was not too difficult. We found a decent-looking one, and in conversation with the owner we asked if there were any jobs available on the tobacco farms.

"Why, yes," he said, "and the tobacco farmers need a lot of help these days. I will phone our councillor right away, because it seems you also need a place to stay for the night."

It was not the councillor who came, but the mayor of Simcoe himself. He knew of a tobacco farmer who would hire immediately. Mr. Sloot and Mr. Touw, anxious upon hearing this news, took the jobs and left for the tobacco farm that night. The mayor saw that Frans and I were hesitating, and we decided to tell him we were not interested in working at any tobacco farm. The mayor understood and invited us to one of his friends' homes, where we stayed for two nights. We planned to search out our list of addresses and phone numbers of job offers that we wrote down from *Canadian Florist* magazine. We were now on our own, and Mr. Johnston was not aware we would never return to his greenhouse business.

Mr. Sloot and Mr. Touw later returned to Sheguiandah to relate the rewarding news of their new jobs. But the information did not land on happy ears when Mr. Johnston found out about it. He knew his stronger working staff would be gone by the middle of August, and he had no one to manage and work at his greenhouses and farm. In retaliation, we thought, he turned off the hydro for two months while Mr. Sloot and Mr. Touw remained with their families to work there for two more months.

The Touw family worked at the tobacco farm for two years, but their story was unusual and unhappy. Unsettled in the tobacco field, they decided to move to a village near Timmins, in northern Ontario, where Mr. Touw worked in a factory for ten years, during which time he and his wife returned to the Netherlands five times. Each time they went to the Netherlands, they yearned for Canada, and each time they were back in Canada, they longed to live in the Netherlands.

The sixth time came, and before they left, they sold the two houses he built for his family and rental purposes. Were they sure they wanted to live in Amsterdam? Mrs. Touw was not sure, and after two days there, the family returned to Canada, but they had no home. They stayed in a motel in Timmins. Frans and I had stayed at this same motel on our visits with them while they were in Canada. We did not know Mr. Touw would die one morning later from a heart attack while taking a shower. We heard much later that Mrs. Touw remarried a widower with six or seven children, and we did not find out where they lived because she did not keep up the friendship.

The Sloot family had a happier story. While remaining in Simcoe working on the tobacco farm, Mr. Sloot became a successful entrepreneur in the tobacco industry. With little official schooling, he had supported the creation of a tobacco auction in Simcoe, a prosperous means of selling product while in season. Tobacco was marketed quickly and efficiently in this way. The Sloots had several children who all developed different interests as they were growing up. One child was musically inclined. Another, who became my goddaughter, became a teacher and married a widowed father of one of her students. One son worked for an irrigation company with whom we later did business. Another son, unfortunately, died early in a car accident. Then Mr. Sloot, at sixty years old, died of a heart attack while driving his tractor. Mrs. Sloot continued to live in an apartment in downtown Simcoe.

July 1948

Frans and I needed to make the most of our time, as it was already the end of July 1948, and we wanted to find work and a place that we could call home. Out of the three interviews we had lined up, Frans managed to succeed in all three. A carnation grower interviewed Frans in Windsor, a town in southern Ontario, and wanted him to join his business. Prudhomme's Nursery in Grimsby, a town situated between Toronto and Niagara Falls, Ontario, was also happy with their interview with Frans and offered him a job and a place to live in the apartment above the office. Mr. Grobba, living in Mimico located in the western part of Toronto, responded positively, and we planned to meet him by the week's end. Undecided about which job to take, we first visited our friend Ep Pothaar in Morrisburg, Ontario.

We hitchhiked to Morrisburg where Ep and his family lived in an apartment above a main street store. In all the commotion of five people living in a tiny apartment, including Ep's war bride sister and husband, Ep's young son Wim captured our attention with his feistiness and endless energy throughout the duration of our visit. Ep and Rita teased Frans that soon he would be pushing the baby carriage.

Frans responded, "You won't catch me doing that!"

We all had a hearty laugh.

While we hitchhiked back to Toronto, as fate would have it, Mr. Prudhomme, the same person who interviewed Frans earlier, stopped to pick us up.

"Where are you going to in Toronto?" he asked.

"We are visiting friends," we replied. We could not tell him of Frans's impending interview with Mr. Grobba at his greenhouses in Mimico.

The interview with Mr. Grobba was successful, and since we wanted to stay closer to the Toronto area, we decided to take that job. Mr. Grobba was quite old, already predeceased by his wife, daughter of the Stensson family who owned the well-established Sheridan Nurseries. Frans would work in the greenhouses and the fields of Grobba Greenhouses. We called off the jobs with Mr. Prudhomme and the carnation grower. We sent our two large crates from the Toronto train station to our newly-found apartment within walking distance of Grobba's.

Upon the arrival of our two large crates, I felt tiny goosebumps forming on my forearms, so anxious to see our homeland treasures and last connections with the Netherlands. Alas, I came upon our Dutch Indian carpets, and with tears in my eyes, immersed in emotion from the sight, the warm and soft feel of one special carpet brought back memories from our family who gave it to us for our wedding. With lingering sighs of relief, Frans and I reacquainted ourselves in a once forgotten happy life.

New Footings in Canada

Frans was happy working at Grobba Greenhouses. In the meantime, our friend Ep was not having the same kind of luck. In Morrisburg, he was working on freight ships, which sailed on the Great Lakes. Often, he came to the Toronto harbour and visited with us in Mimico. In conversation we discovered that he disliked the gambling on the ships, but his co-workers on the boat, in a way, forced him to play gambling games with them all the time. Ep wanted to save money, but it was not possible, because on payday, the excitement of gambling overruled.

Then one day, Ep returned late to the docks after his visit with us and was immediately laid off from work. In hindsight, the situation steered Ep and his family in a better direction. They moved to Toronto, and after they saw that Frans was happy working at Grobba's, Ep asked Frans to help him to get a job there, too. Mr. Grobba needed someone like Ep with talents in the flower and nursery business. Ep eventually created a new system of marketing Mr. Grobba's flowers and nursery material. Ep suggested selling them door to door. It was a successful system. Ep would soon become creatively instrumental in our lives, while returning a favour in one of Frans's aspiring business ideas.

With our new happy footings in Canada, I wanted to accelerate the passing of time by finding something to do. An ad in the local paper caught my eye, whereby a knitting company was searching for knitters. Because I loved to knit, I applied for the job. However, during the interview, I looked around and was stunned to see that the company had upgraded to knitting machines. I was not qualified. While analysing another job lead of ironing clothes, a lady at Grobba's hinted I should not take the job because it demanded I stand up the entire day while ironing. It would not be a good idea for a lady in my pregnant condition, and she talked me into resting and staying at home. I reluctantly accepted my position and rested while waiting for the birth of our first child.

The twenty-fourth of January was Frans's birthday. He wanted to celebrate his first birthday in Canada with two of his friends, Ep Pothaar and the husband of Mr. Grobba's daughter, an accountant for Campbell's Soup Company. After returning from merriment at the bars, I wanted to celebrate with *gebakjes* (Dutch baked goods) that I had purchased for Frans's birthday. Mr. Grobba's daughter gazed at me, advised against it, and said that I was ready to go to the hospital. I never ate my *gebakje*, because I felt the first pangs of labour, and

Ep drove me immediately to the hospital in his very new car.

Sibylleke, a child-name compromised from my name, Sibylla, was born at St. Joseph's Hospital on Lakeshore Boulevard in Toronto at six-thirty in the morning. She weighed eight pounds and four ounces. I woke up in the elevator with a nurse wearing a red sweater, who had Sibylleke in her arms. I never saw such a beautiful and perfect baby. When cuddling her in my arms, I became lost in wonderment just watching her breathe. She was a tiny person with dark brown hair and a beautiful face. Frans was supposed to visit in the morning, but he did not come until the afternoon. I secretly knew that he was recovering from having had too many drinks from his birthday celebration. However, he fell in love with Sibylleke the moment he set eyes on her. And from that very moment, we both entered our new world of pushing the baby carriage.

Frans came to the hospital each day for five days. Without a car, he used our bike to ride to the hospital. Then, one day, while cycling, a small English car stopped on Lakeshore Blvd, and the driver asked:

"Ben je een Nederlander?" ("Are you a Dutchman?")

Surprised at the sound of the Dutch language, Frans responded in Dutch to the driver. His name was Martin Van Zanten. They discussed the district where they lived in the Netherlands, and Frans mentioned visiting me in the hospital with our first child. They exchanged addresses and phone numbers, and ever since this meeting, we continued our friendship with the Van Zanten family.

Our next search was to find godparents for our little newborn. Mr. Grobba informed us of his Catholic neighbours, and Mr. and Mrs. McElroy were delighted to be godparents to Sibylleke. Our first and only baby carriage came from a Dutch lady, another war bride, who married a Canadian soldier, Mr. McIntyre. They had two sons and no plans for more children, and they wholeheartedly gave us their baby carriage.

We were moving forward quickly with our lives in such a short period of time, leaving behind memories of our experiences on the SS *Tabinta*, our first footings in Sheguiandah, and our first home in Mimico. Frans and I wanted to put down roots in Canada, and more urgently, Frans wanted to grow and cultivate any kind of plant that he could. The rules of growing were so mysteriously hidden.

"

I am interested in going to Toronto, and I need a ride, and I have three Dutchmen who are traveling with me as well.

"

By 1951, we established ourselves on the Mount Dennis property. I was contemplating the work that needed to be done in the fields.

Frans with Sibylleke, and I with our newborn Fransje, in late March, 1950.

Frans driving our first truck, in 1950.

Frans tended to the annual flowers and vegetables in the wooden beds in early spring of 1950.

Chapter Ten: Beauty in The Journey

Perhaps our entrepreneurial instinct truly was a family trait. While Frans engaged in growing volumes of trees, evergreens, shrubs and annuals, I was attached to keeping up with the books and the household. We both shared marketing and selling nursery materials with the public through our newly-created garden centre venue. Each day, the potential of our reward felt better. Our circle of friends, family from Europe, and the growth of our own family took root in a new home. Our business plan happened sometimes with intention, and at other times it did not. That was the beauty in the journey.

What Happens When Opportunity Knocks?

All was going fine until Frans and I felt we wanted to be challenged more in our lives, at least in the foreseeable future. It astonished me to see how an esteemed country like Canada offered business opportunities for those who could see and wanted them. Thinking about it got Frans and me out of bed in the morning. We pondered how we both grew up in business surroundings. We both missed it.

Canada provided opportunities to many people who had already immigrated before us, and we wanted to be part of that excitement. There were two reasons. First was the independence that owning a business could give. The second reason was because we wanted to put our specialized knowledge to work. With our driving work ethic, we both knew we could nurture that business. With the seed sown, all we needed to do was to cultivate it.

In the *Canadian Florist* magazine, we spotted a business for sale in the Kenora district and town in northwestern Ontario, 200 kilometres east of Winnipeg, Manitoba. Frans decided to go alone by train. Upon stepping out of the train compartment that winter morning in 1948, he shivered, tucked his woollen scarf closer around his neck, and remembered saying to himself, "Why is it so cold? My ears are frozen!"

Frans liked the little business that was advertised, and thought to grow annual flowers in the greenhouses. He already had it in his mind that I would take care of the bookkeeping, and he would develop a landscaping side.

After he returned, Ep Pothaar confronted Frans with his new proposition. Ep, in his wisdom and foresight, strongly advised against buying the property in Kenora, and suggested we create something near a city, such as Toronto, where we could find better markets. After much temptation in the new direction, Frans and I finally agreed, but we lost our 200 dollar down payment, which was a lot of money at that time. Then, soon after closing the door on Kenora, came another opportunity, and we hastily explored it.

The golden opportunity came with Frans's newly made friend Martin Van Zanten. Martin had the experience of owning greenhouses in the Netherlands, where he had grown tomatoes. During the war, he was rich because of the fresh food he could use to trade. When his firstborn son Hans was one year old, Martin brought him and his wife Freda to Canada to start a new life.

A greenhouse builder in Canada sponsored him, and he and his family lived in Mimico in the same house as his sponsor. Martin was interested in finding land to grow nursery stock, build greenhouses, and start a garden centre. He saw an ad in the paper where Mr. Wilson, living in Mount Dennis, the western area of Toronto, advertised the rental of his ten-acre plot of land. Martin discussed with Frans the endless possibilities of growing vegetables and nursery stock on this parcel of flat, rich land located in the valley where the Humber River flowed. However, the house available for them to live in was old and run-down. Although the land was perfect for growing and fulfilling Martin's business dream, his wife Freda grew unhappy about living in the house. They eventually decided to neither move there nor take advantage of the land rental.

The tables then were turned after Martin informed us of the same offer. We could not believe our luck at the twist of events. We could not refuse the offer. Our seeds were sown, sprouting, and ready to be fertilized. Martin related details to Mr. Wilson, and Frans immediately spoke with him.

“Mr. Wilson, I heard about your land and house rental offer in the Humber Valley. I understand Mr. Van Zanten had declined, but if you permit it, I am available to begin rental as soon as conceivably possible.”

Mr. Wilson was delighted to agree. It was a win-win deal. Consequently, in February 1949, we found a new, pleasant home and an ideal location, where we could begin our very own nursery business. We only spent a short period with Grobba Greenhouses, and although they were sad to see us go, they kindly offered to help us in the first steps in fulfilling our ambitions.

Building the Foundation to Our Business

What were the logistics of starting our business? What would we sell during the spring and summer of 1949 that could give us enough money to support our family and enough money to save for the future? We decided to start with vegetables that everyone was growing: the fast cash food crops such as cauliflower, cabbage heads, and radishes. When the vegetables were ripe, we would bring them to the market and receive our first business income.

Frans had shown the same gardening resourcefulness he demonstrated in the Netherlands, despite his inexperience in growing in the new Canadian weather conditions. With his initial foresight to starting a business, the process began earlier in the winter when we had ordered seeds from Stokes Seeds Company, having found their ad in the *Canadian Florist* magazine.

The process of seeding during that first winter went like this. Since there were no seeding trays in those days, Frans needed to build them himself. He retrieved free wooden boxes from the grape industry owners in the Niagara winemaking regions. When the Niagara vineyards discarded their one-time-use-only storage boxes at the end of October and November, Frans reserved them by phoning in advance, and then made the long trip to pick them up in the early spring. Once home again, he reshaped them using a saw and hammer. We both filled them with our homemade soil mixture and seeded them with our vegetable seeds.

At the side of the barn, Frans next built long, wooden, rectangular flower beds with window frames for coverage and protection from the harsh weather. After the vegetable seeds had sprouted, we transplanted the seedlings to these beds. With the danger of frost eliminated after the land had thawed, Frans then cultivated the fields to prepare for the planting of the mature vegetable plants. We were proud of our first successful crops that quickly brought money to the family and to the business.

When we first moved into our new home in April, Mr. Wilson allowed us to renovate and add more rooms to the existing house. The outside wall, made of white stucco, added a touch of class to the two-story house with a huge basement and ten stairs leading to the main entry into the home. In addition, we built bedrooms adjoining the house next to the bottom of the stairs, to provide sleeping places for some of our future employees from the Netherlands.

My work in the house was arduous. For example, since the water system was outdated, the mere means of acquiring a bucket of water took well over an hour, as I had to pump it manually from the artesian well. I was dependent on that water for cooking, drinking, cleaning, and laundering clothes, including a daily clean of all the diapers for our baby Sibylleke. But after my household chores, I always seemed to have endless energy to help Frans develop the business.

Our Second Child

It was Friday, March 17, 1950, and the snow began to fall, slowly, beautifully at first. It soon fell quickly and blindingly in thick white sheets. It was Mother Nature's last cold blow of that winter season. The wind blew the heavenly white gift everywhere, and the window felt so cold as I touched it.

I wondered—oh, how I worried!—how was I ever going to make it to my doctor, who wanted a final check-up before our second child was to be born. I was to see him at the Maplehurst House for pregnant women, which was in Weston.

The road needed clearing, and it was not just a simple flat road. It was a road with a steep slope that needed all available strong men to shovel. Frans and Mr. Wilson's son living next door, and two others, worked for hours clearing the road. Then in the late evening, the taxi came to pick me up. We drove up the steep hill, and from that point I could not remember how we arrived at a house, perhaps it was the Maplehurst House. I was in the living room, on a table, and I was giving birth to our second child.

Fransje, a compromised name for Frans, entered the world calmly and quietly at five o'clock in the morning on March 18, 1950. His first smiles stretched from ear to ear, emphatically showing their tiny shapes on his completely hairless head. He was beautiful and healthy, and I loved him.

Cousin Wim's Arrival

Our first guest from Europe was my step-cousin Wim Klein Beernink, who wanted to explore Canada before inviting his fiancée, Catherina (Tiny) Vallinga. A company in Kitchener, Ontario, sponsored Wim to work in Canada, but the plans disintegrated, and he decided to look us up. What came next for Wim was a series of lucky twists.

Wim did not have our address, but he had an address to Mr. Wilson's garage business in Toronto. It was early Sunday morning, and the business was closed when he arrived there. But as luck would be with him, he spotted a young-looking man who was out walking in the same area. After retrieving information from him about where Mr. Wilson might live, the man pointed in the direction of Buttonwood Avenue in the valley of Mount Dennis, where Wim should walk. Wim also learned that Mr. Wilson rented one of his properties to a Dutch family.

After an hour of walking, Wim struck up another conversation with an older man, who was smoking a cigarette while sitting under the porch of a house in front of a small greenhouse.

The older man said, "Go to the upstairs of my house, just over there, and ask my son for directions."

Surprised at his friendliness but without hesitation, Wim found his son sleeping in the upstairs bedroom. Wim moved closer, touched him, then shook him on his shoulder to wake him up.

"Sorry to bother you, but your father allowed me into your home," Wim said politely. "I have a question. Do you know where the Peters family is living?" Wim said it all in one breath, hoping for the best.

"Well, who are you? Never mind, my father welcomes everyone into our home! You asked about the Peters family, I heard you say?"

"Yes, do you know them?" Wim questioned.

"I used to work at Frans and Sibylla's nursery centre down in the Humber Valley, for a couple of months. Come with me. I will drive you there."

Wim was more than delighted, and soon he was standing at our front doorstep. He thanked this kind Samaritan and knocked on our outside door.

I was unaware of the time, but I knew that it was very early for a Sunday morning. I was half asleep when I went to open the door, which had a see-through window. I stood there, not worrying about what I looked like, and that image of me was without a single stitch of clothing! After we recognized each other, we just laughed without any more words to say!

Later that morning, since we did not have a car, Frans cycled to church while I looked after Sibylleke and Fransje. Wim and I went to a later mass by walking the five-kilometre stretch starting in our valley, up the steep hill and through the streets of Mount Dennis to my church of Our Lady of Victory. We decided then and there that Wim would become the godfather of our little son Fransje. But the day did not end here, because Wim needed a place to sleep, and there was only one bed in our home. All three of us decided to sleep together in one bed, me on one side, Frans in the middle, and Wim on the other side.

Wim would be married to Tiny Vallinga, who needed a place to stay when she would arrive from the Netherlands, but that would be their story to tell. Since I had brought over my wedding dress from the Netherlands, it was available for Tiny to wear. Wim and Tiny were married in Our Lady of Victory Catholic Church on July 29, 1950, with a reception in the recreation room of the church. The day was so intensely hot and humid that Frans was afraid that some plants back at the nursery would burn. Therefore, he would need to water them immediately. He cycled back to the valley to give care to them and returned to the church in time for the party. Tiny played the Dutch music recording of her guitar-playing brother and piano-playing sister, a little bit of Dutch ambiance that brought tears to the eyes of the Dutch invitees, Martin and Freda Van Zanten and Rita and Ep Pothaar.

Life went on in 1950. We continued our friendships with Wim, Tiny, Martin, Freda, Rita, and Ep. With our developing business, we managed to find time to have some fun on the weekends. One memory that stayed in my mind was when Wim, Ep, and Martin arrived at our place to swim in the Humber River, as they had done five or six times already. Frans and I knew little about the swimming conditions there, because we were not interested. But on that day Martin said, "I smell something awful today! What is that brown stuff I see over there?"

Could you imagine that what they saw was the contents of the run-off area for the local septic tanks? Unbelievable! They never went swimming there again.

Our business was expanding, and we needed more help to manage it. We asked my cousin Wim. He accepted and he became our first employee.

Growing Pains and Gains

Wim was such a dependable employee, but we could not pay his wages. We learned a hard lesson while he was working with us. Our business with cash crops was coming along nicely during the second spring, until we noticed that the radishes that the three of us pulled from the ground, did not turn out to be as productive as the other cash crops. Here was the reason: Wim received seventy-five cents an hour for his work. (We did not pay ourselves.) Our income of sixty cents a crate of radishes could not cover our costs. Since it would take more than an hour of labour for two or more workers to fill up the container with the tiny-sized vegetables, it was not worth our while to continue with that portion of our cash crops.

Then as the months went on, in further despair, we discovered that the growing of cash food crops became too competitive, and we were forced to even charge less money for the sale of our products. The timing of this dilemma matched Frans's increasing restlessness of wanting to work at something else more productive and appealing in the field of horticulture.

This was when Frans looked around the Toronto neighbourhood and noticed that homeowners showed pride in their homes through their gardens. That meant they would want to buy flowers and trees for their gardens. Frans recognized the opportunity where he could make better use of the land by planting trees, evergreens, and shrubs, selling them at a higher priced mark-up than vegetables. Also, to our advantage, there was far less competition in the growing and selling of nursery stock at the time.

Then the question arose, from where was he going to get the nursery stock? Searching again in the *Canadian Florist*, he found some addresses and ordered the familiar tree names from the Netherlands. Frans did not know if the Dutch-growing tree varieties he ordered would be hardy in the harsher Canadian climate. If he had worked immediately in a Canadian nursery and not in a greenhouse, he would have learned a little more about the hardiness of trees and shrubs growing in Canada. But he did not, and our fate was to grow trees by trial and error. Many trees we planted that first year died because of the cold, harsh winter, while others surprisingly survived. It would cost us some money, and we learned another valuable lesson in the nursery trade.

The nursery stock was delivered to our doorstep. The trees needed planting on our rented land, and my story was that I knew little about their names and how they were to be planted. I remembered planting some live sticks into the soil—that I later discovered were weeping willow bushes. Together with Wim and Frans, we continued to plant and cultivate the fields during the summer until we filled every possible space of the land.

Our heritage was Dutch, and we wanted to capitalize on marketing Dutch tulips, daffodils, and crocus bulbs in the fall season. Where would we get these bulbs? The answer came from Mr. Grobba, who was connected to a Dutch firm in the Netherlands that sold bulbs wholesale to him. In conversation, Mr. Grobba mentioned to them that Frans was beginning a retail nursery business in the Mount Dennis valley. Their sales representative, Mr. Van Noort (Senior), agreed to sell us the Dutch bulbs. We gave him our first of many orders and consequently we developed a long-lasting relationship with him and his firm.

Gardens needed plenty of imagination in design. Frans had a natural feel for creation on home garden landscapes. We purchased a truck for his new enterprise, and on the truck door, we advertised:

"Frans Peters, Garden Designer, Rockeries, Bulb Planter, Mount Dennis, Toronto."

When he went to his garden landscaping jobs around Toronto, he would leave the nursery with a truck filled with trees, shrubs, flowers, and tools. With an empty truck upon his return, I would ask him if he had another job for the next day. Most of the time, he would say:

"Yes, because before coming home, I had visited a new customer referred by the people where I was working. I must finalize a landscape plan for them by tomorrow!"

We were both driven by a force for the greater effort of our own business. Therefore, we both agreed upon

Frans's work hours that sacrificed our personal and family time. He would work all day, and after dinner hours, he would visit clients to draw up landscaping plans. Frans would often win his customers by conversing with them about the Netherlands and Germany during the war. Because we were one of the first immigrants who came to Canada after the war, people were eager to learn what had happened at that time. He succeeded in getting on people's radar and developed long-lasting relationships for the business.

On top of my regular business jobs, I had to first and foremost tend to the customers, always at unpredictable times—a new adjustment at home. For instance, if the customer asked for privet hedging, I immediately stopped at what I was doing, and plodded into the field with my shovel and dug up the privet myself for that client. Pleasing the customer was an integral part of the business, and by doing this mindfully right from the start, I would gain their trust, and their return business. As each night passed, while tucking my two children into their cribs, I always thought of the fact that Frans and I had reached the point of no return. We were thankful for our lifestyle choice.

Hard Work and Creativity

We had decent business practices with our growing clientele right from the beginning, in advertising, pricing, and deliveries. We advertised our popular and best-selling hedging items, such as red barberry, privet, and Chinese elm, which sold easily and quickly. In the case of Chinese elm, we captivated higher interest. We sold them inexpensively in our ten-piece bunches, costing only five dollars per bunch, and we delivered them for free even if it would mean going to the far east end of the city, quite a driving distance for Frans in his truck. Our motto was that no order was too small. I would begin the delivery process by first mapping out an easy delivery route for a minimum of five addresses. Frans delivered them once a week after his workday.

We learned how to minimize our cost of supplying annual spring flowers. The growing process started from scratch, first seeding them, then transplanting them early enough in the spring under the covered glass frames. Frans had built wooden stands to display the beautiful annuals when they were ready for sale to the public. Many repeated landscaping jobs included the planting of our home-grown annual flowers, such as the gardens at the tuberculosis sanatorium, located at the summit of our valley. People returned to our nursery because they enjoyed our service, the quality of our stock, and our prices.

In the first few years, I knew little about the names and characteristics of annuals and nursery stock. However, I could beat the drums in sales to earn extra income. I had proven my skills in marketing cigarettes and raincoats during my weekends off when working with the British censorship. So, in the beginning of our business, I decided to sell fresh-cut flowers, where knowledge of plants was not crucial. I traveled by the iconic trolleybus into Toronto to sell them in the areas close to both the hospitals of Saint Joseph's and the Toronto General, where I was guaranteed a market of many buyers. My arms were full at the start of the day with ten flower bunches, each bunch costing seventy-five cents, and I would usually return home with two or three bunches, which I would sell the next day.

Then I became interested in selling budgies. Yes, budgies! Some people at our church asked us if we wanted to adopt them, and since Frans loved breeding them in the Netherlands with his father, we were soon selling the birds to the well-known department stores of Eaton's and Simpsons in downtown Toronto. So, the basement area of our house became an aviary for our first 300 colourful birds, and we put in many work hours involving their identification and pricing.

Our nursery business became prosperous because of our hard work and efforts to save money. Finally, the moment arrived to give an official name. Could it be Buttonwood Nursery because of the name of the street where we lived? The Mount Dennis Nursery had a good ring to it too. Or could it be the Humber Nursery because of the proximity of the Humber River to our business? Since the Humber River was a popular location to the area, and everyone knew where it was, we voted in Humber Nursery.

“

Frans Peters, Garden Designer, Rockeries, Bulb Planter, Mount Dennis, Toronto.

”

After Hurricane Hazel levelled the land of our business in October of 1954, we reconstructed the lath house in June of 1955.

My cousin Wim Kleinbeernink with his wife Tiny, a photo taken many years later at my retirement party. Wim was our first employee.

Chapter Eleven: The Backbone of our Humber Nursery

The backbone of business is its employees, and we provided as much guidance and support as we could to all of them. In the beginning, we had a colourful group, and one employee stood out more than the others. I am going to relate that story.

Then one day in the fall of 1954, Mother Nature delivered a challenge to us. Hurricane Hazel levelled our Mount Dennis property. The business was destroyed, but we all rebounded from this ravaging natural disaster with the endless support of a wide range of people, including our employees.

Our First Employees

How interesting it was to be in business. You could meet a kaleidoscope of amusing human beings. Humber Nursery provided several colourful employees, with my cousin Wim first on the list. After a year working with us, he, together with our friend Ep Pothaar, ambitiously started a landscaping business on their own.

Second on the list of fascinating employees was a group of three Dutchman from the northern province of Friesland in the Netherlands. One was a minister sponsored by his church and looking for work as a preacher in a congregation. His helpful and likable nature relieved me of a few household bed and breakfast duties for the rest of the boarders, for whom we provided three meals a day, laundry, and tidying up. I certainly had fulfilling days taking care of everyone: my family of one husband and two young children, and the immediate needs of our garden centre, which included serving customers.

Third on the list was Bram, a character of mixed personalities who would endlessly entertain us. We sponsored him because he was a brother of Frans's friend who lived in the Netherlands. We knew he would be committed to the demands of our nursery because his father, a policeman, had recommended him. He was a jolly, musical fellow who would tell many tall tales and sing and play a variety of musical instruments, including an ordinary saw. Although we were entertained and kept dangling in laughter with his stories, we became increasingly worried about the things he did during his stay with us. Here was his story.

We had three young bachelors living and working at the nursery when Bram arrived. The trouble started already during the first week of Bram's arrival after all four received their salary cheques. They needed money, so they went to the bank to cash the cheques—all except for Bram, who quite openly admitted he did not need to cash his cheque because he stole the money from the other three! We had to report him to the police, who put him in jail that night. However, the three others did not want him jailed, and they bailed him out simply because they liked Bram and thought he meant no harm.

Then, a few months later, in the middle of the summer, our truck went missing. We immediately suspected Bram had stolen it because he had not come home the night the truck went missing. After a visit with the police again, we decided we could not lay any charges, because he returned the truck after a few days and sincerely apologized for his action. Apology accepted, but we would not tolerate Bram's mishaps and decided to let him go.

Bram found another employer, and we heard he was not only stealing money but also falsifying cheques. The police caught up with him again, and this time he was deported to the Netherlands.

Some very well-educated people on our list came from the Netherlands, whom we sponsored to work in Canada. For example, Jan Zutemelk's brother Koos, a landscape architect, eventually left our nursery to work in the municipal government. He sought upward mobility, but discovered the politics of the already established community were difficult for immigrants to enter. Koos disappointedly returned to the Netherlands.

However, most people we sponsored were satisfied with their new jobs in Canada, and one to mention was Frans's first cousin Riet Besseling (Raayman). Her husband Wim eventually worked with an established Canadian company with branches in the Netherlands and the Dutch government. Unfortunately, Wim died too young, leaving his wife and their two Dutch-born children, Thea and Jules, to work things out independently.

After learning the hard way, vigilance mattered a lot. For instance, we always left our doors unlocked, until the day we discovered that someone was taking money from inside our home. The incident occurred one Sunday, when we drove to church with the entire family in our truck. I was rushing to get everyone ready, and I forgot my purse in the house. I asked one of the employees if he would not mind retrieving it. Seeing that I was in a hurry, keeping everyone waiting, he instead quickly took out some of his own coins from his pocket for me to give to the church charity. When we returned, I looked for some money to return to the employee. I found out that my wallet was empty.

And as for us, the proprietors, Frans and I had both good and bad days. Some conversations were angry and tearful, and some were earnest and positive. For instance, Frans would sometimes forget his driver's licence, since he was not used to driving a vehicle. Frustrated, he would turn the truck around from wherever he was—going to church with the family, or seeing a client—and he would immediately drive back home to retrieve it. Frans was aware of his error of missing appointments, and any comment from me would end in a verbal battle.

And with further regard to his sensitive nature, he disliked the obvious name for his type of work—being called "the gardener." With pride, he would pretend not to hear the expression when someone called him that. He preferred Mr. Peters. The name-calling was a subtle remark, and he did not like it. Later one evening, we discussed the situation, and delightfully our dialogue led to better mutual understanding. His passion for gardening led to a discussion about the horticultural industry in Canada. He admitted that it was his dream to develop higher standards in the industry.

A Conversation Between Mother and Daughter

"So, Mom!" Astrid interrupted the interview, turned off the recorder, and continued with her question. "It seems you and Dad always wanted to leave the Netherlands, but I never understood to what extent. Dad had the dreams that swept him away from his family in Deventer, but he could have inherited the jewelry business, developed it, and all of us would have been born in the Netherlands. Did you not think that life could have been better for you?"

"Astrid," I said, pausing to take a minute to think about my answer. "I always thought about the jewelry business as a prosperous livelihood, but that business would not fulfill our happiness if only one of us were happy. My willingness to join Dad had to do with leaving a war-torn country where there was no future for us. Dad had a real passion for growing trees, and at that time, we had the opportunity to go to Canada. That was why and how we decided to leave the Netherlands."

"Okay. So, what happened to your families, your three crazy brothers, for example? Did they ever think of coming to Canada, too?" Astrid asked while scratching her head in curiosity.

"Oh! Those little scoundrels!" I chuckled and then glowed with pride. "They all settled down. It was difficult to believe my three mischievous brothers finally matured and grew up to be responsible husbands and fathers. Arnold married Gerda Haverkamp on June 12, 1950, and about a month later, Jan married Mien Langhorst. They lived with Guillaume and his wife Gretel in the same house because it was too difficult to find a house to buy or rent after the war. Both families were lucky to find a place and share living spaces in a house on the Oudegoedstraat, owned by Uncle Jacob Janssen and Aunt Dorothea."

Astrid commented, "In my mind, it seemed that after the war, life was not easy, but still easier than during the war. What happened to Dad's siblings after the war?"

"They went back to work," I continued. "Frans's brother Ton left home to start his own jewelry business in the town of Winterswijk. He married Lies Gotink on June 25, 1951, and they had one child, Frans. Frans's younger brother Lou remained with his father in Deventer and later, on June 18, 1953, married Magda Van Eijsden and had three boys."

I showed Astrid one of the many letters I saved from the Netherlands and explained, "I kept up with family news through letter writing, because it was still too expensive to speak on the telephone to Europe."

Astrid went downstairs to retrieve another photo album. After returning to the dining room, she made another cup of coffee for us and continued with her interview. She wanted to know more about when she was born. I began:

"Growing a nursery business was something like planning for a family. You, my little Astrid, were born on April 5, 1952, during the start of the spring season. I wanted everyone to know that timing was everything in planning your birth, because an early spring baby made it easy for me to manage outdoor duties in the busiest time of year in our gardening business. My family physician, Doctor Middlebro, encouraged me to return to Saint Joseph's Hospital, where Sibylleke was born. Your birth was simple, and I recovered after five days. Rita Pothaar's sister was visiting from the Netherlands, and she helped us with the household for three weeks."

"I know we were all quiet and lovable children, right?" Astrid affirmed. "How many children did you and Dad want to have?"

"I wanted a whole baseball team!" I boasted. "In the spring of 1954, we were due to have another child. Guillaume, later to be nicknamed Guy. He was born on April 11, 1954, in the new Humber Memorial Hospital. But I had some difficulties with the birth. The awkward sequence of events went as follows: after arriving at the maternity ward, I heard screams in loud female voices, and I thought I should cry out as well. My screaming attracted a nurse who tried to calm me down. She told me I should not have to cry out loudly with the others, because I already had the experience of three births."

"You must be kidding! That's a wild story!" Astrid interjected.

"I said to the nurse, 'I quite disagree with you, because I am in pain right now.' I did not know it at the time, but as it turned out, this birth was so painful that Doctor Middlebro advised Frans and me not to have any more children. Problems arose from my negative blood, and Frans's positive blood. We were disappointed, but Dad and I were sizzling with happiness to have Guillaume, a healthy little boy."

Astrid stated she was sorry to hear about our crushed plans. Then—*click*—she restarted the tape recorder.

Adversity and Survival

In October 1954, Mother Nature ultimately challenged our family and our business. Hurricane Hazel blasted the Atlantic Coast of the United States as a Category 4 hurricane. After causing fatalities in the United States and Haiti, Hazel struck Canada, where I had not expected Mother Nature to send a hurricane. Toronto had the highest death toll.

We had finished our workday normally. The Dutch bulbs had recently arrived from the Netherlands, and we stored them neatly in our barn beside the house. We had also just finished planting perennials and annuals in the fields.

Guy was only half a year old, and I had woken him up at three in the morning to give him his milk bottle. I heard the heavy rain pounding on the windows throughout the night, but it had stopped abruptly. When I glanced outside, I witnessed full light everywhere, and I suspected that it was a full moon; I did not put on the lights to see what I was doing. Without worrying about the weather, and with the baby fed and Frans and three children soundly sleeping, I quietly stepped back into bed and fell asleep.

In the morning, we turned on the radio to hear the first shocking news of the ongoing events of Hurricane Hazel, mostly about her destruction and damage to our city and the planning of peoples' safety through evacuation measures.

"What are we going to do?" I asked Frans. "Are we safe to stay in our house?"

We heard reports of a tremendous amount of flooding, particularly from the overflows of the rivers that threaded throughout the city, and one was the Humber River. Unfortunately, we were situated much too close for my liking, because the dikes had broken due to high winds and heightened water levels. As a result, water spilled to most of the lowlands of Toronto, putting roads and cars all underwater. The waters rose so rapidly and with such incredible force that a boat of any size sent to help save people could not maintain control.

The hurricane had brought her destructive winds of 110 kilometres per hour, and had dropped eighteen centimetres of rain suddenly and fatefully. There was significant damage to houses and industries in such a short period. Also, the lives of many people, both children and adults, were lost. But worse, Frans, our children, and I were in real danger that dreadful morning, as the next set of dikes were about to break, and we needed to get out of the house and the valley quickly.

I saw through the window that the water level had risen to over a metre high, and I could see that two of the newly-built Wilson houses across the street were unrecognizable. Some people waited in the water to save their belongings, viciously swept down a hurricane-made river. Frans had seen worse: three dead people about 100 meters from our house. A helicopter was in the process of helping, because no one could safely drive down into our trapped valley.

Later we heard that many people we knew believed we were all dead. But, in amazement, the house phone was still working, and Frans immediately called the police to let them know we were alive. They advised us to move out quickly because there was the fear that another dike would soon break and let go a brutal force of water, to drown everything in its path.

The second call Frans made was to his cousin Riet Besseling, who lived close by. We let them know we were alive, but we needed their help because the police advised us to leave the area. I was never so nervous in my life, and I could not think through what to take with us.

"Blankets only, and hurry!" Riet suggested.

I managed to grab a few smaller items with the blankets. We were waiting inside the front door, ready for Wim, who would try to drive down into the valley to rescue us.

And just then, as I was taking a headcount of our children, our little curious four-year-old Fransje could not be accounted for. I was devastated to realize that he had disappeared from the spot where he was standing and waiting just a few moments ago. The only possible way to go out was through the door, which I tore open. Thankfully, I spotted him within a close distance, but sinking in a watery, thick, and deep mud stream. I stepped cautiously towards him, every second counting for a successful rescue. I finally reached and grabbed him quickly with one free arm, grasping the staircase's handrail with my other hand. I cried out in relief when the weight of his tiny body settled in my grasp. I counted my blessings.

In all the excitement, the police concluded that the potential of the dike breaking was over. Could the dike be indestructible, or was the water force greatly diminishing? Should we leave the valley? We decided to stay, and in about ten hours, the water level lowered about a meter. We were lucky to have survived, but we had a horrible mess all around us. We needed to address the situation.

From our home we could see all the damage. Our brown barn with Dutch bulbs tucked in muddy puddles was destroyed; the flowering perennials were floating in the remaining water; the high winds uprooted the trees in the fields; the rich soil had washed away; and the ground appeared useless. What were we going to do? In less than a day, the hurricane destroyed the business beyond repair.

We knew we had to uproot soon and move to another location. We could not do anything in the valley anymore. That was our thinking at that time.

Property For Sale

We had intended to leave the valley and purchase a place of our own, but not because of a natural disaster and not so soon. Upon seeing and ad in the *Canadian Florist* about a greenhouse with a house for sale on Islington Avenue near Dixon Road in the West End of Toronto, we decided to check out the property. We liked the area, happy to find something not too far from the valley where many people knew about Humber Nursery. The extra five acres of land was a bonus, and we saw business potential. When the business would bring in some money, we would rebuild the house and repair the greenhouse. So, we bought the property for 20,000 dollars, although the price was high for the area.

The purchase was our first glittering hope since the hurricane, and we were proud of our first property ownership. Because we could not move into the house right away, we found a rental home nearby to settle and live for a few months over the winter. It was on Buckingham Crescent, close enough to the new property.

No sooner than a few weeks after our move from the valley, our good fortune turned. All the sour clues pointed in the direction of one influential landowner, and as the weeks staggered on, the hurdles grew taller. Here was why: the owner of the surrounding property was a woman who did not want to see a retail nursery and greenhouse business spoiling the quiet and houseless serenity of her land.

This woman went to the City Council meetings and claimed that there should be a by-law to prohibit building a business near her property. By her affluence and strong influence at all the following discussions, we knew that she would get her way. Frans attended two of these council meetings and he saw that she had successfully convinced the members to believe that our business would destroy the area's ambiance. With their new protection by-law in place, they prohibited us from building, and we had no choice but to ask Mr. Wilson if we could return to the valley. He kindly said yes.

Out of Failure Came Strength

When a decision is made, one needs to stand by that decision. Our refreshing opportunity to live in Canada was dampened by the will of Hurricane Hazel and the powers of humankind. Frans and I humbly acknowledged where we were in our lives, considering the damage in the valley after Hurricane Hazel and the failure of building a business on our first property. We decided to restart our business in the valley near the Humber River. We would nurture new seeds and fulfill our dreams.

The list of things to do branched in every direction after the hurricane. We needed to clean up through heavy work where we last left our nursery. With tremendous determination, Frans first reploughed the ruined fields and at the same time saved what trees, shrubs, hedging, and perennials that he could. He then replanted them. Church volunteers helped to rebuild or repair the framed beds, the old barn, and our rental house. Oh, how the list was endless, to start from scratch all over again. But we loved our work, and we believed the business would give us many rewards in return. By late winter and early spring, we seeded our annuals for our business spring season of 1955.

The spirit of survival moved in another small but different direction. Always looking again for ways to supplement our income, we teamed up with a Dutch couple from Winterswijk, the Netherlands, the same town where Frans's brother lived. We met them at the church, to initiate a business in raising a curious kind of animal called the nutria. It could be a lucrative business if done well.

The nutria was a small animal and came in many fur colours. The more variety of colours, the more expensive they became. In January 1955, we purchased a pair of them, costing 400 dollars, from a farm in southern Ontario. Part of the care, especially after the babies were born, was to keep the newborns' vigilance so that they remained on the mother's back, preventing a slight fall that could cost them their lives. Frans and I took turns taking care of them on our property, and the Dutch couple from Winterswijk came to our place biweekly to take over. However, as time passed, raising the animals soon became too much work, so we decided to give up the enterprise. We sold the business after two years, we broke even, and we could say we tried it.

Our business supported our community with jobs and gardening services. And our community supported our business in more thankful ways that we could count. Mr. Wilson kindly allowed us the return to his property; people from the church helped restore the valley to normalcy after the hurricane; and we enjoyed sharing a business venture with the nutria. Our family grew to four children, who were an integral part of our lives. It was 1955, and we were moving forward.

In 1955, I learned how to drive our stick shift Volkswagen Bug. On Saturdays, with our four children in tow, I drove to our 100-acre Caledon farm, where I usually parked in front of the old farmhouse and barn.

A memorable photo of Frans and our dear friend Ben DeBoer in the summer of 1956. The children from left to right were Guy, Astrid, Sibylleke and Fransje.

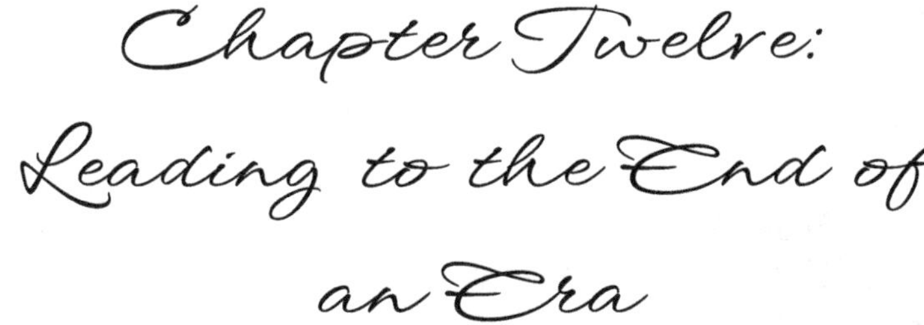

Our children were growing up in the environment of a business, and I captured some memories of my children during this early period of their lives. And for the first time in my life, I was going to travel by plane. My Dutch family waited to see me with my first born. Following that trip was a honeymoon trip to Europe with Frans, but this time I traveled by ship.

Then, in 1959, because of unforeseen situations caused by the growth of our business, we needed to uproot ourselves from the valley. We purchased a ten-acre land property north of Toronto, Ontario, where we would finally build our family home.

Memories of the Children

1. Walking

I usually walked to the bank, church, and grocery stores. The children came with me and cleverly remembered the walking route, which became their route to school, the four kilometres each way, every day, to and from Our Lady of Victory Catholic school in Mount Dennis.

Too young to walk home alone from school after morning kindergarten, Guy needed someone to escort him home. Astrid was old enough at grade one age to accompany him as far as the Buttonwood Avenue hilltop, near the tuberculosis sanatorium hospital. But, needing to return to school for the afternoon, she would only bring him three-quarters of the way home, leaving him at the top of the hill, as he could self-manage his way home from there.

One day, Guy had not arrived home at his usual time, and I was worried about them both. Were they in an accident? Were they detained for something that happened at school? I called the school, and surely they would know, but Guy had already departed with his sister.

"Hey Guy, come with me. I know a shortcut to get home quicker!" Astrid told her brother knowingly.

"Prove it! Prove it! Let's go!" Guy insisted impatiently.

Astrid walked the short-cut route, first taking a well-worn trail in the forest that led to a street. At the end of that trail, however, not recognizing the surroundings, she decided to walk in the direction of an unfamiliar road. Then, in the distance towards the end of the street, a familiar bank sign appeared, the Bank of Nova Scotia, where I always used to go. She planned to make her way to that bank, not to do banking with her mother beside her, but to ask the bank manager to phone home because she and Guy could not find their way. I was relieved to get a phone call from the bank manager. The story ended well. I picked them up in my Volkswagen (more about the car later!), first dropping off Astrid for afternoon school, and Guy came home with me.

Moving forward in time, this same bank manager came to visit me in the spring of 1997 and asked if I remembered him from the Bank of Nova Scotia at the corner of Weston Road, where Astrid and Guy were once lost. I did not recognize him at first, because he had changed in appearance over the years. But as we conversed about the story of my two youngest children, I remembered how thankful I was for his saving phone call.

2. Driving

I could pick up Astrid and Guy from the bank in our brand-new Volkswagen Beetle. Having followed driving lessons three years earlier in a stick shift car, I neatly parked our fancy new Bug in front of the bank. We were in cramped quarters when the whole family was together in this small car, however it provided a new experience of closeness. In that little space, we had the chance to talk, play games, and have some family fun all at once. It brought back memories of the days when I was a young child, traveling with my father and siblings to Germany by train. It was always a treat to be together with the family.

Using the car for errands made my life less stressful, and I gained extra time that I could use elsewhere in my busy day. Then one day, I was more than grateful that I had learned how to drive. Unexpectedly, we had a family emergency. Both Fransje and Astrid had to have their tonsils removed, immediately. Our family doctor recommended that our eldest and youngest should have their tonsils removed, too. So off we journeyed to the hospital, all four children tucked neatly in the Bug, while Frans took care of the business. But while on our way, I was suspicious of inclement weather on the horizon—an oncoming rainstorm.

My children were going to have a strange kind of family closeness sprinkled with a touch of adventure. I felt the scent of the incoming rain, which suddenly fell with a raging force. I slowed down my driving because of the rain. We were almost at the Humber Memorial Hospital, where in a lower part of the main road, small puddles swiftly grew and developed into a large pond. As I maneuvered the Bug through the deep water, I thought about why I was almost floating like a boat with a carload of four anxious children at seven o'clock in the morning! Nevertheless, I made it through, and three of the children had their tonsils removed that day, returning home late that afternoon. Unfortunately, Sibylleke had some difficulty with the procedure and needed to stay in the hospital for three more days.

3. Our Little Work Team

Frans and I continued to work with diligence, every day, in our business in the valley. Our two eldest children—the 'big kids,' as they called themselves—also worked with us, planting and weeding in the fields. In their minds, they thought that they did a lot of work at their age, and as we realized later in our lives, perhaps they did. While the 'little kids,' as they called themselves, were still too young to work, Astrid and Guy spent most of their time in the playpen together. The routine lasted two years.

One day, I lost all four children while working in the fields. The plants and weeds were so thick and high that I could not find the children to gather them in for lunch. Then I saw movement in the bushes. When I came upon them, three were pulling the weeds, and where was the fourth? The three did not know. I looked for Guy, and in the deepest brush, I found him sleeping peacefully, surrounded by greenery. I was relieved. It was not long before Frans and I rewarded our children for their work. We put them on a special business payroll.

Traveling Across the Pond by Air

During the fall of 1957, my father became fatally ill, and I wanted to see him. It would be my first airplane trip across the Atlantic Ocean, from Toronto to Amsterdam. Nine years after our wedding, Frans and I never thought that when we left our homeland in 1948 by ship, that one of us would ever return, let alone take an airplane to get there. We decided that eight-year-old Sibylleke would come with me.

There were many preparations, and aside from packing our clothes and organizing the paperwork for our passports, I needed to undertake the huge process of organizing the seeding boxes. I wanted them to be transplant ready when I returned from the trip. That was the job that I did on my departure date for my first trip back to the Netherlands.

My heart was pounding, and my fear was overwhelming as we got closer to the airport in our car that Frans was driving. I held Sibylleke's hand tightly, and clutched my handbag close to my side, as we walked to the counter to get our tickets. We waited in line to go through the gate, waving last farewells to Frans, and I was thankful to have Sibylleke with me, because she gave me purpose to keep calm. We sat with the other passengers and waited for the boarding call. Then I heard it: "Flight to Schiphol Airport, now boarding."

The flight attendant, wearing a blue dress, welcomed us and guided us to our seats. When everyone settled, the engines roared. Sibylleke sparkled with excitement as she sat beside me, her little doll Annie on her lap.

The plane started to move down the runway, and then we were in the air, with fluffy white clouds surrounding us. About five hours later, after slipping in and out of sleep, we heard a voice from a speaker in the ceiling. All at once everyone quietened down to listen to the pilot of the plane. He said:

"There is an unexpected strong wind, and we have not compensated for the extra fuel that we need to fly to Amsterdam. We must therefore refuel in Iceland."

With the landing gear beginning to take motion, the plane swerved a little to the left and then to the right. I was sure that if Frans was with us, he would have fainted, as he feared flying, just like his father did. A few of the passengers felt uneasy, my little daughter included, and many sympathized with Sibylleke since she was the only child on board. Looking out the window through the clouds, I saw tracings of the island of Iceland, where we needed to land for our refueling.

Safely landing on the runway strip after two bumps, we walked into the receiving area of the airport. It was not tourist-ready, but in its simplicity with a small restaurant and souvenir shop, we could rest, refresh, and regain our ground bearings. Then I realized that we were going to have to do the ascending and descending flight again. I was nervous but got through it, with Sibylleke feeling much better. I convinced myself right then and there that if I did another trip in an airplane, I would not be nervous.

The flight attendant welcomed us again, and we sat in our same seats. The engines roared and the plane started to move down the runway. My hands did not shake as much as they had the first time when the plane accelerated. Then finally we were in the air, and that's when I calmed down again. After forty-five minutes, we descended to the Amsterdam Schiphol Airport.

I could not believe how the Schiphol airport had changed—a reflection of an improved Dutch economy, with brightly-coloured places of business and a rush of travelers moving quickly in every direction. Snippets of foreign languages that I heard—in French, English, German, Spanish, and Danish—made it feel international. The train station was within walking distance inside the airport, and with our two retrieved suitcases in hand, Sibylleke and I made our way by train to Deventer.

Deventer had improved in its own way, maintaining its medieval look and feel. But more about that later.

It had been so many years since I had last seen my father. He looked old, with unkempt graying hair and long wrinkled fingers. However, his first words of warmth and welcome came with a huge smile and then many hugs. He was happy to see me again, and his first grand daughter, Sibylleke. I was much too excited to speak. After calming down, I unravelled the story of my diligence in working at our garden centre until the last minute before departure. Frans and I made and prepared seeding boxes outdoors in those few hours under the blue and sunny Toronto sky. The news stunned him, because he did not understand that our business in

Canada involved so much unprecedented physical labour.

We talked about Frans and my other three children, about life and customs in Canada, and more about the operation and management of Humber Nursery. He nodded and understood all the work efforts of my entrepreneurial spirit and starting and growing a business.

And lastly, he asked, "Are you happy with your life and business in Canada?"

I responded, "Every day I think about my happy childhood. Look at me, Pa. I am just as happy right now."

Sibylleke was soon the centre of attention. With a white bow of considerable size in her hair, which swayed with her every move, her smile would widen as she encountered people whom she had never met before. She made me feel proud that I had done something good in her upbringing. I lost those nervous butterflies in my stomach with her at my side, and the nine-year absence seemed like it had been only nine days.

Our Honeymoon

I enjoyed that trip to the Netherlands so much that I wanted to return to Europe with Frans. It would be our long-awaited honeymoon and a celebration for our tenth wedding anniversary. We were going to travel across the pond by ocean liner, a ship more beautiful (of course!) than the *Tabinta* in 1948. Gertrude, our trusting hand in the nursery, would care for the children and the household.

We transported our car on the ship, and it gave us the freedom to travel where and when we desired to go. From the landing dock in Rotterdam, where we last saw our Dutch relatives in the spring of 1948, we drove immediately to Deventer. Oma and Opa, Frans's parents, opened their arms to welcome the two of us. Lou, his brother, and his wife Magda opened conversation in Dutch. In our mother language, we comfortably unravelled our stories: the birth and growth of our four children, the friends we developed, and the details of our Humber Nursery. Frans was in awe to see how his family had matured, and he remarked that the jewelry store had developed into a thriving business that could support two families.

Deventer kept its medieval feel as we strolled through all our favourite streets and places, remarking on the repaired buildings damaged during the war: the church where we were married, the schools that we had attended, the dance halls where we had taken dance lessons, the local butchers and bakers, the waterfront overlooking the bridges, and all the refurbished cycling paths. We continued to visit more family who lived in Deventer. We knew their addresses by heart; hardly anyone had moved. After all the excitement died down, we left for our European tour.

Expo 58, the name given to the Brussels World Fair in Belgium, marked the return of the World's Fairs, after eighteen years of absence due to World War II. For six months in 1958, from April 17 to October 19, visitors could witness the symbolic giant statue called the Atomium. After four square kilometers of exploration and three days of walking, we were tired out.

Driving onward to the Normandy Beaches in the north of France, we were met with the haunting sight where many soldiers perished during the D-Day invasion. As we drove further south into the wine regions of France, we discovered an unhurried pace of life, particularly in the Mediterranean district. We were appreciably forced into vacation mode and more idle time together.

As we drove further south to Spain, the weather became considerably hotter. In Madrid, the city where we stayed a few nights, the architecture had changed, too, and specifically I was impressed with the swirly black iron-fences on many of the hotel balconies. I went into culture shock when I learned that siesta time lasted three hours in the afternoon. So, naturally, shopping and banking business hours extended noticeably later into the evening.

From the southern coast of Spain, we steered toward Monaco, a country built on layers of mountains that extended to a beautiful valley overlooking the Mediterranean Sea. On the top of the mountain was the royal palace, and there we saw the one and only Prince of Monaco, walking freely with only his bodyguard.

Our trip lasted six weeks, and we longed to see our children in Canada. After our beautiful return trip by ocean liner across the Atlantic Ocean, we drove back to Toronto, our new hometown. As we turned on to the last leg of the trip, Buttonwood Avenue, who did we see walking home from school? We saw Sibylleke and Fransje, surprised and beaming with excitement at the sight of their long-awaited parents.

We bought many souvenirs and gifts for all four children, which gave us great pleasure. They stared breathlessly at one of the large suitcases sitting unopened on the living room floor and asked, "Mom, Dad, what did you bring for us?"

And we were delighted to have something to give to them. I could see that we had taught the children well about the true meaning of gratitude, because their appreciation shone through their sparkling eyes.

The End of an Era in the Humber Valley

We wanted to expand our garden centre, but the question of when kept coming up. To put things into perspective, we were not the only nursery that was seeking expansion at the time. We had associates whose businesses flourished in different ways. As examples were Sheridan and Holloway Nurseries, where we would make long-lasting friendships.

One life-long friend was Dick Veerman, who originally worked in Sheridan's purchasing and distribution department in the Netherlands. Frans enjoyed his passion in the business and his humorous personality. We also befriended Ben DeBoer. Having worked for years at Sheridan, he moved on to work at Solty's and Braun Nurseries in Hamilton before beginning his own wholesale tree-growing business in Uxbridge.

The life story of François Hennin, owner of Holloway Nurseries in southern Ontario, exemplified, in my opinion, pride of extraordinary immigrant success after the war. François was exceptionally hard-working and optimistic, and within a year of arriving to Canada, he managed to save enough money to buy land near the shores of Lake Erie near the town of Sherkston. Here he built his first house and three beach cottages. He maintained them by himself, and later, with the help of a good friend from Germany, Pia Klein, he also managed a large nursery tree farm and nursery. She eventually took care of his four children, who all led tantalizing careers that could fill another four books. François was as proud as any Canadian could be.

In addition to the nursery farm, there were 300 acres of cattle and horse fields and an airway landing strip for his three hobby airplanes. Having acquired flying skills with the French Air Force during the war, François would skilfully fly over the land in his plane, spotting nursery jobs and potential land purchases.

Once, while taking me on a joyride in one of his Cessna planes, François said to me: "Hey Sibylla, we're running out of gas!"

François flew the plane quite low over the water of Lake Erie, and I really believed that we were going to go down. When the plane soared high again to a safer flying height, I knew that he was only making a joke to show off his aerial skills.

François's wife, Paula-Françoise, a professor in French and Russian languages at a Buffalo university (New York State), helped him in the first years of his business, but at heart she did not share his same passion, and she became less interested.

In the meantime, Frans and I preferred to build a garden centre where we could sell our home-grown trees and shrubs. We needed a larger piece of property in which to do that. We were outgrowing our space in the valley, and our story first started with our Islington/Dixon property.

The house and five-acre property that we bought on Islington Avenue and Dixon Road gave us a few headaches. After renting out the house four times, we discovered that we were disinterested in the house rental business. When we put it up for sale, many real estate agents came to look at it because they personally wanted to buy the valuable property and build apartments and condominiums, which were all the rage at the time. We found a buyer and sold our property in 1959 for sixty thousand dollars.

Reinvestment into land was our best business opportunity. Also, our sacrifices on social outings and luxury purchases would soon pay off with this goal in mind. We found and purchased a hundred acres of farmland in Caledon, Ontario, for 100 dollars an acre. This was what the Canadian opportunity was all about. As a matter of fact, another house came with the deal, because our new Caledon investment included an eighty-year-old red brick farmhouse. However, it needed updating in electricity and plumbing. Nevertheless, it was an unexpected piece of beautiful real estate.

In 1959, our house and business in the Humber Valley was beautiful—not the Butchart Gardens of British Columbia, but certainly just as well-maintained. First, Frans landscaped our rented house to give it an attractive curb appeal with a unique rock garden surrounding our newly-constructed white staircase at the house entrance. In addition, he brightened the outside with fresh coats of white paint on the stucco stone wall.

Frans had also prepared the surrounding fields with soil to make it a rich mixture of peat moss, sandy loam, and manure. Then he maintained the fields of nursery stock in outstanding condition for the ten years that we were there. He also built many plants and seedbeds, two greenhouses, and repaired an old barn. In addition to all this exterior work, I was thrilled with the interior renovations of a completely new concrete floor, a beautifully finished bathroom, and a new basement bedroom for our children.

No wonder that we were content in the valley, and the business was growing. With many customers returning in large numbers, especially during the spring season, we could dance to the tune of our success built on hard work each spring. However, as much as we were happy with our living conditions, our landlord, Mr. Wilson, was not as enthusiastic. He did not enjoy the same satisfaction, and he became distraught, more and more with each passing year.

In reality, we recognized that Mr. Wilson disapproved of the window sight of chaos and disruption to his valley from us as business tenants. We knew that he could not even find space in his driveway to park his car during our busy spring seasons. The situation was too overwhelming, and finally, he asked us to leave the valley that year. That spring in 1959 was the last chapter of an era for us in the Humber Valley.

The Move

The first plan was to research an area to the north of Toronto. We wanted to maintain our popularity of goodwill and keep clients happy enough so that they did not need to travel long distances to shop at our nursery after our move. A ten-acre lot of land on Highway 50, a quarter of a mile south of Highway 7, originally in the Township of Toronto Gore (and later changed to Brampton) became our next real estate purchase in Canada.

Frans could envision achieving his horticultural goals on this property, with plans of building a large garden centre store, creating a display of outdoor hedging and other sample gardens, and constructing an increased number of greenhouses. He could also see the immediate use of the Caledon farm, which would supply the new sales station with trees, evergreens, and shrubs. In addition, the business could eventually lead to selling nursery stock wholesale to the growing numbers of landscapers.

Although we were sad about leaving our first business, we were glad to move on with our lives and build something new on land that we owned. In the few months we spent moving, we uprooted and replanted all our nursery stock. Not long after our new land investment, we bought a prefabricated bungalow, a novel way of building a home and all the rage at the time. Our goal was to have it built and completed by Christmas 1959.

After the land survey and digging the huge hole in the ground for a basement, the walls, interior, and roof appeared quickly and easily. Finally, on December 25, Christmas Day, just in time for Christmas dinner, Frans and I put down the linoleum floor in the kitchen, the last of the finishing touches. Our four children were booming with excitement to be living in the new home, and could attest to witnessing our big smiles as we laid down the last floor tile. We were now proud Canadians, paving new paths for our future and that of our family and Humber Nursery.

We hoped for a successful spring in 1960. As it turned out, our children's work efforts were a part of this forecast. From left to right are Astrid, Fransje and Sibylleke.

Sitting with Frans inside our living room in 1962 are Sibylleke, Fransje, Astrid and Guy.

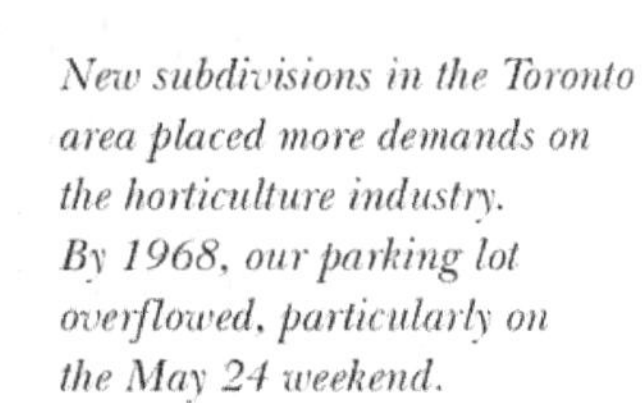

New subdivisions in the Toronto area placed more demands on the horticulture industry. By 1968, our parking lot overflowed, particularly on the May 24 weekend.

By the mid-sixties, our indoor and outdoor sales station greatly expanded to service the needs of our clientele.

Chapter Thirteen: Optimism of the Early 1960s

My life revolved around my family and Humber Nurseries Ltd. The early 1960s were a decade when our children helped in the development and growth of the nursery, although they really did not fully understand that concept at the time. We also guided them to attend Catholic schools and to become involved in music, hobbies and sports. And in the business, Frans and I established ourselves at our new location, but not without budding challenges that highlighted our first year of 1960. In the flow of life, our family routines would weave into our engaging business life. We would also learn to embrace the energized spirit coming from the social changes of the sixties.

1960: A Year of Pains and Gains

Could we make a profit this year? Two factors would be part of the answer to this question. We needed to have personal financial security, and our forecast for economic recovery in Canada was shady.

During the first year in business on the new property in 1960, we had overextended ourselves with our house mortgage. Secondly, we had to deal with the immense spending for supplies to get our business off the ground. We also had the haunting thoughts of bank repayment loans by the end of the spring season, even though we gained the trust of the bank manager through the goodwill we had built up in the business.

The explanation of the second factor had to do with our guesswork at optimistically forecasting a successful spring in 1960. This guesswork had to do with our dependence on the overall recovery of the Canadian economy.

During the years 1948-1949 and all through the 1950s, nursery businesses were almost nonexistent. However there was more competitive development in the early years of the 1960s because of more nursery and landscaping business start-ups. The reason they boomed was because of the sociological changes in the Toronto suburbs, where houses became more affordable. Small urban centres grew around Toronto, where people chose to commute by car to jobs in the city.

The newly-built subdivisions needed trees to line the streets; parks required landscaping; and people's homes needed greenery and flowers. So, nursery and landscaping businesses appeared everywhere. The boost in the industry became competitive in southern Ontario, particularly in the Niagara escarpment region, where business owners had the edge of better growing conditions and richer soils. Competition of nursery products meant lower pricing. The overall goal was to keep clientele happy and returning.

At the selling point, products also took on personalities either as winning propositions or losing deals. For us, we sometimes had a successful learning curve, as in the example of our own development of grass seed mixtures to accommodate various growing conditions. Other times, our losing deals dug heavily into our profits. One error that we made in the winter of 1959-1960 had to do with imports from the Netherlands. The Canadian government required that most trees have their roots washed before arriving into Canada, mostly to prevent diseases. Unfortunately, that winter was an exceptionally harsh one, and many of the trees neither survived the shock of the cleansing, nor the Canadian winter. As a result, we lost a great deal of money. Such was the nature of the nursery business, which I was learning about through Frans.

And what were the logistics of launching our business? In gratitude to my husband's knowledge, I had learned to make intelligent business decisions during the spring of 1960. For instance, I realized that the product (trees, evergreens, and shrubs) could be perishable if not given the correct soil mix; it could be sensitive to temperature changes; and it was subject to the daily effects of too much sun or not enough rain. Therefore, the work and method of propagation of our products had to be done correctly for us to have success in our business.

We propagated our products in three ways: seeding, cuttings, and grafting. Grafting required greater skill than the other two, and there was no certainty of success in any of the three processes. There was also skilled maintenance needed in the pruning of each tree and shrub. I came to realize we could have a successful year one year, and the following season could be a failure, simply because of weather conditions.

Our Humber Nurseries Ltd. survived that first year through the saving graces of selling cash crops. Advertising by word-of-mouth consistently brought in customers, and we gained quick revenue from the sales. Hedging plants, which were all the rage at the time, became our fastest money makers. The Chinese elm, the red barberry, the blue Arctic willow, and the privet were easy and hardy growing hedging plants. I would package them in bundles of ten and sell each bundle for five dollars. On average, I sold approximately ten bundles a week during the spring season, an incredible success story for that year. With our household expenses amounting to no more than fifteen dollars a week, we still had leftover money to put away into savings from that venture alone. I was always careful to keep our business and household expenses low, and at times that meant more work to be done by family members.

Our crop of privet hedging was the king seller, and this was how it worked: I took hundreds, perhaps thousands of cuttings, and Frans planted them in the greenhouse beds where rooting conditions were perfect. After the short rooting period, I transplanted them into our prepared outdoor beds for them to continue to grow. Our two older children weeded and watered them, working four hours a day during the summer growing season. When the privet was ready to be sold, I dug them up, counted them in groups of ten, and then wrapped them in moss and brown paper. They were all ready for market! We performed the work ourselves because it was less costly.

Just as important as word-of-mouth advertising was advertising through the telephone book. Frans consistently and immediately returned phone calls to all customers of potential landscaping jobs. He attained their addresses and visited each customer during afterwork evening hours in the spring and summer. Frans would charm the client, earn their trust, and thereby always get the jobs. I managed daily phone calls, and gave the information needed or took down orders, to be prepared in advance for a client pick-up or delivery.

Daily Routines

Keeping a daily routine was my way of keeping my life focussed every day, starting at five-thirty in the morning. Because we supplied many customers with soil (loam), sod, rockery stone, and patio slabs, I needed to place orders to our wholesale suppliers, Jenkins (for loam), Zander Sod Company (for sod), and Industrial Cast Stone (for patio slabs), always in that order. We marketed our business through our service in the support of these companies, and I needed to put in extra work hours to make it all happen.

I also chose Monday or Tuesday for our own Humber Nurseries' products delivery day. In the mornings on those days, I would prepare delivery lists according to the location and size of the order. I located the customers' addresses on a map to help minimize address search time for our driver Harry Penner (more about him later). Then I would go outside to find and organize all the plant and delivery materials before seven o'clock in the morning.

Frans, in the meantime, would routinely drive in his Ford truck for twenty minutes to the corners of Weston and Albion Roads in Toronto to pick up our employees at seven o'clock for a seven-thirty work start. Sometimes the employees would work on the Caledon farm, which was an extra twenty-minute drive. Frans organized the work on all the fields on both properties, which meant the management of hoeing, watering, planting, and various other maintenance jobs that needed completion. And he always found time in the evenings to research in the horticulture review magazines for new varieties of plants to sell, all of which I would record.

I completed my work just before seven o'clock in the morning, at which time I woke up the children, and dressed and organized them so they could be ready for breakfast and their chores of feeding the dogs and tidying up their bedrooms and kitchen. I would make their lunches and put aside thirty-five cents for their weekly milk money on Mondays. After working at the garden centre in the latter part of the morning with paperwork and serving customers, I would have my lunch with Frans. Most times I followed up with a short nap, which energized me for the rest of the day. The afternoons were always busy at the garden centre, and then the children would come home from school by four o'clock. There was dinner to prepare, summing up the money from the day's business, and the book-keeping that went with the day's events. After that, the children had their evening chores and homework, and soon it was bedtime again.

Balance Between Family and Work

During the 1950s, Frans and I kept an even balance between family and work; figuring out how to be loving parents and, at the same time, trying to be decent at our jobs. However, that balance shifted after the move. Business took on more importance than parenting in our day-to-day lives.

In 1960, there was always work to do and little time to socialize with family and friends. Keeping employment to a minimum kept our expenses in check, but we risked failing to serve our family's needs because Frans and I were both so busy. The children were of great help with their daily chores, but it was painful to miss an event for them, especially during the spring season that year.

Our garden centre was open six days a week, from seven-thirty in the morning until dusk. But the reality was we closed the store only after the last customer was gone. We were closed on Sundays, as were most nurseries in the Toronto area. After Sunday morning mass, we treated the rest of the day as privileged time to visit friends and relatives. However, we rarely left the house before one or two o'clock in the afternoon, because customers, feeling at ease, would knock on the door of our house and make conversation with Frans.

Happy to be of service, Frans would often become engrossed so much in his discussion that he did not realize that four impatient children and I were waiting for him in the car. When we were on our way, he would ask where we wanted to go. Most times, our visits were spontaneous (part of our Dutch culture), and we would arrive unexpectedly on someone's doorstep with four children.

Sometimes we would visit people who were not home, and sometimes they were. We liked to visit the DeBoers in Burlington, the Hennins in Sherkston, the Besselings in Peterborough, or our Toronto area friends and relatives, the Klein Beerninks, the Hoogstratens, and the Van Zantens. On a sunny summer day, we ventured to Niagara Falls. Frans loved the drives; the children enjoyed playing unending games in the car; and everyone usually welcomed us into their homes. Much to my satisfaction, our four children were always well-behaved.

Schooling in the Early Sixties

Neither Frans nor I had the time or even the means to bring our children to school. When living in the valley in the 1950s, walking to school was the only option. In the 1960s, after we moved to the country, we fortunately found car transportation to Our Lady of the Airways school in Malton. The Catholic nuns who taught there kindly drove the children to and from school. In 1962, a new church for our parish of Saint Margaret Mary in Woodbridge was built to replace an old house. We sent the children to the elementary school there, using the municipality's new yellow school bus system. The children simply crossed the street to our neighbour's business, Hudson Welding, where they could stand indoors on rainy or cold days to wait for the bus.

One fine Sunday morning, we celebrated the sacrament of Confirmation for all three children—a religious and social highlight during our busy spring season in that year. Close family and friends would be their sponsors: Tiny Klein Beernink (Sibylleke), Ben DeBoer (Fransje), and Florie DeBoer (Astrid). In a later year, Guy received the sacrament of First Holy Communion and Confirmation in Woodbridge, and Wim Klein Beernink was his sponsor. It was at this time we came to know the parish priest, Father O'Mara, who later became a Monsignor, a higher rank in the Catholic Church. He would be our link to sending our children to private Catholic high schools in Toronto.

Once again, in September of 1963 transportation was the issue when our first teenager in the family, Sibylleke, was of high school age. Frans and I wanted our children to attend a Catholic high school, but we were out of the specified school jurisdiction, and there was no means of transportation in the township where we lived. Father O'Mara's connections to a nun named Sister Imelda Cahill and the principal of an all-girls high school, would be lucky for us.

By a piece of good fortune, two Saint Joseph's nuns who taught at the high school lived around the nearby town of Bolton and kindly picked up Sibylleke and brought her back home each day after school. Sister Imelda allowed our two girls to attend St. Joseph's High School Islington in Toronto. Our two boys attended the all-boys Michael Power High School, which was located next door, in the Dundas-Bloor crossroads of West Toronto, through the same connection. Then when she turned sixteen, Sibylleke received her driver's licence, and she drove her siblings to school. Everything worked out well in our planning of our children's high school years.

A Little Christmas Cheer

Christmas celebrations during the 1960s always included Oma and Opa Peters, Frans's parents, but it was a distant relationship. They sent parcels from the Netherlands to their grandchildren, including traditional Dutch chocolate letters. One year, they sent matching blue cardigan sweaters for all four children that they would wear every Sunday, and everyone would recognize the Peters family children!

Music, Hobbies, and Sports

I wanted the children to grow up with music, swimming, art, and skating. Piano lessons started with Mrs. Peacock, who lived in a small brick house within a ten-minute walk. After four years of giving music lessons, she moved, and we were left with an upright piano and no teacher for the children. Frans had the musical genes in the family, carried on from his father and brother Ton, who played in a music group in Deventer. Frans desired a venue to nurture music in the family, and I wanted the children to continue studying piano because we had already invested in an upright piano. We searched for another teacher during the next few years, and we found a suitable one, but more about that later.

Our family loved the outdoors, and swimming was at the top of the list, especially during the summer months when we drove to different places to enjoy that activity. We traveled as far as Crystal Beach in Sherkston on Lake Erie when visiting François Paula-Françoise Hennin. We also went to a place closer to our home on Highway 7, to an artificial lake built by a company called the Swanik Brothers, which soon dissolved because they could not keep the water clean enough for swimming. We soon found the Italian Gardens in the town of Woodbridge, where they offered swimming lessons in their large concrete pool. The children always wanted a pool at the house, but since there was no water coming from the township, and we used the water from our wells and pond for the nursery, we never invested in a pool.

Would my children ever take art lessons? Yes! The children enjoyed oil painting lessons with Mrs. Snider. The school bus route would pass by an art school on Highway 7 near Woodbridge. The kind bus driver knew to allow four Peters children to exit the bus every Monday night at this art school. To sweeten the event, Mrs. Snider served chocolate cookies and milk before their art lessons. I was not sure if they enjoyed the snacks more than the art lessons!

First, however, they learned all about oil painting, mixing and putting colours creatively together, what brushes to use, and then how to practice painting at home. Then, on winter Saturday mornings, the four children sat around the kitchen table, all painting the same scenery. I thought that the paintings were all so beautiful that I sent some masterpieces to our family in the Netherlands, so they could show off works done by not-yet-famous budding artists!

The children wanted to take skating lessons at the Woodbridge arena with all their friends. But Frans would agree to give them the lessons, "Only if you related your skating experience when you were a little girl still living in Deventer."

With a smile, a wink, and in a light tone, Frans forewarned the children that this would not be a story anywhere near excellence as in the tale of the famous Dutch skater, Hans Brinker!

I started my story with my age:

"You see, I was only ten years old. All my friends were skating, and I felt left out because I could not join them in their fun. Willing to give it a try, I strapped on the borrowed skates. Things already felt weird. Standing up, ankles bending first to the left, then to the right, I struggled to keep my balance. Oops! There I slipped and saw the ice close at my face. Determined, I held on to the sideboard and regained my balance. I decided to walk my hands on the sideboards and follow one step at a time with my new footwear below me, moving ever so slowly on that slippery surface. I moved around the outdoor rink three times without changing my method: my hands first secured my balance on the sideboards, and then I dragged my feet onto the surface of the ice.

"All the time, I thought that skating would be easy to learn; after all, I was Dutch. I did not want to let go of the boards, and it seemed that I could never get my feet and legs to feel the luxury of moving smoothly on ice. The truth of the matter was, I did not want to let go of the boards, even though I could hear the chuckling of my friends when I passed them. I imagined they saw the show of their lives with this silly, monkey-like friend of theirs on the ice. I think you get the picture. I did not learn how to skate that day."

I jokingly asked Frans and my children, "Was I not a good beginner skater?"

And they all knew the answer. "No, Mom, and that's why we would like to take skating lessons!"

Frans agreed. The three eldest children took lessons at the Woodbridge Arena; Guy was too young to participate. During the winter months, I would sometimes drive the children to lessons when I had the time; otherwise, the parents of school family friends, the Armours and the Hendersons, would pick up the children once a week.

Although the arena was the best place to skate, the children found other skating locations. For instance, during one of the first winters, our nursery parking lot turned into a sheet of clear flat ice. The icefield would even be an artist's delight to paint during that memorable cold winter. Later that same winter, the children discovered a stream of water on the farmland behind our property that froze over well enough for skating, although they needed to prepare the ice rink by shoveling off the snow.

A few years later, we built a pond for watering the trees and evergreens in the fields. In the depths of winter, that new pond froze sufficiently for safe skating. The children skated and played hockey there with the neighbours. As they chose their hockey teams, I wondered if one would grow up to be a Toronto Maple Leaf or a Montreal Canadian hockey player?

Frans and I were hopeful about the future. We worked hard. We loved our family and our business. In our new phase of life, in the years from 1960 and into the early 1970s, we leaped into family vacations. Unavoidably, we connected with more people, thereby investing our time to get to know them better.

“

I wanted the children to grow up with music, swimming, art, and skating.

In 1961, I traveled to the Netherlands with my Fransje, then eleven years old. Fransje looked on as his Uncle Jan Janssen (my brother) made handmade clay pots at his pottery factory in Deventer.

We visited his grandfather Opa Peters and my sister-in-law Magda Peters at their jewelry store in Deventer.

Chapter Fourteen: Summer Fun and Interesting People

There would be nothing like a family vacation to make our lives happier. We would all pile into our car, with Frans in the driver's seat, and experience what the world looked like in the improving economy of the 1960s. We would also venture to Europe again. These were times of change, and in our business, we open-mindedly tried new things, even if it meant making mistakes.

Summer Fun

Family vacations during the early 1960s were week-long car trips, usually to the eastern United States. Guy, our youngest, was mostly impressed with once meeting Santa Claus and his elves at work in Santa's North Pole Park in New York State. We visited many other parks built for children in the Adirondack Mountains and Whiteface Mountain areas. Once we traveled to Boston, Massachusetts, to see where the well-known Kennedy family lived, and on another vacation, we explored the Cape Cod area to see the famous Plymouth Rock.

How did we find accommodation with a family of six in August, the busiest vacation time of the year? We had a family routine. I took Fransje with me, holding my hand every time we stepped out of the car, to check for a vacancy at the motel office. I would ask to see the rooms, and Fransje would give me feedback on the suitability of the rooms.

Well, once he said out loud, "Oh, Mom, it's so dirty here. Let's not stay!"

Embarrassed, I declined the rooms, and we traveled on until we found another motel.

Summer camps were all the rage for children to attend, and my two sons were no exception. At the De La Salle summer camp on Lake Simcoe, my sons learned various sports and made new friends. They also learned about carpentry and electricity as part of their crafting activities, and they used to bring home their prized crafts of wooden sailboats and electric lamps. Their days were filled with swimming, canoeing, and camping in outdoor tents.

Astrid also enjoyed her summers at her godfather's, François Hennin, who took her to the Lake Erie beaches with his children. She also learned to horseback ride on one of her favourite riding horses at his farm. Sibylleke was quite content to be at home, sitting cozily on the living room couch, with a tucked pillow supporting her head, looking at a magazine, listening to records on the new stereo system, or watching our newest member of the family, the television.

An Addition to the Family: Television

Our family had their own story about the new TV family member.

The Golden Age of television started in the early 1950s, and we became part of that era by purchasing our first black and white TV in the latter part of that decade. Anxious to watch our prized wooden framed box, the children asked, "Mom, can we watch the television? Can we change the channel?"

To which I usually replied, "When I have finished work!"

Our second black and white television, purchased in the 1960s, became a welcomed seventh family member, but it, too, came with house rules: no watching the television on school days, and if school homework was not done, that meant no TV on weekends. The children watched *Family Theatre* religiously at five o'clock on Saturday nights during the summer, and *Bonanza* was another show they loved to watch at eight. Fransje became our first hockey fan in our family, and he watched all the NHL games on winter Saturday nights.

And oh, what a family event to watch our third purchase, the upstairs colour television. Family reservations, please! On Sunday nights at eight in the evening, our family ritual was born as we watched the infamous *Ed Sullivan Show*. I also loved watching the comedy of *The Red Skelton Show* on Tuesday nights, and I broke the house rule so that the children could watch this comedian and his entertaining show with me. What naturally followed that broken rule was my permission to watch the NHL games on Wednesday nights, and Fransje would be the first to grab the best seat in the basement of our TV room: the new swivel turquoise chair!

Fransje Goes to the Netherlands

I decided to go to the Netherlands again in December 1961, and bring my eleven-year-old Fransje to introduce him to his Dutch relatives. We traveled mostly by train to all the towns where they lived. First was my stepmother Gezina and her relatives, Jan and Wiete Klein Beernink, with their five children. I wanted to see my five siblings, Rie, Jan, Guillaume, Arnold, and Greet, and their families, followed by my visits to my cousins from the Bernards family. My favourite relative, Aunt Jo, living in the convent, was the most ecstatic relative to meet my eldest son. She also updated us on the news from Greet, newly wedded to Louis, both who chose to give social and medical aid to a Dutch community in New Guinea, all supported by the Dutch government. They were experiencing a hot and humid climate, not conducive to energetic work, and Aunt Jo predicted that they would return within a year. And they did.

I liked to recite my favourite Canadian story to every one of my relatives. The story began with the news about Wim Klein Beernink's sister, Yet, who had left the Netherlands and married an American, Om Chhabra, in 1959.

On a cold but sunny wintry day in Toronto, our family attended their wedding. Their honeymoon began the following day, the destination was Niagara Falls, Ontario, and the weather was uncooperative. Unfortunately, a nasty icy drive in a snowstorm put Yet and Om into a snowbank while accidentally slipping off the highway. A passing truck driver saved them. He stopped and brought them to a nearby motel, where they indulged in a lovely meal of leftovers that they had packed with them from their wedding dinner. What excitement! They later traveled safely to Connecticut, in the United States, to establish their home.

On my husband's side of the family, we visited his two brothers: Ton and Lies with their son Frans, and Lou and Magda with their three sons, Frans, Rob, and Eric. Naturally, Fransje mingled well with his cousins, especially the ones with the same namesakes. I could tell that Fransje also liked being with adults, as I saw him trying to converse in Dutch-English when we visited both Frans's sister Ria and his parents, who lived with Lou at the home built above the jewelry store in Deventer. Fransje especially proved to have an adult attitude when we attended a twenty-fifth wedding anniversary celebration in Arnhem for Frans's (my husband's) childless aunt and uncle. He was singled out as the only child there.

Then, there was one special outing to Amsterdam with his brother Ton, a jolly and musical fellow who loved to go out and play piano in music bands. Both Fransje and his uncle danced and sang, arm in arm, in a street in Amsterdam after we had eaten a late meal in a restaurant and visited one too many bars.

Fransje was interested in the now third-generation Janssen family pottery business in Deventer. My father, the second generation, expanded the company with a store where they sold the pottery made in their factory on the street called Ooievaarstraat. The business successfully grew not only in retail but in wholesale as well. My two brothers Jan and Arnold carried on the business, and it thrived for many more years. Fransje was impressed with this family story, and he appreciated his uncle Jan's pottery lesson when he sat at the turner and learned how to shape a flower vase out of fresh clay.

On another note of history, and a highlight to our trip, we visited the Holten Canadian Armed Forces War Cemetery. Many soldiers buried there had died in the last stages of World War II, some of whom were killed in Deventer. Our trip was coming to an end, and

Fransje returned home with the eagerness to talk about his family and Dutch heritage.

Sadness and Fear

July 1962 turned out to be a peculiar month, drawing out emotion from all sides. It came to be quite a coincidence when three people of our close family and friends all died within a few days of each other. My brother Arnold and my brother-in-law Ton had died, both at the age of thirty-nine years. Our close friend Hermann Leudecke's wife also died in July at the age of thirty-nine. Arnold departed his family of five children, leaving Gerda to raise them on her own, and Ton left his wife Lies to manage their only child and their new jewelry store. Hermann's eighteen-year-old daughter took her mother's role as a radio announcer on the Toronto-German Radio Station, where we advertised our nursery.

What came with the sadness over three deaths that summer month was our fear of another war. In October, the Cuban Missile Crisis pointed to fear of an atomic war. Frans and I had experienced the effects of war in our home country and felt that food shortages were an imminent danger. We decided to purchase enormous amounts of canned and dried foods. We stored them in our truck, tucked securely beside other survival goods.

While we were attending Sunday mass at our parish of Our Lady of the Airways, a certain priest and a future long-lasting friend named Father Alfred Paul Caley

(Father Hap), noticed our truck with family and food. He made light of the seriousness of the situation:

"Oh, there's gonna be no war. President John F. Kennedy will take care of both the United States and Canada. And, Sibylla, have faith in the Lord!"

He always had an uplifting manner of solving problems, and a comforting way of calming our worries.

As it turned out, Father Hap was a very musical person who played and taught the piano. He even advocated for candidates to audition for the television series *Tiny Talent Time*. So, I asked him if he could teach my children how to play the piano. He agreed to come every Tuesday night, and the children promised to practice every day. And that was the foundation of our cherished friendship.

Make A Mistake. Try Something New!

1. The Traveling Salesman

The traveling salesman was all the rage during the early 1960s. Naturally, one needed to pull out all the stops for the six-week madness that the spring season brought on, so we were thrilled to hire a door-to-door salesperson to sell nursery stock for our company. We hoped for the best in our new opportunity. We hired our first candidate, who we interviewed right on the spot, and in less than two days, he learned enough about plants and planting to inform our customers of whatever they wanted to know. In addition, he was a fast thinker and talker while giving his sales pitch to the client.

He would convincingly say, for example, "You will need five pounds of grass seed to start your lawn and an extra five pounds in case you made a miscalculation."

Or he would push the need for someone to buy more than one evergreen. "Three of these is always the best way to show in a garden. And then you need some colourful seasonal plants to go with that."

Throughout the season, he sold many nursery items, which was a good thing. But soon enough, the money was not coming in. We received customer complaints because of misunderstood pricing. In addition, the salesman asked the customers to make payments by cheque, which they wrote in his name, and not to Humber Nurseries Ltd. As a result, we needed to involve a lawyer, and in the final analysis, we needed to let him go.

2. Our Grafter

We had some better experiences with truly educated and experienced individuals who worked at the nursery. Our first foreman, Hans Herrmann, lived at our Caledon farm and helped develop Frans's new interests in grafting many varieties of coniferous and deciduous trees, fruit trees, and roses. On Saturday mornings during the summer months, I also participated in the new adventure. However, with the four children in tow and the workload of grafting, I would send the children to the fields to instead learn about the art of hoeing the weeds. I used to bait them with ice cream, and so it would not be long before they begged, "Mom, can we go to the corner and get some ice cream?" The corner was about five kilometers away.

After five years, we decided that grafting was too labour-intensive. We would be better off importing new varieties of young trees and rose bushes from Europe, Canada, and the United States. The work of planting and maintaining the imports was far less. It entailed only four to five years of pruning and fertilizing, watering and weeding, much to Hans's satisfaction and a more profitable return on our investment.

3. The Professor

Herbs had not yet reached popularity in the nursery business. However, at this time, Frans had an ongoing interest in finding new things in horticulture, and he learned more about them through the professor. The professor had immigrated to Canada from Hungary and was a passionate horticulturist. A camaraderie developed between them.

On one Sunday dinner invitation, the professor's wife prepared a spinach dish, where she used many herbs in her cooking, and she said to me:

"Oh, Sibylla, you have to add basil, parsley, or rosemary to complement the flavour, and it's healthy for you, too."

I was never a creative cook, so I did not pay too much attention to her comment, and Frans and the professor both decided that the times were not ready to sell herbs to the homeowner. Unknown to all of us at the time, the whole industry of herbs would explode many years later.

The professor, a business intellectual, carried the immigrant spirit because he discovered other creative means of making a living in this new land of opportunity, some of them worth mentioning. For instance, he discovered how to grow sod, or turf, and create an attractive lawn instantly for the homeowner. The method he used was to first purchase a few acres of healthy land, then enrich the soil to seed the grass at the appropriate time of the year, and then meticulously maintain the new turf through reseeding, fertilizing, and watering. The turf would then be cut, collected, and sold to local nurseries, ours included. Not being of a greedy nature, he could not get used to the growing numbers of people who copied him, made huge business profits, and continued living a life of greed (in his opinion) in the competitive world. He therefore sold his business and sought work elsewhere.

Then the professor's acquaintance with Alexandre Raab from Czechoslovakia proved worthwhile. As a fellow immigrant in the early 1950s, Mr. Raab, with much perseverance and determination, founded the White Rose chain of nurseries, a company sold on the Toronto Stock Exchange. The professor asked him for the management job of one of his many White Rose Garden Centres. When the professor asked his wife to work with him, she showed no interest in his passion for horticulture, and with no children, they soon went their separate waves.

We lost contact with the professor until one day when Frans and I showed interest in purchasing some more real estate. He seemed to just appear at our doorstep out of nowhere. After spending a few years in California, he remarried an opera singer, and they moved to her birthplace of New York City. When Frans traveled to New York City to visit him, he tried to entice us to purchase property in New York, but we never made a real estate investment with him.

4. Delivery Day at Humber

Every Tuesday was the delivery day at Humber Nurseries, and my job was to prepare all aspects of the deliveries. The preparatory work of mapping the journey of addresses, updating our brown suede change purse, and labeling and organizing the materials to be put on the truck, saved an immense amount of time for our driver. And who was that driver? Harry Penner. He was a dedicated and efficient employee, a kind friend, and a staple in our life. He worked for the township for the railway during the day, and on weekends and evenings in the busy spring and fall seasons, he worked for our Humber Nurseries. He took complete control of our deliveries, and he became the specialist salesman for selling fruit trees.

With Harry Penner in the picture, I could accomplish much of my work and family plans. For instance, two of my children took music lessons in Mount Dennis on Weston Road at the Ontario Conservatory of Music. Fransje played the Hawaiian guitar, and Astrid played the accordion. They easily journeyed the long distance from the Woodbridge school by public bus transportation to the music studio in Mount Dennis. However, they needed a ride for their journey home. I would phone Harry the night before to let him know to pick up the children at the bus stop at the corner of Weston Road and Wilson Avenue at about six o'clock, before arriving for work at the nursery (an extra twenty-minute drive). Harry would routinely return to the house after his deliveries, late at night, and have a coffee with us. A long day for all.

No plan, however, was perfect. Sometimes Harry would not be available. The transportation problem popped up once again, but it soon went away after I taught Fransje and Astrid how to hitchhike by themselves from the bus stop corner to the nursery. It was simple for me to explain since I had done hitchhiking many times in Europe during the war when Corrie and I had our cigarette and other enterprises.

I said to the children, "First of all, you put your right thumb up, clear and straight like this." Fransje mimicked me. "And you keep an eye on the cars headed in your direction. You can tell which car will pick you up because it will slow down."

Fransje turned next to Astrid's side and demonstrated what this would look like, extending her arm and straightening her thumb upwards. Astrid added a feature. "But you have to use your thumb together with a pleading smile, like this!" And she acted out the pose with huge satisfaction.

They were always successful at this new venture, and sometimes they came home bursting with, "And we were picked up by the same lady as the last two times!"

The adventures with Harry and the children did not stop here, because sometimes Guy would ask to go on deliveries. Guy liked that very much, because Harry would first treat him at the snack shop with ice cream or other sweets before going on the deliveries. At a curious and young age, Guy was quick to appreciate some business tips from Harry. On one occasion, they drove a long way to the east end of Toronto, where they delivered Chinese elm to six houses in that district.

In conversation, Guy asked Harry, "And how much does each small bundle of Chinese elm cost?"

Surprised by the question, Harry replied, "Each is worth five dollars. But, hey, Guy, and with six deliveries, how much money do you think you would make?"

Guy smartly responded with, "That's a total collection of thirty dollars. But I don't get that it is all delivered for free. How can going all this way for free make any money?"

Harry, amused, replied with a smile. "If you cannot honour the small deliveries, you are not worth the bigger ones. In business, you must start somewhere to build a foundation of trust with all your customers."

And Guy picked up on this valuable lesson in business and life.

Through visits and letter writing with Harry Penner, his wife Thelma, and their only son Keith, we always kept in touch. Moving forward in time, Harry retired with a government and veteran's pension, and he and Thelma regularly enjoyed winters in Florida. Keith became interested in photography, and he started his own business, opening a store in downtown Toronto where he specialized in wedding photography. He later would be the photographer for Astrid's wedding.

Our family and business grew with the times, and we enjoyed the journey. However, there was soon to be trouble at the helm while traveling in Europe. Did I have the strength to get through it?

In San Marco's Square in Venice, Italy, I enjoyed the company of the numerous pigeons on my special trip with Frans to Europe in August of 1963.

Our family photo in 1967. Sibylleke was eighteen, Fransje was seventeen, Astrid was fifteen, and Guy was thirteen.

Chapter Fifteen: Traveling Adventures and Teenagers

Traveling to Europe was a reward of which we had dreamed. Frans and I were going to Europe once again, this time to visit our friends. This was going to be a vacation to keep in my memory always, but not for the reason that you might think. It was a story of an unexpected tragedy that occurred during the summer of 1963.

In 1964, Guy wanted to go to the Netherlands, so we put a red cowboy hat on his head for his Uncle Lou to identify him when he would land, alone, at the Amsterdam Schiphol Airport.

On another day, back in my Brampton home, I had a long dream that I thought to be worthy of telling. It was a dream of how my teenaged children were maturing during the mid-1960s.

My Unexpected Tragedy

August 1963 was the month of my unexpected tragedy. It would be a fourth return trip to Europe, this time to visit our Canadian friends in Monte Carlo. Frans and I were taking Astrid, hoping to leave her with relatives in the Netherlands while traveling throughout Europe. We took the beautiful SS *Rotterdam* across the ocean, and with our car on board the ship, we had the liberty to drive anywhere we wished once landed. We would be free from phones, customers, and business problems to solve. We were confident that our trusting foreman could take care of the business, and that our kind and caring relatives could mind our other three children. Frans and I looked forward to our holiday, almost honeymoon-like, or so I thought at the time.

There were many activities on the ship to make the journey memorable, especially for Astrid. A highlight was the applesauce story. Because we were so busy on weekends at the nursery, we would go out for dinner, particularly to our favourite restaurant at the Four Corners gas station coffee shop, a five-minute drive from the business. The owner, Mr. Parsons, knew to serve our usual order of pork chops, mashed potatoes, green peas, and huge amounts of applesauce. Therefore, when Astrid saw the tiny portion of applesauce on her plate in their ship's restaurant, she politely asked the waiter, "Is there a shortage of applesauce on this big ship?"

Our waiter chuckled and said, "That is not a problem, my young lady. I will bring you some more." For the rest of the trip, he would bring a huge bowl of applesauce at every dinner.

After ten days aboard the ship, we drove to Deventer, visited our relatives, and planned our trip to Monte Carlo to visit our Canadian friends. Astrid was going to stay in the Netherlands, but with whom we did not know.

"Who would like to take care of our little Astrid for the summer?" I asked.

Everyone wanted to take care of her. So, our best choice was to leave her with aunt Lies Peters, whose son Frans was about the same age as Astrid. They could play together in and around their jewelry store, which fronted the house in the town of Dieren. Aunt Lies would love having a daughter, and she wanted to spoil Astrid above anything in the world.

We planned to be in Monte Carlo by August 15. At the end of July, we had some time to drive through Germany, where I knew my brother Guillaume and his wife Gretel and family were vacationing. Earlier they had sent me a postcard from the Black Forest region in southern Germany, and in my wildest dreams, I thought we could locate and visit them without an address or an invitation.

After driving the entire day and arriving in the area where I thought they were staying, we decided to get out of the car for a stretch. It was already about eight o'clock in the evening, and we walked along this long street. I was looking around, thinking I would see them, and then, my eyes settled on a window of one of the houses where we were walking. I remembered so well that I saw someone who resembled Gretel, my sister-in-law. And guess what? It was Gretel! I could not believe the coincidence, and she invited us to stay with them for dinner and overnight for a few days.

The Black Forest region of southern Germany was so beautiful that Frans repeatedly asked me, "Dear Sibylla, where would you like me to build our beautiful villa in these mountains?"

"The thought occurred to me as well!" I answered.

During our visit, the family enjoyed hiking expeditions in the mountains. On one such hike, when we climbed about halfway up the mountain, I started to feel a little sick to my stomach. I blamed it on the high altitudes. I decided to rest while everyone else continued with the hike. I slept a little during my rest, and upon their return, everyone saw that I appeared in better spirits. We were sad to depart our relatives, but we wanted to move on to our next destination, which was Monte Carlo.

The reason why we chose Monte Carlo in Monaco as our destination was to meet our newly-made Canadian friend, Carlos. He invited us to meet and travel with him and his wife in Europe. Carlos and his brother-in-law built a large business in the construction industry and sodding land development in Canada. As builders by trade in Italy, they immigrated to Canada, as we did, to start a new life. We met them through the landscaping portion of our business, whereby we landscaped the finished homes using the sod they supplied. Carlos eventually took over the company as his brother-in-law died in a car accident in Rome, Italy.

When we arrived in Monte Carlo by car, we were warmly received by Carlos, his wife, and his parents in the home where they all used to live. We stayed for a few days there and enjoyed this beautiful place in the world. Then, Carlos suggested a driving trip of 900 kilometres to the Isle of Capri. It was a long but scenic trip with a few overnight stops, and after finding our hotel on the Isle of Capri and resting, we decided to go out for something to eat. Then, while at dinner, I began to feel something strange happening to my health. I had ordered a soup to be followed by the main course. I managed to have the soup, but I felt dizzy and lost my appetite quite quickly as soon as the main course arrived. After that, I knew I could not eat anymore.

Feeling weary and too tired, I announced I had to back out of the planned boat ride after our meal. Frans, Carlos, and his wife went reluctantly without me. We reconnected at the restaurant after a few hours and returned to the hotel.

During our return trip to Monte Carlo, Carlos suggested that we take tours in Rome and Florence, but I mentioned to Frans that I felt too sick to continue our touring holiday with our friends. So Frans and I embarked on our long driving journey to Monte Carlo and rejoined our friends at their home on August 14.

Back in Monte Carlo, Frans and I explained that we wanted to depart immediately for the Netherlands.

While sitting in the car, I felt so ill I could hardly shake hands with Carlos' mother to thank her for her hospitality. As we were driving away that day, I felt even more sick as I could not lie down on the back seat of the car.

Frans then suggested that I rest at a conveniently located hotel in the centre square of Monte Carlo. So, there I was at the bottom of the stairway of the hotel. There were twelve steps to climb to get to the entrance doorway. I could barely walk, let alone climb the stairs. However, even though I felt deathly ill, I made it to the top of the stairs. What happened next was upsetting. I noticed there was blood following me everywhere I walked. Frans did not say anything, but he must have seen it later.

Resting in bed, I somehow made it through the night. I woke up and peeked outside of our hotel window, just in time to see a huge procession in the square. As I inspected more closely, I spotted Carlos and his whole family marching in the parade. It was August 15, the day we had planned, back in Canada, especially to be with Carlos and his family.

As Frans and I were admiring the procession festivities from our window, we saw Carlos, walking towards our car parked in front of our hotel. Carlos mentioned to us later that at that moment of recognizing the car, he asked his wife:

"Didn't Sibylla and Frans not leave for the Netherlands yesterday? They left so abruptly, and I wonder why we see their car here in front of the hotel? Maybe they did not depart for the Netherlands the day before and perhaps wanted to surprise us?"

In disbelief, his wife responded, "I think there is something wrong here. Let's check to find where their room is."

Upon first seeing me in the hotel room, Carlos saw that I had developed a far too unhealthy and sickly appearance since he last saw me. He asked his wife to call a doctor, who came immediately and ordered an ambulance to bring me to the hospital.

The hospital was a new one, and I stayed there for five days. It was a place to rest, but I was still hemorrhaging and I felt exhausted and too weak to leave on my fourth day. On the fifth day there, however, I regained my sense of hunger, which was a good sign, and I asked the French-speaking nuns working there to bring me some "pommes de terre." They understood, but when the dish came to me, I saw the olive oil in the potatoes and could not stand the looks of it. I threw up immediately, and all the food and everything else on the tray fell onto the floor. It was a mess. My room was close to the hospital entrance. To my astonishment, someone cleaned it up with a broom and swept the whole works out of the hospital entrance on to the outside steps!

All in all, I was very well taken care of by the doctors, and thankfully, Frans could stay and sleep with me in my room. The doctors announced I would need an operation. I wanted to go back to the Netherlands, where I felt more comfortable with the medical treatment. Carlos made arrangements to return to the Netherlands, but it would not be an easy journey with a three-hour drive to Rome, where I would catch a three-hour flight to Amsterdam and then take a train or drive to a hospital in Deventer.

Frans and I had our car, but we asked what would happen if Frans would lose his way driving to the airport, and I might miss my flight? Carlos came to the rescue. He was my guardian angel for a second time. In Italian, Carlos asked the doctor to prepare me so I could travel reasonably well. Carlos arrived at six in the morning, and he successfully drove me to the airport for a noon flight in Rome. I went in first-class with the instructions that I should say nothing about my illness. It was the twentieth of August when I arrived in Amsterdam, and the customs officer asked me if I had anything to declare. I had nothing to declare, traveling with only my handbag, which was already too heavy to carry. Since I found myself too weak to walk the small distance from the airport area to the train station, I traveled by cab, costing 100 guilders or seventy Canadian dollars.

The cab drive to the Deventer hospital came with interesting requests to my driver. First, since I was getting cold, I asked for more heat in the car. Then I requested he stop by a hotel for a washroom break. After that break, I decided to tell him about my medical problem in case of an emergency.

The cab driver drove quickly from then on. We passed by some places I recognized, and that led to reminiscing about my past, as in where my brother Andre was buried in the Apeldoorn cemetery and where he lived in the institution just before he died—all sad memories for me. We finally arrived at the Deventer hospital, and I requested he wait for me until I entered, since I saw a lock on the entrance door to the hospital. The nurse who answered was about to refuse me entry until she saw how frustrated and weak I was when showing her my letter from the doctors in Rome. She recognized the urgency of my situation. I went to say goodbye to the kind cab driver who needed to drive back to Amsterdam. While I was waiting at the hospital entrance, they announced that there was no hospital bed or room for me to stay. For my first night, I had a cot in one of the doctor's offices.

They arranged the operation for Saturday. However, two problems arose: I needed a specialist doctor from Nijmegan, a town some distance away, and secondly, I suddenly developed a high fever—that meant postponement. I did not want to phone any family or friend announcing that I returned to Deventer without Frans. But because they told me they could not operate on Saturday, and because it was the weekend, I decided to phone the family. And everyone came to see me!

Where was Frans? And did Astrid know or understand what had happened? And would we make our return booking on our ship to Canada on September 8? It was already late August, and Frans was still driving, en route from Monte Carlo. He did not know what was happening to me, and we needed to get to the Le Havre port in France on time for our departure.

The operation would take place immediately on Monday morning after that weekend. I was recovering, but slowly—the return boat trip to Canada passed by as a dreamy blur. I only remembered two things: seeing my relatives at the hospital, and getting seasick daily because of rough seas, a discomfort to my already serious condition.

Little Astrid, however, enjoyed the children's activities on the SS *Homeric*. We were in the second class, and one day she made friends with a girl, Karen, in first class. Astrid was not allowed to go to that level, but because her friend took a special liking to her, Karen invited her to participate in all the children's first-class functions. It was enjoyable to hear all the stories she told us when she came back every evening to sleep in our cabin. When Karen disembarked in New York City with her family, Astrid was sad, and she only had a picture of them dancing in a contest, taken by the ship's photographer. All in all, Astrid met many Dutch relatives and certainly had a memorable vacation with all of them. For Frans and me, we claimed it was quite an adventure to fall ill in another country.

Speak English

"There he is, there he is, little Guy with the red cowboy hat from Canada!" My brother-in-law Lou shouted. Lou Peters arrived early at the Schiphol Airport in Amsterdam to greet my little ten-year-old son in 1964.

In all the excitement after traveling by air, Guy asked: "And do my cousins speak English? Do Oma and Opa Peters know I am here? And do they speak English, too?"

Lou's three sons knew little English, and Oma and Opa Peters spoke only Dutch. The two families lived at the same house, number 44, on the Langebisschopstraat in Deventer, the address that was store-fronted by the family jewelry business. Guy quickly learned to speak Dutch with them all, and he enjoyed most of his morning walks with Oma while she did all her morning errands to the bakery and butcher stores.

When Guy returned from his trip, our whole family went to pick him up at the Toronto airport. We waited a long time, and suddenly an airline steward appeared with a little boy wearing a bright red cowboy hat, holding his hand. They arrived at the customs station, and we could see that Guy was having difficulty talking with the officials. To our surprise, he was speaking only Dutch to them. The customs officials searched through his suitcases, not as thoroughly as they would do today, and then Guy raced towards us. Just as he pulled out a beautiful gold chain hidden under his shirt, he said:

"Kijk Mam, dit is wat Oma gaf aan mij!" ("Look Mom, this is what Oma gave to me!")

The steward examined him with curiosity and chuckled.

Our whole family celebrated Guy's homecoming with dinner at one of our favourite restaurants that Saturday night. While listening to Guy's stories, half in English and half in Dutch, we learned he visited my stepmother Gezina in a retirement home in Apeldoorn. In addition, he saw the cemetery where my brother Andre was buried. Not long after that, Guy resumed speaking only English.

I Was Falling Asleep

I took off my glasses, rubbed my eyes, and signaled for Astrid to turn off the tape recorder. I needed a bit of time to think through my stories—highlights such as how the business interweaved in our family lives; why individuals like Hans Herrmann, the professor, and Harry Penner, all kind people, showed their care for us as a family; and why Frans and I chose to bring up our children in a business atmosphere, as this was how we were teaching them about honesty and responsibility.

My gaze took me towards a photo album lying open on the dining room table, where I focused on a picture of Sibylleke. My thoughts lingered to the time of her Confirmation at the Church of Saint Margaret Mary in Woodbridge. My eyes grew heavy, an indication that I needed a little nap. Astrid took the signal and quietly went outside for some fresh air while I gathered myself to walk to my bedroom. I saw my bed and lay my head comfortably on my pillow, eyes shut, covers pulled over my shoulders, falling asleep, ready to flow into my dreams.

I was in my dreams.

I was at my elder three children's Confirmation ceremony, when Monsignor O'Mara of Saint Margaret Mary's parish said to me: "You must be Mrs. Peters, mother of Sibyl, Frans and Astrid?"

I was thankful that Monsignor O'Mara recognized me. I was thankful for my good fortune in connecting with other people who chose the religious ministry, like Father Hap and my favourite aunt, Sister Romualda (Aunt Jo). I remembered the endless conversations especially with Aunt Jo about why God chose to have my mother die at such a young age.

Then my dreams wandered to an entirely different scene:

"Sibylleke," I said, "Look at me and the camera!" I was gazing below at the lens of a Brownie camera, holding it as steadily as I could before I snapped the picture. She managed to proudly show the keys to the family car in the photo. She had just turned sixteen on January 25, 1965, and she was already driving a car. Where did the time go?

"With your new driver's licence," I stated, "You can now drive to school and buy all the family groceries."

She agreed to help me with the household and bring her younger siblings to school. However, I knew that she would have preferred driving with her girlfriends, enjoying the chatter about the latest teenage idols, Bobby Vinton or The Beatles, who were all the rage at the time.

I continued to dream about Sibylleke.

The business demanded that I become a full-time worker in the nursery, which led to leaning on family support. Sibylleke was more than willing to help. Here was her routine. On Saturday mornings, she organized the grocery shopping to be done at three stores: the Dutch store, the specialty fruit store called Hastings on Highway 7 in Woodbridge, and finally, the core grocery store at Food City. After returning from shopping and putting everything away, she would help her sister Astrid clean the entire house.

During the week, when peeking into the children's bedrooms, I found my daughters' shared bedroom neat and tidy. It was Sibylleke who did the last job of cleaning up the kitchen before going to school. She was always on time, driving with her brother Fransje to school. When she arrived home, Sibylleke helped me with the business office work, such as working with the employees' wages and checking accounts payable and receivable. She was such a dear and helpful child.

"Mom," Sibylleke would begin each day during the spring season, "How can I help with preparing dinner?"

I taught Sibylleke how to prepare dinner, and together with Astrid, they learned the basics of cooking all except for the main course (the meat), which I would prepare. However, because of my inattention, the main course would sit in the pan until it was overcooked. It became apparent that the novelty frozen TV dinners would replace many of my evening meals. As the years went on, the famous Kentuckey Fried Chicken routinely would find itself on the Saturday night dinner table.

Or we resorted to picking up hamburgers for our family and sales staff. On Sunday evenings, we went to our Four Corners restaurant where Mr. Parsons would prepare our dinners, even if the clock chimed ten o'clock in the evening when we arrived.

My dreams next skipped over into a vision of my two sons.

Fransje, who we would rename Frans Junior (Jr.), would turn sixteen on March 18, 1966. He would learn how to drive, attain his licence, and share the responsibility of driving to school with his sister. He was already diligently learning about (and how to organize) insecticides, fungicides, fertilizers, grass seed, and various gardening tools in the garden centre store.

Guy, our youngest in our family of four, learned about business matters at a young age. His first meaningful business venture was learning how to set up the Coca-Cola machine, a novelty of its time. Then, both brothers would attend to the finer details of nursery work: watering and fertilizing the perennials and deciduous trees, and they would watch Frans, their dad, propagate many varieties of tropical plants and annuals in the greenhouses. These were valuable hands-on lessons that they would use in the future.

I was then reflecting on a Mother's Day gift from my children.

Choosing to leave the Netherlands to start a new life in Canada allowed Frans and me to choose a business lifestyle. Our healthy and supportive family gave us their blessings. I reflected upon how all four children studied hard at school and worked well at home in the nursery. They returned their love for us many times over, and on one Mother's Day in particular—a day I always associated with my first arrival on Canadian soil—they gave an artistically hand-made card that made me burst into tears as I read:

"Now is the day, the happiest day in May, Mom. Thank-you for all that you have done for us. We kiss you and hug you, and we would try to even make you a free turkey dinner with all its trimmings. And now we wish you: Happy Mother's Day! We love you."

I was thankful to understand the depth of these words on that special day.

I felt a cool breeze on my face and neck as I lay on my bed staring at my clothes armoire. I began to feel the draft turning colder and stronger from the air conditioner from underneath my bed. As I was awakening from my sleep, I heard a *Knock, knock, knock!* coming from the kitchen area. The loud banging sound on the door succeeded in attracting my attention. I was quite awake now from my deep sleep and beautiful dreams. I walked and stumbled somewhat to the back kitchen door, opened it, and saw that the person making all that noise was my sweet and harmless Astrid. She had locked herself outside. I opened the door and looked at my watch. It was already three o'clock in the afternoon, and I said, "Let's get started again."

I fortunately remembered to relate my dream(s) to Astrid after I woke up. She asked me to tape record them. Of course, I said yes.

Astrid made a cup of coffee, and placed Speculaas cookies beside my mug. We both got comfortable around the dining room table, and in good time, I was ready to tell another story.

Frans and I were sailing on the SS Statendam, July 25, 1966, the first of my two trips to the Netherlands that year.

Chapter Sixteen: Rewards of Business Success

Our business success came with a reward, and for us, traveling was that reward. To arrive at our destinations, I would enjoy the airplane ride, and Frans would enjoy sailing on a ship because of his fear of flying. When Frans and I first traveled together in the Netherlands, and later in Europe, we always took the ship to get across the Atlantic Ocean, and then we drove to our destinations. When I traveled without Frans, with my children and later with friends, I always took the plane. Then I would rent a car and/or take a train to travel to destinations.

My Two Trips to the Netherlands in 1966

I could remember the excitement of seeing Oma and Opa Peters again. This time I was in much better health, and it was such a festive greeting. Opa decided to take Frans and me out with Oma for a drive in his precious and highly valued car. The invitation was indeed special since Opa rarely took out his car for any occasion, let alone a casual drive.

Opa kept the silver-gray Peugeot 404 in mint condition, and if there were rainfall, he would take the extra time to dry the car sufficiently by hand until it was spotless. That was a daily activity, since it rained nearly every day in the Netherlands. Everyone enjoyed looking at his car when he did drive it, and even when Germany invaded the Netherlands during the war, the German doctors were proud to drive it when on patient rounds. (They returned the vehicle by the end of 1945.)

“And where is the car parked now?” I asked.

“It's just a ten-minute walk to my private garage across the street from that old hotel. I think you remember it, don't you?” Opa replied.

Indeed, I remembered it because that old hotel was the local centre where the working ladies waited in the tall decorative windows in Deventer's red light district. Oma and I were to wait for the car at the corner of the street, where the provocative entrepreneurs behind us were out advertising. Oh, how they could show off! We were not selling our goods, but certainly, we both gave hearty smiles to any spectator who looked with interest in our direction!

Another car story, perhaps not nearly as humorous, included my sister Rie living in Deventer. She lived in the same house as Harry Kruyssen, who owned a gas station and a Fiat car dealership. Harry's gentle nature morphed into a burning desire to take risks when driving cars, his passion in life. On one occasion, when it was raining so hard that I could not see two feet in front of me, I was terror-stricken when sitting in the passenger seat of his car. The roads were as slippery as an ice-skating rink. I survived, but my heart went through my throat more than once.

And then, sometimes Rie would work at the gas station there and pump gas for the clients. I always had to laugh when she told me that Harry made her earn her keep!

Going forward in time, we had invited Rie and Harry to Canada in the summer of the following year, 1967. One of Canada's largest cities, Montreal, hosted the World Exposition, called Expo 67. Astrid and Guy were thrilled to accompany us on our little Canadian holiday. Again, Harry did all the driving, but this time he did not drive too fast, keeping to the exact posted driving speed.

Sibylleke accompanied me on my second trip to Deventer that year. Frans's brother, Lou, and sister-in-law, Magda, celebrated the traditional Dutch twelve and a half years' wedding anniversary in December 1966, and we were going to crash the surprise party.

Taking a taxi to the well-known old restaurant in the town of Gorssel, we arrived without detection from the guests.

"Who just arrived?" asked Magda when her eyes met a tall, grown-up young lady.

"Oh no, this cannot be Sibylleke from Canada? And Sibyl, I know you were behind all this!"

We had an enjoyable time with plenty of dancing, singing, and food. Sibylleke reminded me of my brother-in-law Ton Peters, who used to always enjoy a good party.

Returning to Deventer, we rented a car, and Sibylleke drove to various homes and towns of our family. She loved driving, just as her father enjoyed being behind the wheel. As we arrived in the town of Vledder, I was excited to introduce Sibylleke to my wartime girlfriend, Corrie Cossee. We had kept a close friendship throughout the years, but she, too, did not expect me to appear at her doorstep with my daughter.

"And who is this?" Corrie asked. "You must be lost, but come on inside and I will help you out." She then spotted me sneaking from around the bush and gave me that friendly look that only old-time friends can give. She was teaching German at the local high school in the towns of Enschede and Hengelo, but school was out, and she was on holidays for a week.

After our exchange of stories, we planned the next few days of our holiday in Münster, Germany. Corrie recounted how they completely rebuilt this battle-scarred town within fourteen years after the war.

"And Corrie, so many memories, at the sight of where I used to live and the post office where I worked in the British Army."

"Do you remember, Sibylla, that camera company where we did business in Germany," Corrie added. "And how the owner's son always succeeded in getting your attention when we visited the factory?"

"I do remember that," I replied. "I had not thought about him for such a long time."

In the back of my mind, I thought that since Sibylleke seemed to enjoy the German countryside and the language, I was sure that I could convince her to return to Germany and seek work at his camera factory and company.

Soon we were touring the Münster University, and when I turned to my left, I instantaneously focused on a single-worded sign on the window of the university bookstore. My eyes landed on the word, "S I B Y L L A" printed in colossal size black letters. What a coincidence that there were two "Sibyllas" standing there looking at it. How about that?

We soon parted ways with Corrie, and with Christmas just around the corner, we drove to Deventer to spend time with Frans's family. We visited more of my relatives in the days that followed, always knocking at their doors without invitation, and if they were home, we found that we were always welcomed.

There were two remaining days of our driving vacation, and I wanted to visit Uncle Jacob and Aunt Dora, who was also my godmother. This family carried the creative and artistic genes of our family. Uncle Jacob, my father's brother, initially worked as an electronics teacher before starting a business that resulted from one of his inventions. He invented the machinery used in producing fabricated artificial stones for building materials for homes. Subsequently, Uncle Jacob built a factory to produce considerable quantities of that type of machinery. In 1948, he made all his money, and because his two children had no interest in taking over the business, unfortunately he had to sell it.

We visited one of their children, Arnold Janssen, about five years older than me, living in Arnhem and married with about ten children. His sister's name was Truus Bronkhorst-Janssen, and we were in the same class in Deventer when we were growing up. Surprisingly, I did not know at the time that she was related to me. Going forward in time, Truus's eldest daughter came to Canada in 1999 with Marion Jongewaart, a member of the famous European "Dance Europe." She performed in "Steamover, Festive with Flowers" in Toronto. So, our Janssen family made a name in the world of the arts.

European Tour in 1969

My trip to Europe in 1969 resulted from family gifts to celebrate two occasions: my fiftieth birthday, and Father Hap's twenty-fifth year as a priest.

“You look fantastic for your age, Mom!”

My children declared my youthfulness on my fiftieth birthday on August 2, 1968. I loved the compliment, and being fifty had many more unexpected benefits. I knew that I was over the hill, as they say, but I had also flown past the meadow and on to bigger and better things on the other side! First, there was a small party for me with a few of our friends and family, namely Wim and Tiny Klein Beernink, Father Hap, and our four children. The celebration took place at a new hotel on Lakeshore Road in Toronto, and I remembered that they served my favourite delicious chocolate cake. I was touched by the party, and I felt extremely happy on this beautiful day of my life.

Our long-time friend Father Hap would also celebrate a memorable event, a twenty-five-year celebration as a priest and working as chaplain at the Saint Joseph's Hospital in Toronto. I used to go to his cottage north of Barrie, Ontario, on Lake Couchiching, which gave me vacation time away from the nursery during the summer months. We developed a warm friendship over the years, sustained many times over by his jokes. For instance, there was a joke between us:

“Sibylla, you have proven yourself a hundred times over as the best gardener in the area.”

“I think that you are up to something,” I answered, detecting his subtle sense of humour.

"The reward," he convinced me, "is that I will prepare a lovely dinner every time you do a little gardening around the cottage."

We both agreed, and I think that I received the better end of the deal.

Our family gift to him, we decided, was a trip to Europe, which would become our family highlight in the year 1969. It would be an interesting trip because my son Guy, Father Hap, and I would fly to Europe and meet Frans, who would travel there by ship before us. We also had the idea of meeting with Sibylleke in Germany, who planned to work there and learn the language. So we left the nursery in the trustworthy hands of Frans Jr., aged nineteen, and Astrid, aged seventeen. We had trained our children so well in our business that Frans and I knew they could take care of it in our absence.

The three of us toured Amsterdam, Deventer, and places where I worked with the British Army in Germany. Father Hap drove, I took pictures, and Guy entertained us with curious questions. Guy was in constant awe at discovering new places outside the Netherlands. We went to Salzburg, Austria, and onward to Venice, Rome, and the Isle of Capri in Italy, then we headed back to Germany, to the town of Stuttgart, where Sibylleke was working at a restaurant.

Earlier, when Sibylleke was analyzing what to do and where to go in Germany, I wrote to my acquaintance, the son of the owner of the camera factory where I traded specialized lenses in the Netherlands after the war.

Unfortunately, there was no work in the camera factory store, and he suggested the Inlingua School, where she could learn about art or something else of personal interest. That did not work out for her, and she soon found work in a florist's store and a restaurant in Stuttgart.

When we arrived at her rented apartment, Sibylleke said that Frans had just visited her for a few hours, and just minutes before our arrival, he had departed. Initially, we thought that we could drive quickly and trace him on the highway, but a half-hour had already gone by, and we did not have too much hope of finding him. What an unforgettable adventure! We decided to accept Sibylleke's request and take her with us on our European tour. Sibylleke was delighted to share the driving.

On our way to Berlin, we found many sad-looking sites and cities that had been eradicated during the war. An organized bus tour was the best way to see East Berlin, under communist control, and West Berlin, under democratic rule, divided by the Berlin Wall, with an entrance to each side at Checkpoint Charlie. However, before the tour started, a policeman stepped onto our bus. We did not understand why he was there, because he had already examined our passports a half-hour earlier. Then, as he was looking suspiciously at all of us, he called out the name Guillaume Peters.

"Would you please get off the bus?" he requested sternly.

I was afraid for my little son, Guy. Ten minutes ticked on. Then another five. What was going on? But I had no reason to fear, since suddenly I saw a proud, satisfied smile on Guy's face as he ran towards us. Then, getting on the bus, he shouted out loud for everyone to hear: "I only had to sign my name on the passport!"

The tour started, and I noticed that East Berlin had not changed a bit since the war, even after twenty-three years. On the other side, West Berlin had prospered, and they had completely rebuilt the city.

We continued our trip to Hamburg in northern Germany, and then further north to Copenhagen, Denmark, and then the city of Stockholm in Sweden.

We steered south again to Tilburg, the Netherlands, to visit my sister Rie and her friend Harry Kruyssen. Then we decided to drive to Zeeland, also in the south, to find my brother Jan and his family, who were vacationing in the cottage area of that province. Unfortunately, we did not find them. Our last visit was to see Gezina, my stepmother in Apeldoorn, who was living in a retirement home for people with dementia. Gezina did not recognize me anymore. Later, in February 1970, she died at the age of eighty-six. She was a mentor, mother, grandmother, and a joyful person who worked tirelessly in the home. I had a feeling of sorrow with her gone. I flew back to the Netherlands for the funeral at that time.

I enjoyed my vacation trips to my homeland and Europe. As I was feeling more and more comfortable traveling by plane, I sought out further and more distant lands. Japan was on the horizon.

“

Soon we were touring the Münster University, and when I turned to my left, I instantaneously focused on a single-worded sign on the window of the university bookstore. My eyes landed on the word, “S I B Y L L A.”

”

I met Pita Van Dongen at a meeting of the Landscape Ontario Horticultural Trades Association and we made an instant friendship. Our first of many travels was a trip to Japan in 1970. In the photo, we were walking with a local farmer.

And we had fun all dressed up in traditional kimonos.

Chapter Seventeen: Sibylla and Pita See the World

On one holiday flight, while looking out the small, rounded window of the plane, the fluffy white clouds danced thirty thousand feet in the air. They put a grin on my face, a telltale sign that I enjoyed traveling and sought new places to explore. Discovering other cultures, customs, and sights appealed to me, and I would enjoy doing that with the company of a newly-made friend.

Japan

Landscape Ontario Horticultural Trades Association supported the landscaping industry. It also allowed its members to travel in organized tours worldwide to study garden centres and learn about new horticultural institutions. This year, 1970, they offered an organized tour to Japan, which was hosting the World's Fair. I had the fortunate opportunity to meet a lady, also a member of Landscape Ontario, who was interested in traveling on this specific trip. Going forward in time, she would become my favourite traveling companion and my equal in business. Her name was Pita (Petronella) Van Dongen.

Pita and her husband, Mike, came to Canada from the Netherlands, founded a prosperous nursery business, and brought up their children much in the same way as we had done. My children also came to know the Van Dongen children through the same high schools of Saint Joseph's Islington and Michael Power.

Unfortunately, our husbands, Mike and Frans, did not want to go to Japan, but Pita and I were highly motivated. So it was settled we should travel to Japan, and that was to be the first of many enjoyable trips together.

We looked forward to the well-organized trip. However, there was an unsuspecting glitch that started with our observation of so very few people at the airport. Then, without thinking seriously any further, we successfully completed customs and boarded the plane to meet the rest of the thirty people in our group.

After landing at the end of the first leg in Vancouver, British Columbia, we discovered some terrible news. Immediately before our takeoff, a plane had crashed around the Toronto area, north of our nursery property near Highway 50, and over 200 people had lost their lives in the accident. The Woodbridge Arena was the only available place suitable for a medical response. All our families did not know if that plane was our plane at the time. We let them know we had landed safely in Japan.

Tokyo, Japan, had a population of over twelve million. The Landscape Ontario Association welcomed and escorted us to the Akasaka Hotel, one of the largest hotels I have ever seen. Each room had an attendant who served us in a very polite fashion. He first prepared tea, placing it strategically on a table in front of us, and finishing by taking down the beds from the wall, making sure every crinkle in the sheets was smoothed out. In addition, the attendant taught us the custom of removing shoes in exchange for slippers before entering the bedroom and again before entering the washroom. In the evening, we were welcomed into the Japanese society with a beautiful show of Geisha girls, dressed in colourful and flowing silk costumes, dancing to the sway of Japanese music.

The following day was a free day to acclimatize to our new surroundings. Pita, so excited to be in a new part of the world, said, “Hey, Sibyl, why don't we explore the city on our own? See, over there is the sign that says, ‘Private Tours!’”

"Couldn't be better!" I answered. We both usually saw and agreed upon the same opportunities. That blend of our personalities would lead to heaps of merriment.

Our guide drove us to several places of interest, but he did not speak a word of English. We resolved to gaze out the car window, quite a useless activity because of the pea-soup fog that hovered over grey shapes, prohibiting our proper appreciation of the new surroundings. However, we noticed the morning rush hour as everyone blurred into one huge mass of people walking quickly to get to the workplace, including the school children in their black and white uniforms, who we saw standing in straight lines awaiting their train.

Jetlagged, after an hour of touring in the car, we both showed our need for rest, giggling like school children, first quietly, then more loudly. Our outbursts gained the attention of our driver, who waved with his hand as if asking us (or so we both thought) if we wanted more 'sake' to drink. (Heaven forbid, drinking alcohol in a Japanese taxi, first thing in the morning!) Embarrassed, we apologized and decided to continue to stay with the organized, scheduled tours.

The World's Exposition in Osaka showcased the culture and innovation in which seventy-five countries, including Japan, participated. During the fair, the efforts and unity of the Japanese bonsai community blossomed into one of the most extravagant gardens I had ever seen, with a show of three- and four-hundred-year-old exquisitely shaped bonsais (small trees that mimic the shape and scale of full-sized trees). It was very impressive.

During that evening in Osaka, Pita and I again had another giggling incident, where the tears came sliding down our smiling cheeks. Instigated by the requirement to wear formal Japanese clothing, we tried to wrap a silk housecoat around our bodies. But one problem remained. The robes did not fit around our large sizes, and we could not find properly-sized garments in time for dinner. So we scrambled to secure the robes with safety pins, somewhat successfully, but we were still tardy for dinner. With gregarious laughing and hilarious squeezing through the narrow corridor towards the restaurant, we received the attention of all our traveling group, laughing with us, joining in the fun.

The city of Hiroshima was one of the cities bombed with a nuclear warhead during World War II. I had an eerie feeling as I thought of how the war had destroyed many parts of Europe. Like most European cities, Hiroshima had been completely rebuilt. Its government officials honoured our presence at one of the war memorials with the planting of trees given by our Canadian government. Our tour guide took us to the buildings of the old Hiroshima, where we were overpowered by many pensive moments of sadness, forcing us to reflect on the human cost of war. That evening, we stayed in a hotel where the Japanese emperor and empress had slept. Pita, with her heavy Dutch accent, said, "Hey Sibyl, vee are sleeping vith royalty tonight!"

We visited many more places on our trip, such as our Hong Kong tour, and the Fuji and the Hawaiian Islands. On the last day in Hawaii, we experienced a fearful change in weather when extreme wind with a rainstorm hit us suddenly. I clearly remembered that both Pita and I commenced giggling once again in the safety of our hotel room, perhaps to secure the foundation of our friendship or maybe to let off steam for fear of our lives. On July 28, 1970, we landed in Toronto, and our memorable vacation came to an end. However, we promised each other that we would travel together more often in the future.

Curaçao

Landscape Ontario was planning a trip to Curaçao in the Caribbean, and Pita and I wanted to go. Remembering how well we traveled together in Japan in 1970, we proceeded to plan for this trip together. Curaçao was a Dutch island where many people went to relax under the sun. Pita and I did a bit of that. However, we usually wanted to strike up conversations with the local people.

One such occasion happened when we found ourselves sitting next to a man who appeared distraught because, we learned, he had lost his wife. In his mumbled words, we also learned of his four wives, the countless children he had with each wife, and that he would search for them starting right then and there. On hearing of his plans, Pita and I could not help ourselves engaging in an episode of uproarious laughter. Some things never changed between us. And that poor man sitting beside us had no luck in stopping us.

A Christmas Pilgrimage

A Christmas pilgrimage in the holy land of Israel and Palestine would be a dream come true, but the trip would mean missing all the hustle and bustle of my usual Christmas excitement at home. The advertisement in the *Catholic Register* newspaper explained all that I needed to know about a seventeen-day trip to Israel, Egypt, and Greece. I asked Pita to accompany me, and she gladly said yes.

The lengthy journey to get to our first destination, Cairo, Egypt, had our first landings in Montreal, Canada, and Copenhagen, Denmark. But before we knew it, we were standing in front of the famous Egyptian pyramids looming high above us. First, we saw the largest artificial mountain in the Great Pyramid of Cheops, about 450 feet high. There, we feasted our eyes on another triangular structure, decorated with the Sphinx at its base.

On our next adventure, Pita asked, "And how are we ever supposed to get onto that double-humped creature?"

The camel returned an equal stare at her with long-lashed glossy brown eyes, as if to ask, "And you, how are you ever going to figure that out?"

The camels, trained to bend down, kneeling on their forelegs, lowered themselves enough for us to climb on their backs. During the twenty-minute ride, Pita and I had a huge laughing episode between us.

Our next stop was Tel Aviv, Israel. After we made it through security, a guide drove our tour bus to Jerusalem, where we stayed overnight in a rather basic hotel. The temperature dropped into the single digits during the evening, but we did not worry about that too much after finding extra blankets to keep us warm. Our focus was to appreciate where we were—one of the holiest places in the world, and a place where I had dreamed of being my entire life. They guided us through the holy places of Jerusalem that included shrines on the Way of the Cross, the Garden of Gethsemane, and the Ascension Church. We then went on an excursion to Bethany and to the River Jordan, where there was surprisingly only a trickle of water, not a river flow as we had expected. At a few of the places visited, we said prayers and the holy rosary with our group.

Where else in the world could one hope to be on Christmas Eve, except for the town of Bethlehem where Jesus Christ was born? We attended Christmas midnight mass at the Church of the Nativity. We were in the crowded area, forcing us to stand for the duration of the mass; but we could thankfully watch the mass on a large screen in the square outside of the church. Following this religious experience was the next day's prayer and meditation with our visit to Cana, where Jesus Christ had performed his first miracle. Later that day, we went to other interesting biblical places such as Nazareth, the Sea of Galilee, Haifa, and Mount Carmel.

We spent the last days of our trip in ancient Athens, Greece, where we saw the palaces and the gardens of Plato, the Acropolis, and many other ancient monuments. The entire trip was absorbing, sacred, and historical, shared with my best traveling friend, Pita.

I truly treasured all the memories of my adventures, putting them in photo albums to help remind me of happy experiences in my life. Rarely would I find another means to remember details, except through daily diarizing. For example, in one of my diaries, I wrote down the words of a song, "Faraway Places," sung by the choir at our wedding in 1948. Were the words a prediction of my future? It was a popular tune that I heard on the radio during World War II originally sung by the British singer Vera Lynn. Some of the lyrics were:

"Faraway over the sea, Those faraway places, With the strange soundin' names, Are callin', callin', me."

I recorded these words in my heart, giving me sunshine moments and uplifting dreams whenever I traveled.

Other Destinations

During my life, I was able to take many more and varied trips. The purpose of my next two trips in 1979 was to mark my friendships with two groups of four women. The first group included Pita, her sister-in-law Adrie

Van de Avord, and Florie DeBoer. In the rental car, we drove to many places in Florida, such as Saint Petersburg, Sarasota, Tampa, the Busch Gardens, the Cypress Gardens, Clearwater, and Cape Canaveral with the Kennedy Space Center. On one occasion, at our Sheraton Hotel in Clearwater, there was a special dinner and dance, and Pita and Adrie danced to the music surprisingly well. We all enjoyed our little vacation together.

In the second group, I was entertained by the company of my sisters-in-law Gretel (Guillaume), Mien (Jan), and Gerda (Arnold). The enchanted and beautiful Schwarzwald (the Black Forest) in Germany, was our destination. One evening in the hotel restaurant where we stayed, we were enjoying our discussion about Guillaume and Gretel's thirty-fifth wedding anniversary, a feast held before our trip. All at once, someone announced that there was a phone call for a Gretel Janssen. It was Guillaume. He relayed that he wanted to give her a Kusslang (German slang word for a hug and a kiss)! It meant so much to me to know that they were always in love with each other.

My experiences of traveling placed new perspectives in my life. I saw worlds that I thought never existed. And traveling with good friends and family enriched my relationships with each of them. But this would not have been possible if not for my life-long commitment to the business, Humber Nurseries Ltd.

“

Faraway over the sea,
Those faraway places.

”

Expansion in the early 1970s to our Humber Nurseries Ltd. sales station included the purchase of a ten-acre lot to the north of our existing property.

Frans turned sixty-five on January 24, 1965, and we celebrated with our family at The Old Mill restaurant in Toronto. In the photo are seven of our nine grandchildren. From left to right are Henk, Anita, Travis (bottom), Monica, Wesley, Frans (JR) and Peter. (Missing: Sephra and Brandon)

A snapshot taken in 1968. We all loved our canine and feline pets, particularly our three German Shepherds. From left to right were Kip, Princess and Lady.

I recalled the 1970s with great fondness and pride, and I cherished the numerous friendships along the way. As time marched on in this decade, my family grew in numbers and the business expanded. Amazingly, as time moved further on into the 1980s, Humber Nurseries Ltd. evolved from a three-season garden centre into an all-season garden centre. I expressed my view of the world in my stories, but my smooth ride was also met with adversity, once while traveling with my cousin, and once with Humber Nurseries Ltd.

The Early Roaring Seventies

We expanded the Humber Nurseries Ltd. sales-station area, purchasing a ten-acre lot to the north of our existing retail station. These cattle-grazing farmlands originally belonged to our neighbours, Donald and Rita Fines. Mrs. Fines offered the land to us first for our purchase, a promise that she made with her husband before he died. Initially, we used the land for the cultivation and growing of nursery stock, and in time, we used more land for the growing of perennials, Frans's developing interest.

We continued to build plastic-covered greenhouses to display spring seasonal annuals and vegetables sold around the May 24 weekend. Expansion continued with constructing two arch-styled steel Quonset storage barns for winterizing our growing number of trucks and other heavy landscaping equipment. In addition, we installed gas pumps to supply the fuel for these vehicles. We also excelled in sod, loam, and stonework specialty areas, and Frans continued to seek new growing methods and creative landscaping designs. Clients supported our excellent service and quality goods during the last twenty-two years of business.

Simultaneously, we blended in the raising of our family. In their early teenage years, our children embraced all that there was to learn about the nursery business by working after school, on weekends, and during the summer months. They improved their office-duty skills, which included accounting, labour organization, inventory, and ordering garden supplies. They also learned outdoor nursery work such as rose budding, taking cuttings, seeding, and planting.

We entertained many young relatives from the Netherlands who took advantage of our invitations to stay with us in our bungalow basement guest room. Some wanted to learn about our nursery and improve their English skills, and others wanted to see how we lived in Canada.

Andre Janssen was our first guest, aged twenty, the fourth child of my brother Guillaume and his wife, Gretel. While working at Humber Nurseries Ltd., he learned about the hard work behind the scenes of a growing small business operation. He experienced more hard work in the Canadian Christmas season, working at the Yorkdale Shopping Mall closer to Toronto. All this would be part of his learning foundation, leading to the takeover of his father's awning and security systems business in the Netherlands.

Another young relative was Giel Janssen, the eldest son of my brother, Arnold, and his wife, Gerda. He worked at the business for only a few weeks, since his plan was to travel by car to the United States with Frans Jr. and his friend Grant Sherman. They came back with many stories, and one that I remembered well was the story when they went to New York City. They drove to a dangerous area of Harlem and witnessed some gangsters removing car hubcaps in broad daylight. A tall tale for Giel to tell his grandchildren!

Everyone's mother is special, and Frans's mother was no different. She would turn eighty years of age on

April 20, 1973, so we invited her to visit us during the Christmas season of 1972. Opa was reluctant to come with her. He had a fear of flying ever since he had witnessed a plane, one of the first, crash before his eyes.

Seeing Oma walking around our home and nursery was a dream come true, especially for Frans. We stayed up late each night to talk about our humble beginnings and the stories of building our lives in Canada. Would she ever understand how hard it was to spend our first night in Canada in the lonely village of Sheguiandah on Manitoulin Island, sleeping on a straw bed?

We visited many relatives and friends, many of whom had families of their own. Two people of whom Oma longed to see were her niece, Riet Raayman who supported our rescue during Hurricane Hazel, and my cousin, Wim Klein Beernink. But most of all, Oma enjoyed being in our home with her eldest son, Frans, our four children, and all our canine and feline pets.

Who Was at The Door?

On Saturday, March 17, 1973, a cold and miserable day with snow still on the ground, Frans and I had the surprise of our lives. Our day began as usual, with jobs needing completion before the day's end. Frans and I were working in the greenhouses—I was working with the transplanting of annuals, and Frans was watering all the young plants. At the end of the day, still in my work clothes because I was too tired to change, I had fallen asleep in front of the television in the living room, not an unusual thing for me to do. Frans was seeing to some paperwork in his home office. The time was about seven in the evening when we heard banging on the back patio door, followed by a bombardment of continuous knocks. Who in the world was at the door?

The door slid open, and we heard loud singing:

"Lang zal ze leven (That they may live a long life)," a traditional Dutch party song, followed by many voices singing the words:

"Happy anniversary to you!" to the English tune of "Happy Birthday."

It was true that we had been married for twenty-five years, but the wedding date was April 12, and Frans and I had given little thought as to how we would celebrate our milestone anniversary. There were so many friendly and familiar faces hiding on the back patio, and we greeted them all with open arms as they marched into the kitchen area, carrying food, drink, and gifts. All the champagne, food, and music of the James Last Big Band (Frans's favourite) was pre-organized by our children. Frans and I were not even suspicious of the popping of the champagne bottles hidden downstairs during our supper hour. It was a huge surprise.

Weddings of Our Children

During the early expansion of our nursery, our children had many impressive accomplishments of their own. Sibylleke became an elementary school teacher after studying at Western University and Teachers' College in London, Ontario. Frans Jr. received a degree in horticulture at the University of Guelph. He followed in his father's footsteps at Humber Nurseries Ltd. Astrid attended the University of Toronto to study languages and music and pursued a high school teaching career. Guy attended the University of Guelph to study horticulture and followed in his father's footsteps.

Frans and I were happy that our two sons were ready for marriage: Guy to Dorothy Van Zanten, daughter of our friends, Freda and Martin, on July 5, 1974, in Saint Gregory's Catholic church; and Frans Jr. to Vita Skvereckas on July 12, 1975, at Our Lady of Mercy Lithuanian Catholic church in Hamilton, Ontario. Vita, Astrid's best friend at university, was first introduced into the family through Astrid's invitation for a summer job to work at the nursery. Here she met her brother Frans Jr.

The third family wedding occurred between Sibylleke and Henk Sikking, a grower in the tulip bulb and cut flowers industry in Saint Catharines, Ontario. Through Frans's best friend and business associate in the bulb and flower industry, Dick Veerman, Sibylleke met Henk on a blind date. They were married at the Saint Margaret Mary Church in Woodbridge on October 16, 1976.

Was There a Handbook for Grandparents?

No one wrote a handbook for new grandparents, and therefore, we newbies would react individually. For me, the sight of my first grandchild left me amazed by the real miracle of life. At six thirty in the morning, on September 21, 1977, he was born to Dorothy and Guy and weighed a healthy eight pounds six ounces. Wesley was a little bumbling bundle of autumn joy.

In the year 1978, we were blessed with two more awesome grandchildren. Baby Henk was born to Sibylleke and Henk, on March 21 at five thirty-six in the evening, weighing a healthy nine pounds and four ounces. He was a cute spring bud, and I pictured him blooming into a handsome young man.

Vita and Frans Jr. were blessed with a beautiful daughter of nearly seven pounds on June 23. They named her Monica. She would remind me of the energy of summer with endless smiles of happiness.

In November 1980, there were more grandchildren added to our family. I received an announcement from my son-in-law Henk:

"We have beautiful twins, a girl and a boy!"

I cried in happiness, with tears rolling down my face, because this was indeed a miracle of two lives, born within eighteen minutes of each other. Anita came first that morning of November 29, weighing five pounds and four ounces, and Peter weighed five pounds and eleven ounces. Their soft bodies were so tiny that they needed to be kept in the hospital for a few weeks until they gained weight.

Our sixth grandchild was born to Vita and Frans on February 5, 1981. He was named Frans, taking the name of his father and his three forefathers. Just think that each Frans was the first-born male to each of these families. Imagine that heritage!

Our seventh grandchild, Travis, was born to Dorothy and Guy, on May 30, 1982, in the middle of the spring season. Happy about the new arrival, we were still busy with the nursery and unable to fully appreciate the occasion. After the busy season, we truly welcomed him into our family.

Our All-Season Garden Centre

Our nursery business grew steadily from a three-season into an all-season garden centre. One reason for this came from growing nursery stock in plastic containers in the 1980s. Below is the explanation of the process.

We did most business in early spring and late fall in our formative years. We would sell almost all deciduous stock in a dormant bare-root stage. The next stage of the selling process was calling the customers, informing them of delivery dates. We then dug the nursery stock from the fields, wrapped the trees, shrubs, and hedging in moss and paper, and finally placed them into a large or small truck for delivery at prescribed dates and

In 1988, we had a year-round promotional anniversary sale to celebrate our forty years in business.

Every spring season provided a huge splash of colour, a great motivation for our clientele to visit our nursery surroundings.

'Buy From A Grower, Buy The Best' was our commitment to our clients. Most of our trees, shrubs and evergreens were sold in container-grown pots.

The new method of growing trees, shrubs, and evergreens was easier and faster. The method came with the expanding use of plastics in many other industries. In the spring, we would immediately transplant the nursery material into plastic containers, and they would be neatly and completely ready for sale.

There was nothing like seeing rows and rows of container-grown trees, shrubs, and evergreens that easily enabled the customers to view on site and purchase during any season of the year. This efficient method of growing and marketing made business more profitable, and it was also more convenient for the client. Soon, our nursery developed into a well-recognized name, becoming Ontario's largest and best servicing "All Season Garden Centre."

We functioned and achieved maximum productivity with a permanent staff of thirty-five employees year-round and over a hundred during the peak spring season. All were well-trained and effective to the new Humber Nurseries Ltd. commitment to its clients: "Buy from a grower. Buy the best."

Our Humber Nurseries Ltd. provided year-round service, responding to the diverse needs from its nearest Brampton community to as far as the town of Oakville, the city of Toronto, and the area of Scarborough.

In approximately three decades, our business had grown from a small community nursery to the largest single horticultural facility of its kind in Ontario. Humber Nurseries Ltd. represented a fulfillment of our dream, first planted in our minds in 1948. And together with goal-oriented and creative direction from our two sons, we managed our multifaceted business. Frans Jr. and Guy were developing a vision of their own for Humber Nureries Ltd. Frans Jr. pursuing the wholesale operations, and Guy the retail operations. It would be a natural step for them to take on the reins for our sucession.

Eventually, our nursery evolved into four distinct departments. First, in our landscaping department we had our twelve-month indoor design and idea centre, displaying landscape themes from water features to patios and lighting. We had three full-time designers on staff. Outdoors, numerous display gardens were used from the ordinary to the unusual, in plant materials and hardgoods.

Secondly, there was increasingly new technology in the greenhouse department. Here was the production of thousands of flats of annuals and perennials, herbs, and aquatic plants, with varieties that were not commonly available at other nurseries. Frans's developing interest was to seek worldwide varieties that could withstand the southern Ontario climate. As a result, Humber grew over 225 different ornamental types of grass, 3,200 different perennials, 300 types of herbs, and 150 aquatic plants. It was an amazing accomplishment.

The third department was the garden centre store, which expanded into a 25,000-square-foot indoor retail store and buildings under plastic. It carried a large selection of giftware, pottery, fertilizers, insecticides, lawn fixtures, hand tools, soils, and quality nursery stock at competitive prices, ranging from boxes of petunias to twelve-foot blue spruces.

Lastly, the wholesale department grew because of the self-supplying 100-acre nursery farm in Caledon, which supported the supply and demand for trees, shrubs, and evergreens, expanding from the most common to the most exotic varieties and which included the propagation of stock for Humber.

Near-Death Experience

Have you ever been somewhere in your life and survived a near-death experience? Here is an updated story on our first Humber employee.

My cousin Wim Klein Beernink wished to have a vacation before the spring season started up again. He was studying for his career change in the fall of 1972 and wanted to take advantage of the opportunity of school break time to do some traveling. His wife Tiny gave her full support to see him go, as he would gain new, revitalized perspectives on life. I took this also as an opportunity to see Europe again, and of course, to see my relatives. Together, Wim and I reviewed the newspapers for train trips across Europe. We came upon the Eurail Pass, a ticket which allowed us to travel anywhere in Europe by train. We bought our tickets in Canada before our departure at a low price of 125 Canadian dollars. We both purchased unlimited first-class travel, and we planned for a three-week holiday.

From our point of departure in London, England, we traveled all over Europe, including the Netherlands, Belgium, France, Denmark, Monaco, Germany, Italy, and Switzerland. The easy part about the Eurail Pass was that no destination planning was necessary. However, in retrospect, it might have been a good idea if we had told someone of our plans. What happened next nearly cost us our lives, and no one in our circle of friends and family would have known if we were alive or dead, at least for the duration of our trip.

The train had abruptly stopped. There were two army officers dressed in camouflaged dark brown uniforms, sitting across from where we were seated. Both Wim and I suspected that they were with the Libyan Army. Suddenly we heard a loud and demanding voice speaking English from a speaker in the first-class wagon car where we were sitting:

"All passengers must immediately leave the train. Take no baggage with you. Leave at the exit points closest to you."

Each passenger rushed, pushing, and shoving to get to the exit, where we quickly disembarked the train. Fortunately, no one was hurt. There was a bomb scare. Where the bomb was, nobody knew. But Wim and I figured out that there was a problem with the two of us sitting near those two soldiers, who we suspected were the potential human targets. We thought that someone had planted the bomb in our compartment.

Later we read in the newspaper that the bomb was found, removed from the train, and put into the water, but we would never know from which compartment. Our time was not up yet.

Why Us? Another Disaster.

We were, however, in for another surprise in June of 1973. Sadly, the surprise was a huge disaster during one mid-week evening after a long workday of clean up at the nursery. Again, the memory of terrible times during Hurricane Hazel came into play.

This spring season had been a prosperous one for our business, and we were now winding down operations. All heavy and light equipment used in landscaping and deliveries were already cleaned, repaired, and stored in our two Quonset buildings. Unexpectedly, a burst of flame shot out from the very depths of one of these buildings, traveling quickly, heating up, burning, and destroying everything in its path. Could anyone understand the terror of losing our home situated twenty feet away from this murderous flame? How long would it take for the gas tanks located ten feet in front of the Quonset building to catch fire and explode?

The saving grace was that the firemen with their well-equipped fire trucks arrived within minutes and first sought the family's safety inside the home. Then my son Guy, quick to react, grabbed the keys of all the trucks from the kitchen key cupboard, and both he and Frans Jr. dared to drive them as far away as possible from the gas tanks.

We analyzed the devastation, and it was enormous. Although the outside steel frame of the Quonset building was not damaged, everything inside had burned to ashes, leaving clouds of black smoke emitting from the arched entrance for many days after. There were the lost memories of hearty stories that came with the death of all the equipment, machinery, and tools used since the birth of the nursery, including our beloved wooden-stone knife sharpener.

However, everyone was safe and alive, and our home remained standing. For months however, the burnt smell in the air reminded us of the tragedy. Frans and I prayed to overcome our adversity, and we were determined to keep our dream alive, and we did.

As we entered the new decade of the 1980s, our nursery became less isolated. People were drawn towards the extensive variety of gardening and services offered by Humber Nurseries Ltd. What went on in the sphere of its influence, involved the company as never before. The business was expanding and undergoing many changes, and I felt that my leadership was gratefully supported by my sons, who were both gladly taking over the organization.

I enjoyed my new flexible schedule of retirement living. At age sixty-five, I was honoured with a surprise party on my birthday.

Ten years later, I was honoured again with another surprise birthday party. My sons presented a Hybrid Tea Rose, named after me, Mrs. S. Peters.

This lovely fragrant rose was sold at our nursery.

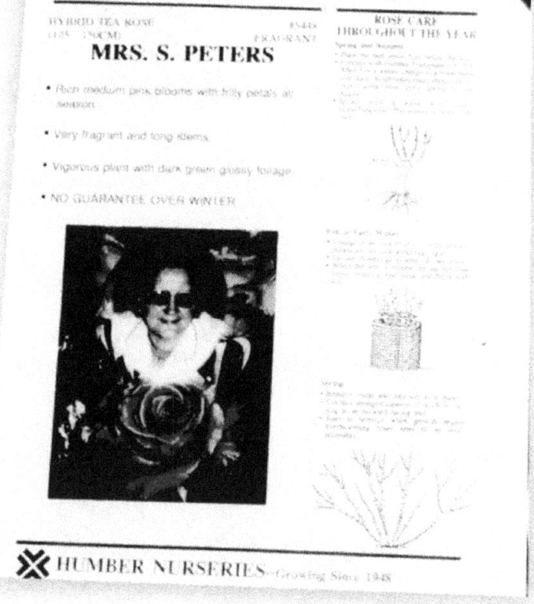

Chapter Nineteen: The Flow of Retirement

I was turning sixty-five, an official retirement age. At this time, I suspected that I would highlight more family interactions in both Canada and the Netherlands. Frans and I also felt comfortable with the security of the future of our business, brought on thankfully by our two sons who fulfilled our business succession plan. With that in mind, I had the option of either a full or a part-time job status at Humber. I liked having that choice, since my work was evolving into a hobby that I very much enjoyed.

And then ten years later, I would be honoured for all my accomplishments and service in the horticulture industry in a special and rewarding way, with the Mrs. S. Peters Hybrid Tea Rose.

To Retire or Not to Retire?

To retire or not to retire? That was my question. Retirement could provide more time for me to do the things that I liked to do. But work-related projects provided a daily focus, something to look forward to as I awoke each morning. Retirement to me was not a stop-all-work sign in life, as it was for many people. For me, it became the enjoyment of a blend of work-play. An example was when I took spontaneous time off work for a family celebration. It involved my eldest daughter.

Sibylleke had the opportunity to make a surprise visit to her Oma and Opa Peters in Deventer. She appeared suddenly at their doorstep with a bundle of fresh flowers, congratulating them on their sixty-fifth wedding anniversary (June 17, 1983). It was an unimaginable tribute from Canada. Unknown to Sibylleke, I, too, flew to Deventer in a spontaneous decision to congratulate my parents-in-law. I knocked on the same door with flowers in hand. Was this a coincidence or a planned surprise by my daughter? Whatever the answer, it was a satisfying experience, and proof that mother and daughter were thinking alike. How about that?

During that trip, I capitalized on the freedom to extend my overseas visit in Europe to mend a family rift. The division of families came about because of an incident that happened at the beginning of World War II. My brother Jan, with the same plan in mind, would travel with me to Germany.

Jan and I first visited Tegelen, a village where our grandfather Joseph Laurentius Janssen's family laid down roots in the pottery industry. We next explored our ancestral German city of Breyll, near the border, and where our Stinkes (the surname of our family in Germany) family lived. Our grandmother's name was Sibilla Stinkes; she married my grandfather, Andreas Arnoldus Janssen, in her second marriage. We had not seen the family descendants since as far back as 1947.

Not notifying the family in advance of our arrival gave us the advantage of surprise, but when we arrived at their address, we continued to have lingering doubts as to whether we were doing the right thing. Nevertheless, we rang the doorbell. We immediately recognized the man who opened the door. His name was Hans Stinkes, my grandmother's great-nephew. No words could explain the strength of his warm hugs and his soothing tears of comfort as we exchanged greetings.

Hans said in German, "Sibylla, Jan, es war zu lang. Willkomen zu Hause!" ("Sibylla, Jan, it's been too long. Welcome home!")

I also heard expressions of surprise and welcome from his wife's voice from the back of the long hallway where she was propped in a wheelchair, anxiously waving for us to enter the house. They overwhelmingly and warmly welcomed Jan and me.

And this was how our German side of the family received their Dutch family into their home. From that moment on, our families kept in contact with each other regularly.

I enjoyed the freedom of my time, and that would imply retirement at age sixty-five. The official date was August 2, 1983. But wasn't I too young to retire? During that summer, after my return from the Netherlands, I planned a visit to Father Hap's cottage on Lake Couchiching, as I had been doing quite often in the past few years, every other weekend. While in the car I thought of my upcoming relaxing weekend, but I stopped dreaming when I noticed Father Hap taking a route that I was not used to seeing. Then I realized we were heading towards Frans and Vita's home in Caledon, and I noticed a decorative sign with fancy print which read: "To Peters House." Why were we going to my son's house?

Surprise! The gathering was for me! A party for my sixty-fifth birthday! There were so many people there, some of whom I had not seen in a long time. I remembered even my parish priest Father Nolan from Our Lady of the Airways parish, who asked if this really would be a retirement beginning for me. Everyone was hoping I would say yes after so many years of working with the business. But I could answer them later. There was a party to attend, and it was all for me. I changed into party attire that Vita had prepared for me, and under the large tent, there were people to greet, catered food to eat, and music for dancing.

Our nursery foreman George, the bartender, handed me a glass of wine and said, "What a great tribute to you, Mrs. P.!"

I laughed and then cried, because I knew my answer: no full retirement for me. I was too young to retire!

My Retirement Trip

Pita Van Dongen would accompany me on my retirement trip to Europe. And what would that mean to both of us? The answer lay in our history of travel. We would have long tall humorous tales to tell upon our return.

Landscape Ontario offered a study tour, starting with a visit to Germany's Munich International Horticultural Exposition and its famous Oktoberfest, then to Switzerland's exquisitely landscaped sites in Zurich, then Austria's Schoenbrunn Castle in Vienna. That evening in Vienna, we chose to attend an opera with our friends Casey and Monica van Maris and Lore Litz. While driving in our minibus after the show, and after a little wine, we sang the famous Viennese song, "Wien, Wien, Nur du Allein (Vienna, Vienna, Just You Alone)."

Lore Litz tearfully said, "I was born in Vienna, and there are so many happy memories of my life growing up here, until the war that changed everything." Then she sang: "Edelweiss," a song about a delicate mountain flower with furry white petals, and sung in the famous movie *The Sound of Music*. Everyone joined her in her happiness. The minibus took the long route back to the hotel while we prolonged our enjoyment.

Our next eventful stop was Venice, Italy, where a group of us made our way to the Casino di Venezia. Suddenly from no direction, a voice commanded us,

“Stop please! You are not dressed properly, ladies and gentlemen!”

Disappointed that we could not enter this famous place, I asked the group, “Who wants to join Pita and me? We know of another casino with no dress code.”

I was unsuccessful in my persuasion, and they left Pita and me on our own, a big mistake. How would they know what kind of mischief the two of us could create? The next morning, we decided to play a joke. We carried our largest suitcases and, pretending that they had inflated weight, we proceeded slowly toward the breakfast room. As we neared the entrance, we were dragging the bags and exaggerating our steps, so that everyone would notice our grandiose entry. Then, in between huge huffs and puffs, we shouted:

Pita: “Oh, our suitcases are so very heavy!”

Me: “Is there anyone who can help us carry them?”

Pita: “We spent half the night into the morning at the casino!”

Me: “And we were lucky at every game. Can't you tell?”

Pita: “Search our suitcases and take what you want for a tip!”

And with that came an uproar of laughter from our intended audience.

After the farewell dinner at our beautiful villa on Lake Constance, Pita and I would depart, each of us in different destinations—I was headed for the Netherlands, and she was returning to Canada. I worried about Pita because when on holiday, she lost all sense of timing. Later I heard Pita was talking and laughing so much on the phone at the airport that she missed her plane. Fortunately, our friend Casey van Maris looked after her luggage in Toronto as she arrived on a later plane.

I Would Write a Letter

Dear Gretel, July 1987

How long has it been since I last wrote to you? Well, I am about to update you on the latest.

First, news on the children: Frans Jr. and Guy work diligently, agree on all work-related decisions, and they love doing the business. In Saint Catharines, Ontario, Henk and Sibylleke are successful in running their wholesale flowers business, where their product is completely grown in year-round greenhouses. Astrid is enjoying her studies in Grenoble, France (as I write this letter). And my Frans is still as passionate as ever about all his plants.

At Humber, most of the craziness of our busiest months of April, May, and June is over, and the commercial jobs will keep a steady flow of income into the business during the summer months. I was especially proud this year because of a visit by Pope Paul II to Toronto. In preparation for his arrival, one of our more sizable landscaping jobs displayed rainbows of flower colour at Saint Michael's Cathedral in Toronto, supplied by the annuals from our very own Humber Nurseries Ltd., of which I had personally grown and transplanted in our greenhouses.

The store closes at six o'clock, a change from our former "wait 'til the last customer leaves" theory. We feel we work long and hard enough, and by closing at a specific time, we can limit the number of escapades that somehow always erupt at the very end of the day.

Christmas will continue to be a special time of year for us; however, our family numbers are multiplying, just like yours, which compels us to make some changes. I love my grandchildren dearly, but the Christmas celebrations are getting too much for Frans and me to handle. It involves cooking turkey with all the trimmings, the enjoyment and excitement of our sing-a-longs and participating in a zealous hype over what Santa is bringing to everyone. Even the space in our home seems to shrink with every upcoming Christmas season.

So, we decided to change the celebration date pointing primarily towards the Sunday closest before Christmas Day. On that Sunday, we hope to have more time to luxuriate in our exchange of gifts over a dinner, buffet style. We would call it the Peters Family Christmas. Consequently, on Christmas Day, Frans Jr. and Guy could enjoy family plans in their homes, and Frans and I would drive with Astrid to Sibylleke and Henk's in Saint Catharines for the day.

We already talked about the marriage breakdown between Guy and Dorothy, and we met Guy's new girlfriend, Alex Kennedy, at one of our grandchildren's birthday parties. Guy invited Alex to work in the office with Vita, and she became a familiar face during those long fourteen-hour workdays at Humber in the spring, working alongside Frans Jr., Guy, and Vita. Alex used to be a nurse administrator at Saint Joseph's Hospital in Toronto, where she worked hard with whole heart and soul. The job change was a difficult choice for her. I know the wedding bells will soon ring, and perhaps you should think of making another trip to Canada for that. Why not? Or you should come for our fortieth wedding anniversary next year. I would love to go dancing at this restaurant in Toronto with an extensive buffet and a huge dance floor!

But I'm going to the Netherlands next year and the year after that again; perhaps I will see you sooner.

Dear Gretel, August 1989

We must have just missed each other, and I think you were out the day I came for a visit. So, I will update you on the latest in this letter.

On July 29, 1989, Guy and Alex married at a service in the Old Mill Chapel in Toronto, and they celebrated with a reception on the boat called The Yankee Lady II in the Toronto harbour. Amongst friends and family were four of my grandchildren: Wesley, Travis, Monica, and Frans, dressed in formal clothes, as in tuxedos for the boys and a beautiful pink and white dress for Monica. What handsome little children! And they even behaved like adults for most of the time. Frans Jr. was the best man, and Vita was the maiden of honour. Tiny and Wim Klein Beernink were there too, who were also celebrating their thirty-ninth wedding anniversary. It was a beautiful celebration.

Now a story about Jan, my brother, your brother-in-law. Sometimes, I think he hides his talents way too much, and I am sure you do not know that he became intensely involved in researching Dutch history. After retirement, he dedicated much of his time to giving tours of the city he loved, Deventer. You probably know more about closing the three-generational pottery business that existed for over ninety years. He was perhaps so distraught without a successor after dedicating his entire life to the industry.

When Jan, Mien and I went on a trip by train to Vlissingen, Zeeland, there was a beautiful piece of art in the hallway of the railway station. Unfortunately, in front of it was a huge and ugly advertisement that destroyed its view. Jan was incredibly upset, and he wrote a persuasive letter to the Dutch railway office about his deep concern.

Within a few weeks, the Utrecht administration indicated they would remove the ugly sign that blocked that fascinating piece of artwork. At the same time, they offered to pay for his train trips between Deventer and Vlissingen. Jan always seemed to have a convincing influence on people everywhere he went, and he always looked for improvement to society in one form or another.

During my November 1989 trip to the Netherlands (and what I want to now relate to you, is a bit upsetting), I noticed Jan was not looking healthy. However, his children confirmed while I was visiting that the doctors found nothing medically wrong with him at the time. However, later, he was diagnosed with terminal cancer. Did you know that? I hope you will visit him in these trying times.

Dear Gretel, July 1990

Thank you for sending the prayer card for our Jan, who had seventy joyous years of life. I often think of the words of the poem from Goethe, the German poet and blessing from God:

"That God made the first man on earth out of clay, and that the pottery maker was made good and strong to start mankind."

The pottery business had taken on a symbol of strength for our Janssen family. I hoped that God would bless us all.

Recalling the 1990s: Two Stories

1. Landscape Ontario

During the 1990s, fresh winds were blowing in. Our two sons were bringing on innovations in the expansion of our nursery business. Our Humber Nurseries Ltd. became popular within the industry, with much of the credit going to them, and their influence carried on into a social circle. Every summer, for example, in the late eighties and early nineties, Frans and Guy hosted well-organized golf tournaments for the Landscape Ontario Association (Landscape Ontario). Much fun under the sun resonated amongst the players after golf in Frans Jr.'s backyard pool and garden. His home served as the best location for everyone to socialize while swimming, to enjoy delicious food and beverage, and to receive creative golf-related prizes.

The horticultural community gave Frans Jr. and Guy significant recognition for their generosity throughout those years. Frans Jr. also performed duties as the longest-serving president of Landscape Ontario, comprising the years 1993, 1994, and 1995. Guy served on the board of directors of Landscape Ontario's Garden Centre Commodity Group for eight years.

2. My Own Rose

For one of my eventful rounds as the matriarch of a thriving and successful garden centre, I was going to be honoured on my seventy-fifth birthday. On August 2,

1993, an extraordinary flower was going to bloom. Yes, my sons gave the direction to create a real flower of distinction in my honour. It was a pink fragrant hybrid tea rose, called "Mrs. S. Peters." I could not imagine all the planning involved in producing such a perennial flower, and the work of budding roses would bring back memories of Frans's first job on Manitoulin Island in the spring of 1948.

I felt deeply privileged to see dozens of these roses, spilling out a sweet fragrance and radiant beauty. They were decorating the inside of the large convention centre at the Doctor's House, in Kleinburg, Ontario. My rose was an extraordinary commemoration of all the work that I had done over the years in the development of Humber Nurseries Ltd.

How grateful I was to all of those who made this birthday an unforgettable one. What a surprise party! Magda (Peters), Gretel (Janssen), my nephew and niece, Andre and Maria Janssen, came from the Netherlands to join the big party of family and friends in Canada. I sincerely hoped that God would bless everyone to witness their seventy-fifth birthday, and I prayed for those whose hearts would grow dark in their lives.

The culminating festivity on my seventy-fifth birthday summed up where I was in life, what accomplishments I attained, and a foreshadow of what was yet to come. I imagined another decade of life filled with more exploration of the world, with family and friends.

Special keepsake memories were made when I traveled to the Netherlands in 1984 with my son Frans Jr., my grandson Frans (JR) and my husband Frans. In Frans's birth home Deventer, a memorable photo was taken of the four Franses.

Chapter Twenty: Blooming of a Rose

Always keep your glass half full, rather than half empty. I learned to accentuate the positives in life, rather than complain about it. I intended to enjoy life and to work on my youthful spirit. It was my way of staying young. For instance, I attended the latest and most fashionable garden and flower festival in which Humber also participated; I traveled to a part of Canada I would never have thought to see; and I continued to share special keepsake memories.

Canada Blooms

In the last decade of the twentieth century, Landscape Ontario, together with the Garden Club of Toronto, created a world-class floral design and garden festival called Canada Blooms. All the proceeds would go to support community projects that promoted horticulture in Ontario, as well as horticultural scholarships. Two participants in this opening year were our own Humber Nurseries Ltd. in Brampton, and Pioneer Flower Farm in Saint Catharines, Ontario (Sibylleke and Henk Sikking's flourishing greenhouse business). The first show took place in the spring of 1997.

Our Humber Garden presentation theme was "Colour in Motion," designed by our landscape architect Peter Stevens. The garden included the work from my sons' business colleagues, Frank Andrioli of Lawn Barber Landscaping and Frank Soave of North Star Landscaping, a true community spirit.

The colour burst at the main entrance and throughout main areas—created from thousands of tulips and daffodils—was designed and donated for opening ceremonies by Pioneer Flower Farm. Canada Blooms was a success and continued in Toronto for many years to come.

My Youthful Spirit

During that opening year of Canada Blooms, my daughter Astrid accompanied me to see all the flower and horticultural presentations. I was overwhelmed with the creativity and enormity of gardening ideas. Truly, gardening had evolved into a fashion all its own. I admitted that starting a business in the gardening industry of this day and age, would challenge a budding horticulturist in a different way than it was for Frans and I. Different opportunities and unique circumstances surrounded us in those days.

Unfortunately, at my life and health stage, my asthma and other health issues were slowing me down and contributed to depending on a wheelchair for long distances—which I accepted without complaint. In reflection on this vast new world of aging, I analyzed at where I was. I recalled a conversation that I had with Astrid, who was eager to listen to my thoughts and questions.

"I am lucky to have one strong woman to push me around in a wheelchair today!" I began. And thinking of my appearance in the wheelchair, I asked Astrid, "Do you think I look like an old woman now?"

I hoped that my provocative question did not disturb her. She smartly requested what I meant by "old."

I thought about it. "Well, 'old' is complaining about aches and pains (*but I didn't*). 'Old' is when you admit to sleeping more (*but I enjoyed getting up at seven-thirty in the morning these days, and that was not because I thought that I needed my sleep*). And 'old' is the enjoyment of watching more television (*but I watched TV because I was excited about watching the many new shows offered*)." I chuckled. "Is watching more television setting me up for new retirement plans?"

"Yes, you should watch more television," Astrid answered. "And I like your explanation of 'old.'" She paused, took a deep breath, and then said thoughtfully, "I think of using the word 'youth' to describe you, Mom, because your youth shines in your sparkling brown eyes, your alert mind, and your eager curiosity to try new things." She chuckled and teasingly added, "Like watching new television shows!"

"Yeah, I like that new show called *Judge Judy*!" I said.

Astrid continued. "You tire a little more these days, but really, Mom, you don't need to keep up with your grandchildren! At seventy-eight, you have lots of time for exciting escapades."

I then teased my daughter in return. "I am lucky to have one smart woman to push me around!"

Astrid guided the wheelchair through the doors of the next garden presentation. Then, somewhat changing the direction of the conversation, she said:

"Mom, let me remind you that you and Dad have come a long way since you left Europe. You were part of the growth of the landscaping industry in southern Ontario since 1948. The nursery business developed a beautiful path because of your inputs over the years. And that, I think, is a life reward. In addition, I think that in your present youthful stage in life, it won't take *you* long to figure out what to do next in the coming years. So, let's now enjoy Canada Blooms!"

The truth was, they no longer *needed* me in our nursery, but my sons showed their appreciation of my work when they asked me to teach the employees about transplanting and cuttings, which at heart, I continued to enjoy. I gained satisfaction while putting in a full day of work, and I thought that I deserved my vacation trips.

And on that topic of traveling, I was excited to answer the call of Newfoundland, a province on the eastern Canadian seaboard. Indeed, there was also a thirty-year-old problem that I wanted to solve on this large island.

Humber in Newfoundland

Humber Nurseries Ltd. had been receiving invoices for products that had never been delivered to our business in Brampton or in Caledon, for over thirty years. We, therefore, did not pay them. I needed to find the destination where the deliveries were made. As the mystery continued throughout the years, one day, in conversation with our friends at Sheridan Nurseries, I discovered the address of the destination to where the nursery material was sent. Sheridan had sent product to a Humber Nursery address in Cornerbrook, Newfoundland, and mistakenly sent bills to our Brampton address. I asked that they readdress their mail to Cornerbrook, Newfoundland. However, after that request, invoices still made their way to our doorstep. They remained unpaid.

I was suspicious of the mail system that never distinguished our nursery from any other nursery in Canada of the same name. (Being so popular did have its drawbacks!)

Newfoundland, I thought to myself. That was the first sight of land in Canada that we saw from the SS *Tabinta*. And that was so long ago, and Newfoundland was so far away.

Then I saw an opportunity to be effective in working on a project for Humber Nurseries Ltd. I decided that I wanted to see where this other Humber Nursery existed, which would mean a trip to Newfoundland where that mail was intended.

Wim and Tiny Klein Beernink had never been to Newfoundland, and neither had I. They were happy to join me on my tour. We departed with DeNure Tours on September 2, 1997. After a few days on the road, we discovered how incredibly similar the island of Newfoundland, and specifically the town of Saint Anthony's, was to the Dutch province of Drenthe.

Here were homes with mud-turfed roofs compacted in peat that the Dutch people found from the area's swamps, bogs, and forests. The dwellings of Saint Anthony's replicated the same type of homes, but the roofs were made more from a grass-sod material. These homes gave us an idea of what the eleventh century Viking village L'Anse aux Meadows would have looked like, and this National Historic Park site was considered as the only known Viking colony in all North America.

After that northerly adventure, we traveled southwest to the town of Cornerbrook, where we stayed at an appropriately named hotel for us, the Wind Mill Inn.

Thirty or even forty years ago, Cornerbrook had a nursery and garden centre called Humber Nursery. Because of the identical name with our nursery, and only because of that very name, our Humber Nurseries Ltd. received those invoices from many Ontario companies for products that we had never ordered. I would not pay them, and during the period after I discovered the destination of the product, I immediately redirected the bills to the Humber Nursery in Cornerbrook, Newfoundland. I would receive no communication from the Newfoundland garden centre.

In a casual conversation with my daughter a few weeks prior to our trip, Sibylleke said:

"I must mention that a few of our employees at Pioneer Flowers Farm were born in Cornerbrook. They used to work at this Humber Nursery. So, there's your proof that the nursery existed."

I knew then that I had to see the nursery for myself.

Tiny, Wim, and I researched where Humber Nursery could be located by making inquiries at our hotel and searching in the phone book. We came up empty-handed—there was no such nursery. But I was even more driven to find the location. I decided to take a taxi from the hotel and planned to ask the driver to take me to any nursery in the area. It was my lucky day, because the driver knew of only one nursery in the area, and we drove for an hour to get there.

When we arrived, I saw that there was no Humber Nursery sign. I stepped out of the car, caught a glimpse of about an acre of perennials, trees, and shrubs planted in the backyard, and proceeded to enter a small building that looked like a retail florist store. I said to myself, not too loudly, and under my breath:

"Why do I see only artificial flowers and artificial tropical plants here in this store? Where are the real ones? I would never think of making a living with these products."

At that moment, a gentleman stepped forward to greet me and said, "Welcome to my store. What can I do for you today?"

"I am traveling in Newfoundland," I explained, "and I was hoping to meet the owner of this store, with whom I was somewhat acquainted for over thirty years!"

The owner gave a curious look. "Please explain?"

I unfolded part of my story to him as he showed me around his store and outdoor nursery. He then commented:

"I have recently taken over from that previous owner, and I have changed some of the products, as you can see, with all these colourful artificial plants and flowers. Here in Newfoundland, we have a short growing season, and I now maintain only ten percent in real seasonal and tropical plants. I have a variety of perennials, shrubs, and trees in my outdoor field, which I import and maintain for clients who ask for them."

I was disappointed to hear this news, because I wanted to hear the story from the first owner of the business. I knew that the present owner would not understand the real reason why I was there; however, I was still happy to see that he had a substantial variety of nursery materials. He wanted to know more about me, sensing that I had more horticultural knowledge than the average customer.

"Do you have a nursery business in Toronto?" he asked.

I decided to tell him a brief history of Humber Nurseries Ltd., and to unravel the mystery of the mix-up between the two addresses of the Humber Nurseries. Finally, we were both content, and we wished each other well. I returned to the hotel with a satisfactory conclusion to my story and a promise of no more invoices.

We followed the Trans-Canada Highway back to the town of Gander to see its large airport, and then headed to our last destination, St. John's. Here we enjoyed the town's Cabot 500 celebration of John Cabot's voyage to the island in 1497, 500 years ago. Wim, Tiny, and I had a wonderful time on this interesting and revealing ten-day trip, perfect for the three of us. And I particularly felt a great deal of pride to have solved a business accounting mystery.

One Happy Letter, Two Short Stories, and One Longer Story

1. A short letter to Pita Van Dongen:

Dear Pita,

I hope you have recovered from our memorable trip to the Bahamas. I think the slot machines at the casinos have never been so active after we were there, and do you believe Nassau would ever hear such laughter again? Did we worry about how loud we talked and giggled when we "tiptoed" through the casino to get to breakfast? If we were too loud, not our fault that we had a blast! Right, Pita?

I have enclosed a video made with the help of Astrid. During the videotaping, I have reminisced about all the times we traveled together, about twenty-five years! It is a tribute to our camaraderie, and I hope it brings back memories. Enjoy the viewing!

2. Short Story of a Problem Solved

I was always thinking of Humber Nurseries Ltd. in Brampton on all my travels. In Newfoundland, I solved a persistent mail delivery problem, and later that year, in November, I wanted to solve an entrance fee problem. Would our nursery ever become a show garden, where people wishing to explore our nursery would need to pay an entrance fee?

Frans gave me the address of the Jan Boomkamp Gardens in Borne, a town in the eastern part of the Netherlands near the German border. I took a train and a cab to get there. I was surprised to see over twenty manicured show gardens, reminding me of the Butchart Gardens in Victoria, British Columbia, Canada. This privately-owned company also had provisions for landscaping, and the selling of many nursery products. They also provided a coffee shop and a restaurant for people's leisure. The cost to see the gardens was twenty dollars. It was so well maintained and organized that I immediately discovered why Frans had recommended visiting this nursery.

Although our nursery was comparable in size, perhaps even larger, I resolved that our next direction would not have a permanent show garden. Frans and I did not want to give the extent of attention and work needed to develop the nursery into an entrance paying establishment.

3. A Short Story on Royalty

I seemed to have a special heavenly connection, if I could be so bold to say. One of those connections came from Father Nino of Saint Benedict's Catholic parish. Father Nino was somewhat of a comedian who spoke in riddles many times. He once wrote a humorous note to Frans Jr.:

"And give my love to your mother, who is to Humber Nurseries, what the Queen Mother is to the British Empire!"

In another letter, Father Nino wrote:

"To our Queen, Lady Peters, and Prince Frans and Prince Guy, and the Humber Nurseries Empire: Thank you for your kind Christmas remembrance and all that you do for our church."

My husband Frans, from that time on, used to tease me with: "Dear, nothing could be better than being part of the Peters 'Royal' family!"

4. The Frans Tradition Story (A Little Longer Story!)

Have you ever taken videos of your family? I would hope the answer is yes. On January 24, 1996, we watched old homemade family movies after a dinner celebration for Frans's birthday. The movies contained events about his family in the Netherlands, and the beginnings of Humber Nurseries Ltd.

Movie making was a hobby of Frans', most of them taken on eight and sixteen-millimetre films. They were all neatly stored on a shelf in Frans's home office. Secretly, Sibylleke chronologically organized them, analyzing each film as she viewed them on our old film projector. Then she had them all professionally reproduced into videos. And there we were, all sixteen of us who scrambled to find a cozy viewing spot in front of the television to watch all the videos.

Then with much interest and laughter, we took out old photo albums of Frans and traced his life from a baby to a nice old fellow. Many memories came up, and there were many questions from the children and the grandchildren.

One question from my grandson Frans came about: "Opa," he asked, "Could you explain why the name Frans, my namesake, was handed down from one generation to the next, always to the first born?"

My husband Frans prepared himself for a long answer. He replied:

"As a tradition, the name Frans was passed down to the eldest boy in each Peters family. It started with the first Frans, who learned the trade of watchmaking in Rotterdam, and then moved to Deventer to open a watch repair and jewelry store. My father Frans, the second generation, carried on his father's work. I was the third generation, but I did not want to work in the shop, because after the war, business was not good, and when I met your mom, we decided to come to Canada to work with plants, a passion in my life. The tradition of passing on the jewelry business to the eldest son then changed because of my life choice. (Nevertheless the name Frans continued to be passed on to the eldest son.)

"Therefore, my younger brother Lou took over my father's jewelry business, and two of his three sons took it over after him. When my youngest brother Lou married Magda, they shared living quarters with Oma and Opa, my parents, on the second and third floors of the store-home. With their three sons in tow, their dwelling seemed to shrink as each year passed. In the late 1960s, Lou took on most responsibilities in our father's business, and by 1979 Lou and Magda took over the company completely.

"They needed renovations, product upgrades, installation of locks and alarm systems, and to purchase large insurances. Gone were the old days of over 100 years ago, when one could leave the door open until late into the evening. Times had changed. The streets would be empty of customers by six o'clock during all evenings of the business week. Nevertheless, the older two sons, Frans and Rob, would grow an interest in the business. That family jewelry business has been around since 1886, and in 1986, Lou organized a 100th birthday celebration in Deventer, an event celebrated by the whole town.

"Fixed on tradition, however, and even though we were on new soil, your grandmother and I decided to call our eldest son, your dad, Frans. Then you, Frans were born to Frans and Vita, and became the eldest boy in my eldest son's family. You were named in honour of that tradition. Incidentally, you became the fifth generation in our family line of Franses."

My husband Frans paused, thought for a bit, took hold of a picture that was displayed on the mantelpiece of our living room.

"Do you remember when your grandmother and your father took you to the Netherlands in September 1984? I had traveled by boat to meet you all in Deventer."

My grandson Frans shook his head. "I really cannot remember, Opa, because I was only three years old at the time!"

Frans then pointed to the photograph he had in his hand. It was in colour and taken by a professional photographer in the foyer near the narrow stairway of his parents' home in Deventer.

He asked his grandson:

"Do you see yourself in this picture? You are one of the four generations of Franses: two of us were born in the Netherlands, and the other two in Canada. Here is your great grandfather at ninety-three years old; here is me, your grandfather; here is your father; and here is you, of course, at three years old. This picture is now in all our family's homes. Don't you think that the picture is a creative way to remember a tribute to family tradition?"

His grandson, tucking away precious information, nodded yes in satisfaction.

"And if you have a boy later in life, I trust that you may call him Frans, too," Frans added. "He would be Frans the sixth by that time. I would certainly like that!"

In addition to that gathering in Deventer when that memorable photograph was taken, Frans and I traveled to Belgium to visit the commemorative historical centre in Bastogne, a scene of heavy fighting during World War II in the Battle of the Bulge. Rows and rows of white crosses were a sight to see and an experience full of emotion for us. We then returned home to Canada, me by plane and Frans by ship. However, not long after Frans returned home, we received a phone call.

Frans and I received some incredibly sad news. Lou informed us that Oma had died, of natural causes, as her health was already in decline. I decided to fly to the Netherlands to attend the funeral. However, after Frans picked me up from the Toronto airport from my flight home, and after stepping in the doorway of our home, the phone was ringing. It was Lou again with more sad news. Opa had passed away, perhaps of natural causes, perhaps in sorrow of losing his loved one of so many years. I decided to represent Frans and our family, once again, with our condolences.

When we were settled in our living room after my return from the funeral in Deventer, Frans and I stared at the photograph of the four Franses on the mantelpiece. There were moments when you needed parents to hold your hand, navigate into your sorrow, and stay there for awhile. This moment was an oasis of quiet time for the both of us.

Time moved on from garden shows to personal reflections of 'old,' and from solving problems in Newfoundland to learning to appreciate family traditions. These were part of many high points in my life, but one unmentioned highlight was about to come, and no one on this earth would ever want to miss this one.

Humber Nurseries Ltd. Catalogue History. Growing since 1948.

My special day, August second, 1998: I reached the age of 80; Frans and I celebrated fifty years of marriage; our nursery turned fifty. My sons, Frans Jr. and Guy organized a celebration and presented a large and beautiful cake.

More than 500 guests were invited to the party. Actually it was open to all clients, employees and bystanders to enjoy the entertainment, speeches and refreshments.

Chapter Twenty-One: A Commemorative Year: 1998

Every year in life was a special year. As a matter of fact, every day was special. I was going to highlight however, one year, and one day in particular—the year of my eightieth birthday. Some words of wisdom evolved over those eighty years: learn to know thyself; learn to communicate honestly; and, if gifted with good health, persevere in hard work. Life rewards would be granted with humour, happiness and satisfaction.

Fifty Years of Living and Working Together

Fifty years of living and working together would manifest into a festive celebration on August 2, 1998. It was my milestone eightieth birthday; it was the year of our fiftieth wedding anniversary; and it was our fiftieth year in business.

In our sea of matrimony, Frans was my true partner in friendship and business. I would not describe our relationship as a relaxing cruise on the "Love Boat," because much of our time ranged from minor squalls to blowing hurricanes. As owners of a family business, we saw many unpredictable circumstances. After leaving our seaport in Rotterdam, it was a "two in the lifeboat" journey with no tour guide to lead the way. There was no room for the idea of abandoning the ship, because we both looked at life positively, setting mutual goals and believing most of the time that the glass was always half-filled.

During a private family celebration, we announced our resolve that one of the crucial elements of a long-lasting marriage and business partnership was to always communicate personal desires and beliefs to each other without inhibition. With the gift of health and persevering hard work, we were rewarded with humour, happiness, and satisfaction.

Our wedding anniversary day always landed on a day when our nursery business was at its busiest. Rarely did we celebrate it on that exact date, but on April 12, 1998, our fiftieth wedding anniversary, we decided to take the day off for the momentous occasion. We reserved a private room for our immediate family members at the beautiful Marriott Inn restaurant near the Toronto Pearson International Airport.

The ongoing fiftieth anniversary celebrations of Humber Nurseries Ltd. began in February at the Canada Blooms Show in Toronto.

Our garden presentation, titled “A Train Ride into Spring,” won the award for the “Most Outstanding Medium-Size Garden,” where Frans Jr. used his backyard automated train set to highlight movement in the garden. In addition to the celebration this year, our own company initiated a Canada Blooms trophy, awarded to the “Best Innovation in Garden Design.” We also produced a special golden anniversary catalogue, which we displayed throughout the Canada Blooms Show.

On August 2, my two sons planned to celebrate all three festivities with an enormous party, one from which would take a lifetime to recover!

August 2, 1998

Boom! Bang! What was going on?

Early in the morning of that eventful day, I woke suddenly to the sound of hammers and the movement of large equipment outside my bedroom window. There was something unusual going on. Peeking outside, I saw tents set up close to the house; many chairs and tables with umbrellas were already displayed on the lawn. At ten o’clock in the morning, our four children entered the house in an eager mood. I was in awe when I opened their gift, a gold necklace for my eightieth birthday. Guy then put a video tape into the television, and I was deeply moved to see a family-themed movie that they had made. I was on the verge of tears, and with Kleenex in one hand and my arm tucked under Frans Jr.'s, we exited the house through the front door.

The sight of the cake took my breath away. It was the largest cake (about six feet by five feet in size!) that I have ever seen in my entire life. On it were the words: "Celebrating Fifty Years of Growing." There was a huge monarch butterfly dressed in many colours at the corner of the cake. Beside the cake was a slowly melting ice sculpture about four feet in height, with a large-sized number 50 at the top with simulated butterflies on the inside of the ice. Under the next tent was a trio of musicians playing classical music. A clown with oversized shoes, a red nose, and a fuzzy-looking moustache burst out of nowhere and said, "You are so beautiful today, Mrs. Peters!"

I laughed, and just then, I caught a glimpse of a magician with a tilted top hat, introducing himself to three attentive children, whom I did not recognize. With painted faces, they admired each other and then watched the magician as he played a card trick with them. I also caught sight of two professional-looking photographers who captured all these sights and more!

Many people were waiting to congratulate Frans and me. One of the first was our Brampton Mayor Peter Robertson and his wife, whom we knew for years when he was councillor to Brampton. In a flash of excitement, I greeted Henk and Ans Hoogstraten with their daughter Diane, her husband, and their twin children visiting from Australia. Suddenly my sister Greet and her daughter Sibylla from the Netherlands appeared in front of me. What a surprise! Following them was a line of familiar faces, waiting to see Frans and me, and all resonating sincere congratulations, and stimulating emotion within me. Suddenly, the crowd momentarily stopped upon the sound of a voice over a loudspeaker, saying:

"There are many articles for you to view at the auction and on which to bid. Don't miss the chance for a real bargain on many specialized items!"

And then we heard: "Would Mr. and Mrs. Peters please find your places of honour right here in front of the podium."

They had the podium decorated with the Canadian, the Dutch, and the city of Deventer flags. In addition, our friends' authentic flower shop in Bramalea had made two tropical flower arrangements, and that was where we found our places to sit.

Mayor Peter Robertson was the first to congratulate Frans and me with a plaque to honour our business, Humber Nurseries Ltd., and he introduced the formal opening of Humber's own butterfly conservatory. Following his speech was a representative speaking on behalf of mayor Hazel McCallion of Mississauga, who praised us on our diligent work efforts. Mr. John Hastings from the Ontario government articulated how our family contributed to the growth in Ontario's business sector.

A representative from the prime minister's office, Mr. Singh from Brampton, expressed our country's appreciation for our business leadership in the community. Many more officials from Bramalea, Gore, and Malton congratulated us as well. *De Nederlandse Krant* (The Dutch newspaper, Wim van Duyn), the *Brampton Guardian* (Don Ford, business editor) and the reporter to the *Horticultural Review* later wrote favourable reports of the full day.

Not to be forgotten were presentations from our family and friends, namely Frans Jr., who spoke of our early beginnings in a land of opportunity. Wim Klein Beernink related his story as the first employee of Humber Nurseries Ltd. The master of ceremonies, George Kash, entertained us with clever anecdotes end games, provoking continuous laughter, and then he toasted us with glasses raised to me for my eightieth birthday. At the end of the speeches, I awaited the last and most spectacular gift of all: a bouquet of eighty variously-coloured, sweetly-scented roses from Frans and my four children, Sibylleke, Frans Jr., Astrid, and Guy. It was something out of this world!

After the formal ceremonies, Astrid advised me to take a rest in our air-conditioned house. However, first, I needed to walk around to absorb all that was happening on our transformed front garden lawn and driveway—an entertainment platform decorated with ribbons, balloons, and signs of "Happy 80th Birthday,

Happy 50th Anniversary, and Happy 50 Years of Growing." Round dinner tables covered with white linen tablecloths, each with umbrellas and dotted with chrysanthemum flower arrangements, set a formal scene to the whole affair.

And from where did all the people come? The people came because they had received one of the 500 personal invitations sent months before the occasion. And for all I knew, with the flow of eager-to-participate customers who were shopping at the business that sunny day, there could have been 800 people there at one time.

Who was this lady all dressed in Dutch costume? I did not recognize her at the outset, but Zena came closer to greet me and said:

"Hello, Mrs. Peters. I know that I represent many of the staff when I say you have done so many remarkable and unforgettable things in your lifetime. You are worthy of much honour for all you have done here today and in the past. Congratulations, and Happy Eightieth Birthday!"

Zena was working in the food department all day long. Free catered food, and drinks of wine, coffee, and sodas were available throughout the day.

I did not want the day to end. There was still so much more to see. And while I was pondering that thought, a policeman mounted on a horse appeared from the direction of the parking lot. I supposed he wanted to see what was going on, too, and he was riding in style!

The silent auction, set up outdoors with displays on tables on our home driveway, was wrapping up. The proceeds would go to the children's ward of the Peel Memorial Hospital. (I heard later that they raised over fifteen thousand dollars.) On the left side of the auction was a children's playground with huge balloon-cushioned constructions in which to romp around. And further to the left of the playground, I saw a small crowd of people surrounding a trailer. Curious to know what was going on, I peeked beyond the trailer door, and I saw a jovial group of people surrounding a small bar with a busy bartender.

"Happy Birthday Mrs. P.!" they all chimed together!

Satisfied to acquire this knowledge, I cheered them on and left them to their fun.

My Reflections

I woke up from my nap and reflected upon what had just happened during the last five to six hours.

My first reflection: How did I physically survive, always standing, and sometimes sitting in a wheelchair under the hot sun for that length of time? And I remembered listening more than talking. When I would begin to say something, people would interrupt and excitedly tell me about themselves with stories about how they met me, or I would hear a recent account of their gardening progress. For instance:

"Mrs. Peters, do you remember me? I was the one who asked where I could find that one new variety of geranium that I read about in the paper. You answered with great information about it, and more importantly, that I could find that new variety in row thirty-four in the annual greenhouse. I could always count on Humber to have every variety in the world!"

I recognized many admiring faces, because I would have seen them in the office or around the nursery as I was still working every day in the greenhouse, taking cuttings, transplanting, cleaning the plants and sorting out labels. I never thought our business would attract such a diverse clientele, but we were certainly doing something right in our lives.

In my second reflection, I thought of the 500 invitations that our office had sent out. Unfortunately, I did not accurately account for the final numbers, because the signing-in book was not in a central location for people to see and write their names. However, I remembered a few people's names: Harry Churchill-Smith's parents, Jess and Dave; our Danish jeweler Henning, who also had his birthday on August 2; Harry and Thelma Penner; our neighbours Mrs. Fines and Lois and Gerald Livingston; the whole Wilson family from Mount Dennis; Om and Yet Klein Beernink from Connecticut (U.S.); Joan and Harry (Alex's parents); Mrs. Skvereckas, Vita's mother; and many of the employees, some working at the party and others not. Everyone greeted me with congratulations! I also thought of all the people working that day at the party.

My third reflection: I was glad to have Catholic masses read in our Church of Our Lady of the Airways by Father Burns and Father Steve, who came to celebrate with two other priests. One priest came from Saint Andrew's parish in Orillia; and my dear friend Father Steven Kopfensteiner also came to give his blessing.

A fourth reflection came to mind when I thought of a specific coincidence between my sister Greet, her daughter Sibylla, and my twin grandchildren Peter and Anita, upon their arrival from the Netherlands. Peter and Anita were working in the bulb industry for three weeks in the Netherlands. By coincidence, they were flying back to Canada on the same plane as Greet and Sibylla who were coming for the celebration. At the airport, they did not recognize each other, but Sibylleke introduced the family to the family right then and there. An unbelievable coincidence.

And for my last reflection, I thought of the Mrs. Sibylla Peters Hybrid Tea Rose created for me for my seventy-fifth birthday. Someone placed a memorable life-size picture in front of the podium. And during the celebration, they had the actual rose at Humber Nurseries Ltd. for people to purchase and enjoy in their garden. I was so happy my sons had done that for me.

And That Evening

That night we had another celebration, but only for the close family—a celebration for my eightieth birthday at the Marriott Inn. The long white limousine would accommodate ten family members, including Wim's sister, Yet, and her husband, Om, from Connecticut. The champagne helped us let go of our inhibitions in the limo, and we all sang the traditional Dutch birthday song: "Lang zal ze leven! (That she may live a long life!)"

The rest of the family were waiting at the restaurant, and when all settled in, Vita's mother sat beside me. She made one of her homemade unique layered cakes for my birthday and managed to help me cut a piece of cake for everyone. We were all in a festive mood, and I felt like a young girl bursting from within. In addition, without admitting I was elderly or old, I felt privileged to be at the octogenarian age of wisdom with all its perks!

Viva Las Vegas!

We packed our bags, all five of us: Sibylleke, Astrid, Greet, Greet's daughter Sibylla, and me. We would experience one of the most exciting cities in the world. Oh, oh, what a fabulous 1998! We had so much fun on that trip.

Las Vegas was not the city it used to be, since my trip there with Pita about twenty years ago. They replaced the hotel landscape of relatively fewer and smaller hotels with many enormously-sized hotels designed for nothing but luxury. Although gambling was a high attraction, the city emerged as a centre to attract tourists for shopping, fine dining, extraordinary entertainment, and night life.

One evening as we were walking by the Treasure Island hotel, we heard and announcement:

"In ten minutes, pirates will be at war with the British. There will be shooting and bomb-throwing. I urge you to find a safe place to hide."

And we did just that. We found seats with a good view in an air-conditioned restaurant, ordered our ice cream, and became spectators of the re-enactment of a battle in the 1800s between two opposing ships floating in a huge pond of water. After the show, we walked down the Main Street and indulged in the atmosphere of busy New York City, then Paris's French cafes, and finally Cairo's beating pulse. This was the new Las Vegas!

The theatre shows were spectacular, particularly a Cirque du Soleil presentation. There were acrobatic clowns who would animate the audience, and one peculiar-looking clown asked if there was an eighty-year-old in the audience (and I did not know how he found me out). Everyone in the audience of thousands of people centred their attention on me. Not feeling intimidated, I joined the clown's lead who joked around through conversation and silly actions. I could hear the hearty laughter of the audience in response.

There were many types of wandering entertainers in the casinos congested with card tables and slot machines. There were musicians, music bands, magicians, gymnasts, dancers, impersonators of famous people—

all of whom attracted the tourists' attention. For example, when two people dressed in costume enticed Astrid, Sibylleke, Greet, and Sibylla to play a game presented to them, they immediately joined in, and an audience formed a circle around them to watch the performance.

"It's a simple game. Come over here!" the actors said.

Greet detected a Dutch accent in the lady's voice and asked, "Waar kom je uit Nederland? (Where are you from in the Netherlands?)"

The actress, surprised to hear her native language spoken, replied: "Ik kom uit Indonesie. (I come from Indonesia.)"

Greet and the actor exchanged stories of Dutch Indonesia, and Greet felt a little homesick but delighted to have met someone Dutch right in the middle of a desert! Sibylleke, Astrid, Greet, and Sibylla were all given a memorable T-shirt for their participation in the game.

The next day, I said to Astrid that I would like to have a professional tour of Las Vegas. So, as it turned out, she and Sibylleke found a friendly young man with a long quite touring limousine and asked him if he could take five tourists on tour. He accepted and we drove around the city for two hours. We had more fun inside the limo, because we laughed so hard at our own jokes and embellished life stories about our grandfathers and grandmothers. What unpredictable fun we had!

We discovered one of the most iconic hotels in Vegas, Caesar's Palace. An unusual attraction in itself because of its indoor moving statues of Greek gods, white clouds on blue-skied ceilings, and many replicas of Greek statues and fountains scattered everywhere, we felt we were in the country of Greece itself. We also discovered that Las Vegas was a city of love with its many wedding chapels. We even witnessed an attractive bride waiting in front of one of them.

We welcomed the air-conditioned monorails that whisked us away to many places when it was too hot to walk. We discouraged taxis in the heavy slow traffic so that we could enjoy people-watching. However, by the day's end, the taxi did come as a relief for a lady of eighty years of age! And soon enough, the trip came to an end, and Greet and Sibylla returned to the Netherlands with many enticing stories to tell.

Photo Album Number Eighty

I liked taking pictures, mainly of my family and my travels, placing them carefully into albums that I labeled and numbered. Photo album numbers seventy-eight and seventy-nine retold a story in pictures of the three 1998 celebrations. The eightieth album told the story of my eightieth year of life events. How coincidental. I had expanded my photo hobby by making one photo album for each of my children, once a year, giving them as Christmas gifts. So naturally, this year, they all received an additional one from that extraordinary day of August 2, 1998.

An entertainment platform decorated with ribbons, balloons, and signs of "Happy 80th Birthday, Happy 50th Anniversary, and Happy 50 Years of Growing."

Two sisters and two ages. Sibylleke was six and Astrid was three.

Sibylleke was forty-nine and Astrid was forty-six. They shared many interests, discussed over a glass of wine.

In my eighties, I enjoyed my hobby of transplanting annuals and perennials, in both the locations of the foyer of our two original Mount Dennis greenhouses, and in the kitchen of our original home. I would listen to talk shows and music from my yellow transistor radio.

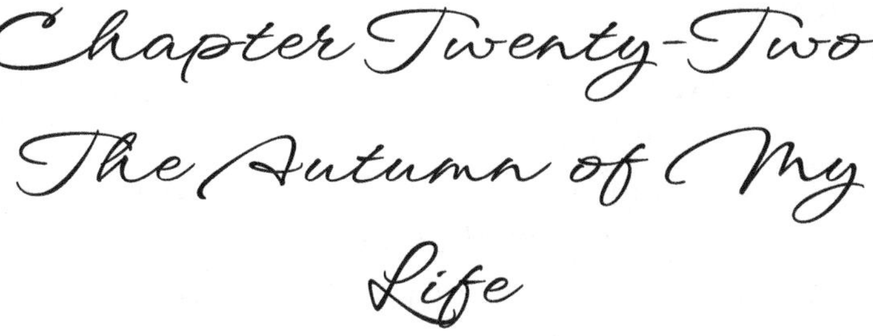

I was aging and slowly moving into the autumn of my life. I reflected upon the changing seasons of the year. The spring season produced flowers in full bright colours, and they grew more beautiful in the summer because of the longer days. And then those bright colours faded in the autumn to shades of gold and orange. The gold shades, for me, registered two things: how beautifully Mother Nature presented leaf colour changes in deciduous trees, and secondly, gold represented longevity in my marriage.

As the turn of the century approached, I often wondered, as many people did at the time, if life would come to an end in the year 2000. For me, one precious life would come to an end, one so very close to me. This tragedy threw me off track in my life journey.

After much bereavement, I rediscovered my vibrant walk of life. I continued along that path, but reflecting more often about the past. Then I decided to look at the big picture of my life: I was only in my early eighties and I was actively working every day in the greenhouses, where I would listen to talk shows and to music from my yellow transistor radio.

Sibylleke

My daughter Sibylleke turned fifty on January 24, 1999. I was filled with awe and emotion as I looked at her during a family birthday dinner at Astrid's home. That little girl who aimed to please had finally reached the age of wisdom. She received fifty freshly cut red roses, whose fragrance carried everywhere. She was the life of the party.

Little did Sibylleke know there was another surprise birthday party planned for her during the summer. Her eldest son, Henk, having graduated from Guelph university that June, had just enough time to make all the preparations, excusing himself from home, most times under the pretense of jet skiing with friends, to avoid suspicion.

Sibylleke returned from a long weekend holiday in Huntsville, with Tiny and Gerd, her sister-in-law and husband, who were visiting from the Netherlands. She stepped out of the car, and her eyes widened as she met a life-sized doll strategically placed on the house side lawn. Henk, her son, had made a traditional Dutch "Sarah" doll, a symbol of wisdom in the Dutch tradition. To describe that doll: it was an enlarged photo of Sibylleke's real face placed on a stuffed body wearing Sibylleke's clothes. This body was sitting on a toilet seat (Dutch humour!) waiting for the real birthday girl to arrive.

Sibylleke walked into a dream world of festivities and guests. People from the Netherlands, high school and university friends, business associates, and our family, enjoyed the celebration with her. The party went well into the morning of the next day, and many stayed overnight. Her son Henk did a superb job in organizing a memorable party for his mother.

I was excited about reaching fifty years of marriage in my own relationship, but in the summer of 1999, Pita and Mike Van Dongen, and Tiny and Wim Klein Beernink also reached their significant golden milestones. Reaching that number in their marriage and my daughter's birthday signified to me the existence of lifelong trust relationships in healthy handfuls of love.

The End of Time?

The year 1999 was the concluding year of the twentieth century, and many people believed the world would end. Perhaps in a one percent chance of angst that the world might end on the last day of 1999, Frans gave a homemade Christmas gift that year to each of our family members. With research in the Netherlands to find his family origins, he put together his results on an artistically-mapped genealogical tree. We had written proof that our Peters family existed!

The world did not end on December 31, and Frans successfully turned seventy-eight on January 24, 2000. His sister-in-law, Magda Peters, arrived from the Netherlands on our doorstep to celebrate his birthday.

Magda and I decided to travel together that winter. First, we went to Las Vegas, immediately followed by a cruise in the Caribbean. We both loved traveling, and despite the thirteen-year age difference, we enjoyed each other's company. We always immersed ourselves in deep conversations about business, people, and life, and in so doing I discovered in her an intuitive faculty to perceive and understand what others usually could not.

After our return from our holidays and just before Magda returned to the Netherlands, I decided to bring Magda to visit Sibylleke, Henk, and their children in St.Catharines and to see the incredible Niagara Falls. We had a lovely time, or so I thought at the time.

When we were home again, while Magda prepared her bags for the next day's flight, I was curious to know why she had made no comment about our recent visit. There appeared to be something wrong after our excursion. So, without hesitation, I questioned her about her mood.

Magda answered, “It was Sibylleke. She was not laughing, nor participating wholeheartedly in our conversations. She seemed to be dreaming and always in deep thought. And those normally sparkling brown eyes were dull and almost lifeless. Even though she looked at us, I could tell that she really was not listening. She had changed dramatically. She was not her jovial self. I detected that something was wrong and deeply bothering her.”

This unexpected response led to a feeling of guilt and sudden change in my demeanor. Why had I not made the same observations? It appeared that we had a good visit, and I had never expected Magda’s conclusive and negative remarks. I resolved to Magda that I would pay more attention to Sibylleke the next time we were together. I promised to keep Magda up to date.

A devastating event took place a week before Mother's Day, the busiest time of year for those in the flower industry, and a continuing busy time of year for those in the nursery business.

May 2, 2000. This was the date of a horrifying and heartbreaking experience. I would never forget my fear. I felt my heart pulsing in my throat when I heard the news. Each family member would tell you exactly what they were doing on that evening when my first-born child, Sibylleke, took her own life.

At his mass at the Cathedral of Saint Catherine of Alexandria, in St. Catharines, Bishop O'Mara expressed:

"While her death was tragic, I am confident the good Lord has welcomed her into His Kingdom. We never know what another is thinking and the extent to which they are struggling to cope with the events that burdened them. We do the best we can to support them with our love and prayers, leaving the rest to the Lord, who is full of mercy and compassion."

Bishop O'Mara was like a guardian angel in our lives, especially to Sibylleke, first as pastor at St. Margaret Mary's church in Woodbridge, where Sibylleke went to school and was also married. He had also helped her with admission to Saint Joseph's Catholic private school; he confirmed her children when he was Bishop of Saint Catherine's diocese; and lastly, he presided over her funeral mass in St. Catharines, where hundreds of people gave last respects and final farewells.

I deeply missed my Sibylleke. I knew in my heart that no parent should ever have to bury their child before them. How cruel life could be with hidden mysteries.

Life continued without Sibylleke, so difficult in the beginning. Frans and I spent time with Henk and our three grandchildren. Henk's sister and brother-in-law from the Netherlands also stayed with the family for a few months. During the Christmas season, Sibylleke's favourite time of year, we celebrated without her, sorrowfully, because we missed her love, laughter, and excitement. But personally, I felt at that time that family and friends could not heal the lingering wound of my daughter's absence. In the final analysis, I slowly recognized that we all grieved in diverse ways. I eventually learned to accept with humble gratitude what God delivered to me on my plate each day for the rest of my life.

The Healing Takes Place

I would go to the Netherlands again to visit my relatives. The trip would give me time to reflect on Sibylleke, and it was helpful for me to take Astrid along with me. I would continue the healing process over the loss of my eldest daughter.

We started with a river cruise on the Rhine River, inviting two sisters-in-law, Gretel and Mien. The Dutch ship, the MPS *Serena*, journeyed from Arnhem and through the flatlands of the Netherlands and on into the picturesque hills of Germany. We developed a daily routine. After breakfast each day, we proceeded to the open deck to experience beautiful weather and scenery; we would dock at a port and walk or take a tour of the city sites or winery or museum; and we ended the day watching the evening entertainment. Like a budding journalist, Astrid would always be the first to stir up conversation and dig for stories of our past lives. We enjoyed her interest in our lives.

For example, during one tour in Cologne, Germany, staring at the mighty gothic spiraled columns of its famous cathedral, Astrid questioned us:

"This is a pretty special place. When and with whom were you all here?"

I answered first. "This beautiful place stirs up memories with your dad after the war. I met him here once on one of my weekends off while working in the British Army. We stood right here in awe, dreaming together in wonder of the cathedral's survival through the passage of time."

Astrid insisted that we talk about that story in more detail after dinner that evening. I began again, but without the inspiration of the historical presence of the cathedral.

"I had never discussed this story with anyone," I began, "because I only rated it as just an ordinary untold war story. I did not understand it at the time, when your dad left for Germany for three years during the war and did not connect with us, not even his mother. He explained to me that it was a fascinating time for him but also somewhat dangerous. It had to do with a friendship that he developed with some German soldiers."

Astrid interrupted:

"And how does this story include the spirals of the Cologne cathedral?"

I responded, "The answer to that question involved his road trips that began in Deventer and ended in many towns across the border to Germany before the war, when he delivered and picked up jewelry for his father's store. He had no idea of the growing seriousness of the politics in Germany at the time, and neither did his German friends. As a matter of fact, they did not take Hitler's politics seriously. And to have some fun, your dad's friends found a German uniform that would fit him. He used to change into that uniform and visit the local beer parlours with his newly trusted buddies, pretending to be a German soldier. Some of his friends were from this town of Cologne, and they invited him to stay with them while he was on overnight deliveries.

"After your dad and I were married, we came here on one of our trips, and he told me that story as we were standing in the same place we did earlier today. He showed me one of the beer parlours that he visited with his friends."

Astrid, happy to have torn away one of the carefully-tended walls of my life, could see another side of her father and a new angle on our early lives together. Indeed, all three of us lived during such historic times. As the ship maneuvered down the river, so did our stories, as each historic place would spike our interest and another round of storytelling.

Astrid and I continued our trip with visits to many other family and friends, and it was uplifting to talk about Sibylleke with each of them. We first visited Greet's daughter, Sibylla, and her friend, Mark, in their home that he built. Then I guided Astrid, who was driving in our rented car, to see Tegelen, the town where the Janssen family originated. We visited Hans and Gertie Stinkes with Hans's daughter Ursula, and then Ernst-Joachim Stinkes in Germany. We visited Gretel's daughter Marian in Nijmegen, where Astrid was impressed with the thousands of books on shelves on every wall of her house. We saw Andre Janssen's huge factory in Zwolle; and we drove to Wim Janssen's, son of my brother Guillaume, home in Groningen where he worked at the university and where I worked during the war. We visited with Lies Peters in Ulft; we saw the Peters family in Deventer; we visited with Albert, son of my brother Arnold, who opened an art store in Deventer; we visited with Jack Hoogstraten and Gerda (Arnold's wife) who lived on the same street in Deventer, the Zwolseweg; and we visited my old girlfriends Corrie Cossee and Ilse van Geuns. Then we saw Maria and Liesbeth, my brother Jan's children; we saw Jan and Riekie Engels in Enschede; and finally, we visited with Greet in Vlaardingen.

It was a busy trip to see so many relatives and my friends, but it was also a rewarding experience for

Astrid and me, as we felt the support and love in our bereavement for Sibylleke.

Life Begins After Eighty

Once you have reached eighty, life seems to become a series of parties. And for the first memorable party Frans and Vita celebrated their twenty-fifth wedding anniversary during the early summer of 2000. They hosted their celebration with a huge boat party, departing from the Toronto Harbour and sailing throughout the Toronto islands in Lake Ontario. For a highlight, Vita put on her wedding dress, worthy of taking a formal and memorable picture of her family of five sisters and mother at that time.

My Yellow Transistor

I carried my yellow transistor radio everywhere. The usual landing place was in my work area in the foyer of the aluminum and the wooden greenhouses (the originals that we built in the Humber Valley in Mount Dennis). Here, I would take cuttings, transplant young annuals, clean all the mature perennials, and sort small labels. My day started at eight in the morning, and I listened all day to the talk shows, news, or music on my transistor radio, feeling the comfort to allow my mind to drift away. On one exceptional day, I thought of a variety of things. My thoughts first wandered to family.

My thoughts first came to thinking about Guy's second marriage, and why it had broken up with Alex. He soon met Elaine Lister, mother of two children, Sephra and Brandon, and I had predicted marriage on the horizon. Through Guy's remarriage and adoption, the two children would become our beautiful eighth and ninth grandchildren.

I also thought of when Harry Churchill-Smith and Astrid announced their engagement at Christmas. Soon we met the Churchill-Smith family and Harry's close friends, the Woods' families, at a meet-and-greet party at their cottage in Shanty Bay, north of Orillia, Ontario. I would never forget the sight of my son, Guy, with Elaine, both dressed in black leather riding gear, descending from a Harley motorbike after driving 120 kilometres to the occasion. What an impression he made on the whole family! Astrid and Harry were married on August 4, 2001, returning from their honeymoon in Tahiti only two weeks before the sad historical event of 9/11 in the United States.

Time was marching on, and before I knew it, two of my grandchildren, Monica and Anita, announced their engagements to be married within a year. And then when Frans turned eighty years old, I asked myself, "What did you give someone who had everything?" We decided to dine out in style, escorting Frans in a black limousine. Frans enjoyed all the attention that came with it.

My thoughts next wandered to the International Horticultural Trades Association. These members were horticulturalists who came from around the world to see an example of a well-run Canadian all-season nursery and garden centre. They would also be witnessing the largest self-supporting one in southern Ontario. We featured our show gardens, greenhouses, storage barns, sales station store, trucks, and machinery. And everyone pitched in to make it sufficiently presentable. Over five busloads of nursery and nursery-related tourists from all over the world would enjoy and appreciate our astounding efforts in this business.

I then gave thought to an article written on the theme of butterflies, raised in our butterfly conservatory. In the spring of 2001, the *Toronto Sun* newspaper printed an article written by Janet Davis titled: "Butterfly Kisses at Humber Nurseries Ltd." Here she claimed that "there was no better way to introduce and teach children and adults about the latest scientific highlight in nature than to bring them to the natural habitat."

Raising butterflies started with the work of our chief horticulturalist Tom Thomson. He shared his knowledge on butterflies and moths to children on school field trips in the in-house classroom in the Humber Butterfly Conservatory. The latest theme was about the natural habitat of those brightly coloured and strikingly patterned creatures. In his lessons, he taught about nectar-producing perennials and annuals which attracted them.

I also became personally involved in the culture of the butterfly, having learned everything I knew from Tom. I helped during the importation stage of these lovely creatures into the conservatory. Having received them (in my kitchen) in their cocoon stage, it was my job to pin each of them to a corkboard, that was subsequently properly carried and displayed in the butterfly conservatory. The butterflies would come out of their cocoons during their transformation to a butterfly, where a specifically designed exercise platform helped them stretch and strengthen their wings before they learned how to fly and care for themselves. I was honoured to witness one of nature's pure miracles of life every time one flew into the air for the very first time.

As I stopped my work of transplanting petunias, so that I could reach for another tray of young plants to be planted, I thought of the many employees that I had taught how to do various jobs around the nursery. I often thought of myself as the chief of the business, or in the fashionable term of the day, a Chief Executive Officer. But I was not a patient and calm boss, as were my husband and even my sons.

We all sailed in the same boat but with different oars. In my situation, during my workday, I would often take time during my coffee break to stroll around the nursery in the store or outside. I always noticed how the employees worked; it was on my mind that I expected high work standards from our employees because I expected those same standards for myself. Sometimes, I would grab a teaching moment, and perhaps inappropriately bark out how I would accomplish certain jobs more efficiently. For example, I would burst out with a comment such as:

"If you are walking to the brown barn empty-handed, a very long distance, as you may know, you must think about what you can carry with you while walking there. Take a tool with you, for instance, that you see lying around. Never waste time by going empty-handed. Always think ahead on how you can use your time wisely and efficiently!"

All the seasoned employees knew who I was, and the newer employees learned about me very quickly. When you owned your own business, there came personal love, dedication, and pride in it, as I had maintained throughout my life, and it showed in my daily conversations with personnel.

I would receive a different kind of respect from the customers. I made myself available to them during the busy spring season, when I would greet them from my dedicated seat at the information station in the perennial greenhouse. Many clients would express something like, "So good to see you, Mrs. Peters! I want to tell you about my latest gardening project." And many customers over the years, who became closer acquaintances, would add an update on their family lives, their travels, and their jobs.

Sometimes, while listening to something spoken on my yellow transistor radio, I would break into laughter. One time I thought of my dear and late cousin Wim, who had recently died in April of 2002. In life, Wim and I often acted as though we were two young children, behaving like two peas in a pod. I remembered we received inhalers for our asthma at about the same time, and we pranked around about how the puffer was supposed to work. We threw the puffers in the air and poked each other in our noses with them. We joked around so much that we almost died laughing then and there.

Times were changing in the world of technology, and certainly, my radio had outdated itself. It was the day and age of the Internet. Many of our family members adapted to this communication method as it opened more advertising doors for the business and contributed to speedy personal messaging.

For example, my niece Marian, only daughter of my brother Guillaume and Gretel, Professor of English at the Radboud University of Nijmegen, the Netherlands, and director of external relations, had invited the Canadian Governor General to her university. It was important for her to learn a little more about Canada, and so she browsed through the Internet. She remembered that our Humber Nurseries Ltd. would probably have a website. So she typed into her computer: "Humber Nurseries Ltd." and found a lot of information about its founders, Frans and I, including many pictures. She was proud to be better informed when her honoured guest arrived.

I depended, however, on others to keep me updated on the latest news on technology. I was most content to listen to the talk show stations, music, and news presented on my yellow transistor radio.

I was in my mid-eighties, and I learned from many of my family and friends about life. The twenty-first century was bringing about a new face and rhythm to our business, and the age of the Internet further painted a new look into communication. I was feeling a need to prepare for my next life phase. It would include a celebration for my ninetieth birthday, and a celebration of Frans's life.

“

I was honoured to witness one of nature's pure miracles of life every time one flew into the air for the very first time.

Frans and Frans Jr. made the first cut on the three-dimensional cake - notice the windmill on the upper right corner of the cake! - made for the celebration of my ninetieth birthday, our sixtieth wedding anniversary and Humber Nurseries Ltd.'s sixty years of business.

Our celebrations were completed with a visit from our nephew Andre and niece Maria from the Netherlands. From left to right were Frans, Astrid, Maria, Guy, Andre, Frans Jr. and me with my right leg in a cast!

Chapter Twenty-Three: My Train of Life

As I traveled through the changing stages of my life, I shared my dreams, hopes, sorrows, and laughter in my journey. What did I learn from my family, friends, and business associates along the way? I knew, in reflection, that I loved, I gave, and I have forgiven in my life. I revealed much in my storytelling that I recounted in my memoir.

In 2008, I reached my ninetieth birthday; Frans and I celebrated our sixtieth anniversary; and Humber Nurseries Ltd. reached its sixtieth year. And without a doubt, the occasions came with huge celebrations. Not long after, however, I would be in mourning for the loss of another precious person in my life.

My Train of Life

Life is like a train journey with all its stops and changes in routes. When I was young, I remembered the train rides to Germany with my father and believed that he would always be there, but he stepped off one day, leaving me on this life journey alone. I have learned a lot about life since then, maturing into a responsible young adult when boarding mini trains in the Netherlands and Germany during and after the war. In marriage, Frans and I vacated our train seats in the Netherlands and pursued unexpected adventures in a new land.

In my mid-life, many travel destinations included the use of the train. I specifically remembered the freedom that the Eurail Pass had provided for my cousin Wim and me. But the train of life that I was on in my ninth decade evolved into something different. I knew that God would not allow me to know when and where I would eventually disembark the train, so, my attitude was to keep active, to stay on my train of life for as long as I could.

My Plans

I planned to get to know the next family generation. I invited the younger generation from Europe to Canada. My first guest was Ernst-Joachim Stinkes, who wanted to see how life was in Canada. Ernst, my fourth cousin, became a Catholic priest and he fell in love with our country. He would have chosen to work in our nursery, or even our local Catholic cemetary if he had the choice, as he loved to garden, just like his father, Hans. His church work in Germany was too overwhelming at the time, because he dealt with daily frustrations from the growing number of parishioners in the two parishes to which he was assigned.

My second guest was my nephew, Andre Janssen, who had not visited Canada for many years. He enjoyed seeing how life was getting on at our business in Brampton and at Henk's Pioneer Flower Farm in St. Catharines. Andre was in for a surprise, as both companies had changed. My two sons, Frans Jr. and Guy, had taken over operations at Humber, and Henk's two sons, Henk Jr. and Peter, had taken over more important business roles at Pioneer Flower Farm. Andre himself was looking to expand his customer foundation in pursuing his own business in the Toronto area. Then he continued his journey throughout various cities in the United States. He successfully marketed, produced, and expanded the company that his father, Guillaume, had started years ago.

More Events in 2006, 2007, 2008

I was moving on in age as I approached August 2, 2006, my eighty-eighth birthday. However, the remaining part of this decade would provide some of the best family times in my life. For one event, since I could still sensibly walk and talk, I attended my birthday celebration barbecue at Astrid and Harry's in Brampton. I felt even more special when I read aloud their message in a card, in between sobs and flowing tears of happiness:

"A mom gives advice when you need it; A mom cares about the things that mean the most to you; A mom shares your happiness, because you never outgrow a mother's love."

I was deeply moved by all the family love that day.

Then about a month later, on September 9, 2006, a new family member was born to my grandson Travis and his wife Anna. She was a beautiful and healthy baby named Katelyn, our first great-granddaughter. I welcomed her with love into our family.

I always loved to travel, but my pace had slowed down, and I asked Astrid to travel to the Netherlands in September (as she had just retired from her teaching job) with my list of addresses and phone numbers of friends and relatives. She flew to Amsterdam, rented a car, and visited my sisters-in-law, Gretel, Mien, Gerda, Magda, and my sister Greet. She also visited her cousins of her own age. I relived my past trips to the Netherlands when I listened to her stories after her return to Canada. I felt as if I had gone on that trip with her.

Would you ever think of receiving a park bench for a Christmas gift? In 2006, our children presented a commemorative park bench installed in the Chinguacousy Park in Brampton to Frans and me. The dedication on a bronze plaque read: "To our loving parents Sibylla and Frans Peters. May you always be happy together. From your children, with love. Christmas 2006."

Then with great pride, we were blessed with a second great-grandchild, Declan, born to my nephew Wesley and his wife Kelly, on January 12, 2007. Declan came bumbling into the world, healthy and with great baby laughter.

One could think that life would be a succession of birthday celebrations. However, if you survived your eighty-ninth birthday, one could celebrate milestone wedding anniversaries, too. Frans and I reached our milestone sixtieth wedding anniversary on April 12, 2008.

Through Our Lady of the Airways Catholic parish, we received the Apostolic blessing imparted with a painting from His Holiness Benedict XVI. We also received a formal letter from Queen Elizabeth II congratulating us on our diamond wedding anniversary and best wishes from the Governor-General of Canada, Michaelle Jean. And additionally there were some letters from Prime Minister Stephen Harper, our MPP Dr. Kuldip S. Kular, the MPP Greg Sorbara, and our mayor of Brampton, Susan Fennell. We certainly had a festive celebration on that Saturday night when Astrid organized a dinner at the Terra Cotta Inn in Terra Cotta, Ontario, a small town north of Brampton. All our friends and family gave tributes to us, including my grandchildren and one of my great grandchildren, Katelyn.

One day, my life train took some time off for repairs and cleaning. On May 3, 2008, I had an extremely serious accident. I had fallen in my bathroom, broke my foot and ankle, and bruised everything else in my body.

Frans found me crying in pain, and immediately, an ambulance took me to the hospital, where the doctors took care of me. However, I needed to spend four months in a convalescent home, recovering from my injuries. Immobile, with the loss of my independence, and picking up the contagious MRSA, I was not happy, but I put up with it. When my children and grandchildren came for visits, I managed a smile or two, particularly when I saw them dressed in the required yellow protective garments and masks. I supposed the sight deserved a healthy laugh.

My Ninetieth Birthday and Humber's Sixtieth

I was still living in the recovery convalescent home at the time of the celebration of my ninetieth birthday and Humber's sixtieth year in business in 2008. My sons had many festivities planned. The huge event replicated the 1998 triple celebration ten years prior, with all the catered food, including a gigantic cake, music, and interesting speeches, all taking place in our gorgeously decorated front garden under white tents. My nephew, Andre, son of my brother Guillaume, and my niece, Maria, daughter of my brother Jan, came to Canada for the celebration. A remarkable write-up by Stephanie Smith in the magazine *Horticulture Review: The Voice of Landscape Ontario* highlighted details of the event. Part of the article read:

"Music, food, a silent auction, laughter, visiting among friends and family, and much joy were all part of Sibylla Peters ninetieth birthday celebration on August second. It was also a day to celebrate Humber Nurseries sixtieth anniversary.

"Among the 300 people who enjoyed the event were Brampton City Councillor John Hutton, who brought his best wishes; Mayor Susan Fennell also passed on her best wishes; MP for Bramalea-Gore-Malton Gurbax Malhi was on hand to present his congratulations; Landscape Ontario President Bob Adams and executive director Tony DiGiovanni were present to offer best wishes from the association. We received congratulatory messages from Premier Dalton McGinty and Prime Minister Stephen Harper.

"Although heavy rain fell early, threatening the celebrations, the dark clouds disappeared, and sunshine allowed the party to carry on for the rest of the day. One of the highlights was the cutting of the massive cake that depicted Humber Nurseries Ltd., complete with edible photographs displaying the history of the family business."

The day ended after a private dinner party with the family.

Dancing at Ninety

Who said that one could not dance in a wheelchair? On October 4, 2008, Mike and Pita Van Dongen's daughter, Suzanne, was promised marriage to Ian Muffett. It was a beautiful weekend wedding held at the Hockley Valley Resort in Orangeville, Ontario. I remembered clearly that Suzanne and Ian wanted to dance with me, but I could not because I was in a wheelchair. Nevertheless, they insisted and pushed me in my wheelchair on to the dance floor so that I could move my arms to the rhythm of the music. That was how I danced when I was ninety years old. I predicted that the next decade of my life would bring on more eventful parties that I did not want to miss.

And the next breath of vibrant new life came with the birth of our third great-grandchild, born on March 21, 2009. I never ceased to wonder how small a newborn human being could be. Anita, my granddaughter, and Richard Scholman were happy with their healthy baby boy, named Carter.

Frans

Although my life train was back on track, it was moving more slowly. Since the accident, my daily routines had changed, and I was resting more often and for longer periods. Frans also had his health issues, with his sight worsening each month with macular degeneration. It was not easy with the two of us in the house and our daily needs bidding for more attention. At last, we hired a woman to come into the house to help prepare meals and upkeep the household. We also had an occupational therapist and a nurse kindly sent from the government assistance program to help with modifications to the home and medication delivery.

We discovered Frans's more severe illness in an unusual, but somewhat funny way. It happened when my son, Frans Jr., took us out for breakfast at Frans's favourite restaurant called Denny's in Brampton. My son drove us there, dropped us off at the entrance area of the restaurant, and we were to wait there while he parked his car. Not wanting to wait idly, Frans and I decided to enter the restaurant to find a place to sit. However, we did not make it inside the restaurant. Frans could not see where he was going and accidentally tripped on a rubber carpet. He tumbled hopelessly and hard onto the ground. In the middle of his falling episode and in my efforts to help Frans, I accidentally let go of my walker.

The next thing that happened was quite funny. The walker stumbled and rolled away from us, all by itself, towards the other side of the parking lot. That walker took on a life of its own, catching every bumpy obstacle in its way, always maintaining perfect balance. It was a strikingly hilarious sight! When Frans Jr. returned, he saw that we were in trouble. He helped Frans get onto his feet, and he retrieved the naughty, lifeless walker. During our breakfast, Frans complained that his ribs were sore, and my son suggested that we go to the hospital or the family physician Dr. Kacer. Frans chose to see Dr. Kacer.

What happened next was quite unexpected. While inspecting Frans's bruised ribs, Dr. Kacer discovered a large black lump on the top middle of his back. It turned out to be cancerous. Treatment of radiation and chemotherapy followed, and I was certain that the discovery deeply bothered him. On Father's Day, because he was sick and unhappy with both his blindness and his cancer, we cheered him up with a family party. The children presented a new CD player to play his CD's, as he loved listening to music.

Frans and I closed this year with a fantastic Christmas, celebrated first at the nursery with our employees, and then at the Peters Family Christmas celebration at Astrid and Harry's home in Brampton, followed by a celebration at Henk's on Christmas Day. But it would be Frans's last Christmas.

Father Steve of Saint Marguerite D'Youville parish in Brampton had given the sacrament of the last rites around mid-February while Frans was in the hospital for his cancer. It was the last time that our immediate family was together, and, surprisingly, during this religious time, we all told uplifting and hilariously funny family stories. We laughed a lot, cried a bit, and Frans joined in on the fun. He said with a huge smile to Father Steve:

"At age eighty-nine, I think that I had a pretty good life with this family!"

With that comment, he seemed to know that the end was near. The last few weeks of his life were difficult because of his painful and fragile health. With emergency treatments in the hospital and convalescing at both home and at a convalescent home, it was when he went into a coma that we all knew he would soon be gone.

Nothing could prepare me for the loss of my husband. On April 10, 2010, Frans, my beloved Frans, died. I wished that I could go back, if only for a few hours, to ask him some last few questions and to tell him that I loved him after all these years of living together.

There was a funeral mass on April 14, 2010, at our parish, Our Lady of the Airways Catholic Church in Malton. He was buried at the Queen of Heaven Catholic Cemetery in Woodridge, Ontario, less than five kilometres from our Humber Nurseries Ltd.

Memories of my Husband

I eased into bereavement with the help of visitors from the Netherlands, Magda and her daughter-in-law Wilma. We talked about highlights of Frans's life in the Netherlands and Canada. We traced his busy life in photographs as a young man in Deventer, his arrival to Manitoulin Island, and our move to Toronto. I reflected with Magda and Wilma about how learned Frans became over the years, acquiring much knowledge through his stubborn pursuit of a wide array of subjects through reading and traveling. He had such a sharp, inquisitive mind.

Customers discovered that they could find any plant in the world at Humber Nurseries Ltd. because of Frans, and he would be the person to talk easily, happily, and endlessly about his new finds. His hidden interest in alternative medicine grew into expert knowledge in growing herbs. With herbal medications, he managed to keep himself in nearly perfect health until the age of eighty-eight. So, he was not too happy when he needed help from conventional medicine to correct his vision and treat his cancer.

What a wonderful long life Frans had lived. I hoped and prayed he was watching over us as we went about our lives. Magda, Wilma, Astrid, my two sons, and I enjoyed conversing with our nursery employees as we invited them to talk about Frans. We did some touring in southern Ontario, and when it was time for Magda and Wilma to depart, a natural disaster prevented them from leaving. Unfortunately, there was a volcanic eruption on the island of Iceland, and no airline was allowed to fly across the ocean. So Magda and Wilma remained in Canada for another two weeks, and in the long run, I was grateful for their company.

Each day, in the depths of my soul, I found Frans. My supportive children insisted that I go out on excursions. As I was feeling better, I recognized that adventures, although small, were awaiting me during that summer of 2010. And why not, while I was still healthy enough to do so? Frans would have liked that.

My Outings

The first excursion was to Frans and Vita's home to celebrate my ninety-second birthday. My children, grandchildren, and great-grandchildren all attended with a cake presentation and lovely gifts. Vita also created a gift-giving game where each person had to pull out a ticket from a beautifully decorated gift box, and on that ticket was written a type of gift to give to me.

One of the gifts was to take me to the shopping mall, but the hook was that I had to pay for all my purchases!

A second outing was a luncheon with Astrid's girlfriends and their mothers. Astrid had kept in contact with her St. Joseph's high school girlfriends all these years, and I thought we made a fantastic-looking group in the many pictures taken. We also enjoyed great conversation, and I was thinking, if only the mothers were all a bit younger!

A third excursion was going to be an overnight stay near Orillia, Ontario, with Astrid. I wanted to go to Casino Rama and see how it was there. When we first arrived, we played the slot machines, and I won about 200 dollars. Then we went for a drive, and for my memory's sake, we drove to Father Hap's old cottage on Lake Couchiching north of Orillia, where I spent many vacations during the summer. Astrid and I continued our drive to see Wasaga Beach, about which I had always heard. We also had a lovely visit with Hans and Barb Van Zanten, who lived in the town of Wasaga. We stayed overnight at the Best Western Hotel at the Casino Rama, and during the next morning, we went to the casino for one last gamble at the slot machines. I only broke even this time.

The fourth excursion was my visit with Tiny Klein Beernink at her apartment at Oakview Terrace in Richmond Hill. The timing was good because her sister, Gonny, was visiting from the Netherlands. We had the chance to discuss the world changes in the Netherlands over the years. We also had the opportunity to bereave over Frans. I would remember my thoughts on how little Frans, and I thought about who would be the first to die, leaving the other behind to muddle through life alone. I then related the 'make-me-feel-good story' when Guy and Elaine presented a special birthday gift: a green Humber cap with the name "Mrs. Peters" printed in gold. It matched the green Humber apron with the inscription: "I'm Still the Boss" printed in large white letters!

After my summer excursions were done, I settled into a daily home routine once again. I was satisfied to work on my transplanting and cleaning plants in the kitchen of my home each day. It was not an exciting life, but a quiet and stress-free one that made me feel content. With these full, active days, I counted my blessings in life, sitting comfortably in my 'train seat'. I was working for my favourite nursery, Humber Nurseries Ltd., and Frans Jr. always reminded me that I was never too old to transplant baby plants. If I asked for more work, he would tease me and say, "Yes, Mom. You're the boss!"

A Difficult Decision

Although August was always an enjoyable month, I felt less of this excitement because my health was deteriorating. I felt tired each day because of congestive heart issues, serious allergies to foods, and asthma. I was breathing with difficulty, and my short walks in the house took extra effort. My longer walks became limited because I walked at a snail's pace using a walker and then, my sense of balance disturbed me more often. I used a wheelchair to get around more easily outside and I used an oxygen tank to help with my breathing more comfortably at nighttime.

Soon, I depended on Astrid to bring me to the hospital emergency department, many times at two or three in the morning. I would unexpectedly have an allergy attack, particularly in my throat, causing a thickening which made my breathing difficult. Then on one occasion, I felt the need to call the paramedics to immediately assist me, whereby they gave me two antihistamine injections before going to the hospital. I decided that I was not well, and I was quite frightened by the whole incident.

As each day passed in late summer of that year, and early autumn I realized that I needed to make changes in my living conditions. One day I felt that I was making headway in my decision after reading an article in one of my favourite newspapers, the Catholic Register.

The specific article highlighted influential people of the past. An anonymous person discovered Michelango's depiction of strength and beauty in his paintings of women. On the Sistine Chapel ceiling, Michelangelo painted a particular female figure named the Libyan Sibyl, a Pagan prophetess. I always clung to the meaning of my name, Sibylla—a prophetess that instigated the idea that my name gave me strength and that I could predict the future. After reading the newspaper article, I was convinced to pack my things from my homestead and move to a safer place.

I admitted some facts to myself: I no longer could manage my household; my health was deteriorating; I needed to move to a safer place where I could easily receive medical attention and more personal care; and finally, and most importantly, I no longer wanted to rely wholly on my family for everything. I needed to release my reins of dependence on them and give up my independence. I predicted, therefore, for all the above reasons, that I would move from my home of nearly fifty years to a retirement home with a higher level of personal and medical care. Emotionally, my choice was difficult, but rationally for me, it was the right decision to make. I had bought the one-way train ticket, and the destination was a retirement home.

Afterword

On November 11, Remembrance Day, I brought Mom to Woodhall Retirement Park in Brampton. It was a small room, number 105, with the bedroom and living quarters in open air space. At the entrance was a coat/clothes closet on the left and the washroom was on the right. Her occupational therapist set up the room, giving attention to her toilet needs. Guy planned the interior design of her new home, and together with Frans Jr., they brought her favourite furniture pieces, her clothes, and some of her favourite wall hangings.

It was a cozy and happy place for Mom. The residents were all at the same level, all managing independently but with medical needs provided by the nurses and doctors in the home. There were many social activities, special events, and exercise classes. If Mom participated, she could have had a full day, but most times, she was happy to go for meals, watch some television, read, and sleep. Our family and friends often visited, and I would keep her updated on her mail and financial commitments.

We celebrated the Peters Family Christmas that year at Guy and Elaine's home in Brampton. The happy family experience with all her children and grandchildren gave a healthy uplifting for Mom. It was our first Christmas without Dad, and truly we could feel that under her happy face, mom felt sad. We sang our traditional song of "The Twelve Days of Christmas" and played our conventional gift trading game. The food and decorations were also so beautiful. It was our family's favourite time of year. And so, the visitors came to see her repeatedly, in her new home at Woodhall. However, Mom's health was weakening at this time, and I knew that she would soon need to use an oxygen tank both day and night.

When she fell and broke her hip at the retirement home, this last accident pushed her to her fate sooner than expected. She had tripped over the oxygen line of the oxygen tank while going to the washroom in the early morning hours. Spending forty-eight hours in the emergency unit of the hospital was a painful experience for Mom. My sister's daughter, Anita, and I waited over ten hours for results during the hip replacement operation, hoping for the best. Unfortunately, the best did not come, because a hip replacement would not be possible since Mom's bones were too brittle. The surgeon removed only the broken bones. It was almost a miracle that Mom had not died on the operation table, as her blood pressure was so low.

Mom returned to the Woodhall retirement home, and we upgraded her care with a team of nurses and personal care workers, working shifts for twenty-four hours each day. We visited her often, and a Catholic priest came to give her the last sacrament. She then slipped into and out of a coma-like state. When she showed more clarity one day, we decided to show some old videos of her past life. They were Dad's eight- and sixteen-millimetre films that our dear sister had organized chronologically and transferred to videos for our parents' birthdays and anniversaries. The video started with stories of their lives in Europe and their holiday travels with Oma and Opa in the Netherlands and Germany. While watching the videos, Mom would smile some of the time, and we guessed that she recognized the people and places.

It was a sunny Thursday morning during the spring, and with a feeling of premonition, I wanted to arrive early to spend the day with Mom. I was present at her side, during the early evening, when Mom took a deep breath, followed by a lighter one, and then no more. Mom was gone and had joined Dad and Sibylleke in heaven, and I thank our dear Lord that she was rid of her painful body and was finally resting peacefully with Him.

Mom left us on May 12, 2011, because of congestive heart failure. I thought that her final act on earth was only the physical end of her life, because her vibrant soul and spirit would always live on.

The funeral mass was held at Our Lady of Airways Catholic Church in Malton, and Mom was buried with Dad at the Queen of Heaven Cemetery. So many flower arrangements made the spring funeral look bright and happy. We received many condolences and good wishes for our family from many people, many of whom had known Mom for years.

One letter that I received was from Mom's dear old friend from the war years, Corrie Cossee, who wrote: "It was such a shock for me to receive your letter. Your mother and I have spent the most important years of our youth together. We even visited the Nuremberg Trials in Germany after the war and had pictures taken of us with Russian soldiers. She used to call me by telephone, and after our life-updates, we always found ourselves engrossed in conversation over our memories."

Another letter from an anonymous customer of Humber Nurseries Ltd. said: "I was saddened to hear of Mrs. Peters death. I loved coming to Humber because the family atmosphere and your mother were such a large part of that. I shall never be able to enter the greenhouse without seeing her image meticulously making her cuttings. Jean Cocteau, a French philosopher, once wrote, 'Death is always a shock, even when we expect it. It takes time for healing.'"

Aunt Gretel wrote a letter of condolences: "I send, with a heavy heart, my sympathies for beloved Sibylla, wife, mother, grandmother, and great grandmother. She has brought many tears to you all at her life's end. And there will be many major changes for you to face in the future. I wish you much strength for that. I will think of you all and pray for Sibylla."

After writing my mother's memoir, I honestly believed that she lived a full life. I wrote her tales of people and events to share this belief with family, friends, and interested readers. One would learn that Mom was a person who cared about life and relationships, and that she planted her love in the hearts of everyone who knew her. We would all miss her. She always intended to be happy in life, and she achieved it. I know that she would predict that you could do that, too.

At 91 years of age, my children declared that I was still the boss.

Sibylla Janssen-Peters.

Perhaps her favourite achievement was founding Humber Nurseries Ltd. with her husband, Frans. The business became Ontario's largest self-supporting nursery in its time. She lived during the historical periods of the Roaring Twenties, the Depression of the Thirties, and during World War II. She was always clear on two aspects throughout her life: what was important and what didn't matter. She fell in love with a man who would change her life, and their lives of adventure together led to the birth of four children and a prosperous business. Her reward was the opportunity to travel the world.

About the author

Born in Toronto and the daughter of the principal character Sibylla Janssen-Peters, Astrid Peters is a first-time book author. She is a retired French and music high school teacher who received three degrees at the University of Toronto. Out of her many interests, historical genealogy evolved and took precedence during her retirement in Brampton, Ontario. She lives with her husband, Harry Churchill-Smith, and her pet dog, Jana.

Sibylla, One Story at a Time is based on true stories. May the life that Sibylla lived speak for the love of her family.

Acknowledgments

I wish to thank you all who contacted my mother, whether you are mentioned or implied. You shaped her life, and I could not have written this memoir without you.

CPSIA information can be obtained
at www.ICGtesting.com
Printed in the USA
BVHW061106200522
637016BV00007B/7

9 781777 969103